A History of Ecclesiastical Dress

A HISTORY OF
ECCLESIASTICAL DRESS

Janet Mayo

B. T. BATSFORD LTD. LONDON

To my parents, Gordon and Sheila

ISBN 0 7134 3764 2

Designed by Alan Hamp
Typeset by Keyspools Ltd., Golborne, Lancs.
and printed in Great Britain by
Butler and Tanner Ltd,
London and Frome
for the publishers B. T. Batsford Ltd.
4 Fitzhardinge Street, London W1H 0AH

Frontispiece: William Warham, Archbishop of Canterbury.
After Hans Holbein, 1527.

Contents

Acknowledgment

I would like to offer my thanks to the many people who have helped me in the preparation of this book, by reading all or part of the manuscript and giving me help and encouragement: Dr Aileen Ribeiro of the History of Dress Department at the Courtauld Institute; Michael Dillon; T. A. Heslop of the University of East Anglia; Henry O'Hagan of Westminster Cathedral; Jill Kerr of the Corpus Vitrearum Medii Aevi, Great Britain; Professor J. G. Davies of Birmingham University; Dr G. Cope; the Rev. Donald Reeves; Dr Christopher Wilson; the Rev. Gordon Mayo and Sheila Mayo; Sebastian Birch; Timothy Auger and Belinda Baker of Batsford.

I would like to thank the library staff of the British Library; the Victoria and Albert Museum Library; Lambeth Palace Library; Arthur Barker, the archivist at S.P.C.K.; Jenine Hickson at the Salvation Army Headquarters; the Catholic Central Library; the library staff of the Society of Friends, Euston Road; F. H. Thompson, General Secretary of the Society of Antiquaries of London.

Finally, my special thanks go to Georgina Perrott, who patiently typed and retyped the manuscript, often at very short notice, and to Janice Pullen, the Wardrobe Director at the Royal Opera House, who gave me every help when I first started writing.

List of Illustrations

Introduction

The history of ecclesiastical dress covers nearly 1,950 years and the Christian religion has spread all over the globe in its various forms. In this book, which can only serve as an introduction to a large subject, it has seemed sensible to confine the history – after the sixth century – to the British Isles. Although only a small part of the world, Britain has had an unbroken Christian tradition since the end of the second century and has witnessed and introduced many sects within the Western Church. The Eastern Orthodox vestments have only been dealt with briefly, and are in the glossary for purposes of cross-reference.

As a costume history it is necessary to approach the subject chronologically and discuss the clothes worn by ecclesiastics in the context of contemporary society, although this book is not a history of the Church. As many of the names of the garments may be unfamiliar, and to avoid repetition in the text, an illustrated glossary is provided. Some sects and branches of the Church may not receive a mention, which is no reflection on their part in the history of Christianity, but rather because their contribution to the dress of the ministers has been minimal.

One of the problems of the study of ecclesiastical dress is that the development is so slow that contemporary writers do not feel the need to describe it. Where they do, they describe anomalies or extraordinary details and assume a knowledge of the everyday and Sunday wear of the clergy from the earliest written sources up until the present day. When I was endeavouring to find out if there were any directives for clergy on the clothes to wear on overseas missions, my enquiries only brought me the advice given to a clergyman going to Nigeria in the 1940s, which was to take 'evening dress and thigh length waders'.

A further problem is that for many clergy dress is not considered an important part of their ministry and throughout history there are examples of clergy who left aside parts of the prescribed dress or who embellished or altered their vestments for particular reasons suitable to the time and place. This history tries to contain information about what clergy *should* wear as well as what they *did* wear, and can only act as a guide for a type of dress which, although deliberately distinctive, is not and never has been a uniform in the military sense.

Laity, who have always had a part in the liturgies and celebrations of the Christian Church, are mentioned when special dress is worn to distinguish their functions, but the lay dress of the clergy is only briefly touched on as there are other costume books which deal with the secular dress of particular periods. The dress of women in the Church is perhaps not well represented, but the cassock, the alb, the surplice and the cassock–alb which they wear follow the pattern of those traditionally worn by ministers and no specific 'female' garments have evolved.

This book will, I hope, serve as an introduction to a complex subject which may be daunting to the uninitiated because of the strangeness of the names and the shapes of the clothes. An example of the layman's problems with these terms was pointed out in the *Church Times* (15 February 1980) under the headline 'laundry list': 'A columnist in the *Christian Century* reports that a retired American bishop, John Baumgaertner, sent four vestments to the cleaner – namely an alb, cincture, stole and amice. They were beautifully done and the slip indicated that the Rev. Baumgaertner was charged for one dress, long; one scarf; one rope; and one apron.'

1 Fifth-century ivory box. Detail of the Crucifixion panel. On the left, Judas has hung himself from a tree and the bag containing the 30 pieces of silver is at his feet. He wears the long tunic (*chiton poderes*) with long sleeves turned back and a simple neckline cut straight across. He wears sandals and a mantle, possible a pallium. Mary wears a palla, a mantle which is the female version of the pallium and usually worn pulled over the head and covering the right arm. Her long tunic is visible at the hem and she wears shoes. St John wears a full length, long-sleeved tunic under his pallium which is worn over his left shoulder, brought round under his right arm and then draped over his left forearm. He is bare-headed and wears sandals. Christ wears only the ventrale, the simplest form of loincloth, which is a broad band of cloth, tied at the centre front with the two ends hanging down. The soldier wears a type of clothing adapted from Barbarian dress by labourers and military and universally worn in the Roman Empire, although not one article was adopted by the Church. The hat (*pileus*) was used in art to indicate foreigners and in this case a Jew (only messengers and people who worked outside in the sun wore hats in the Roman world). The cloak fastened on the right shoulder is the chlamys, worn generally by soldiers but adopted by civilians as court dress and frequently seen in portraits of high officials. The short tunic was a natural adaptation of the long version for soldiers, labourers and the young and under this he wears braccae or trousers which were not worn by clergy until the nineteenth century.

CHAPTER ONE

The Early Christians

The Origins of Ecclesiastical Dress

CHRISTIANITY IS an historical cult based on the life and teaching of one man, and was from the first a missionary religion. However, although the birth of the Christian religion occurred in a province within the Roman Empire, it was unheralded by any contemporary historian. Tacitus, writing at the beginning of the second century AD, made the famous remark that in Judaea 'Under Tiberius all [was] quiet'[1] and indeed, Christianity came into the Empire at the beginning of a long period of peace. On 11 January 27 BC Octavian had closed the doors of the Temple of Janus to mark the return of peace – for the first time in 200 years. Apart from local, though severe, conflicts such as the Jewish War of 66–73, the provinces away from the frontiers enjoyed almost unbroken peace between 30 BC and AD 193, and then from 197 to 235.

Ease of communications and trade encouraged the rapid spread of Christianity, despite sporadic persecution. Men could travel between different countries freely and at will, and the missionary journeys of the disciples and apostles started very soon after the Crucifixion, which is generally dated between AD 30 and 33. Paul's missionary journeys took place in the 40s and by 60 he was in Rome.

The Acts of the Apostles state that 'There were dwelling in Jerusalem, devout men from every nation under heaven' (Acts 2:5) and in verse 10 we are told that these included visitors from Rome, both Jews and proselytes (those who had been converted from paganism). In 57 Paul could write of the Roman community as one whose 'faith is spoken of throughout the world' (Romans 1:8). This ease of communication continued generally and a century later (c. 180) Irenaeus, Bishop of Lyons, wrote 'The World has peace thanks to the Romans. Even the Christians can walk without fear on the roads and travel whithersoever they please.'[2]

In the first century we have to rely on the works and writings of the early Christians, mainly found in the New Testament, to learn the early history of the Church. The first Christians were waiting for the second coming of Christ, which they expected in their own lifetime and so made no attempt to formalize their religion: they certainly had no desire to adapt or create specifically Christian clothing. Before the executions of SS Peter and Paul in Rome in 64, there would have been no reason to create formal wear for religious ceremonies because of the imminence of the expected coming of the Kingdom of God.

After the deaths of these two most important men, during the time of the persecution of Christians by Nero, distinctive clothes would have been positively dangerous. The persecution of the Christians began just as it was becoming clear that the Church would outlast the lives of the men who had known Jesus Christ in his lifetime, and the early Church had to blend into the Roman community to survive. After the Nerovian persecution of 64 there was an uneasy peace until 95 when Diocletian began taking action against the aristocratic Christians in Rome; in Asia at this time there was also a persecution of both Christians and Jews.

A consideration of ecclesiastical vestments will reveal that they had their origins in secular Roman dress. The view that vestments were of Levitical origin and came from Jewish priestly garments is a later idea and will be discussed in the correct context of the eighth and ninth centuries. Clement, Bishop of Rome 90–100, represents St Peter as saying 'My dress is what you see, a tunic with a pallium.'[3] This form of dress would have been worn in Judaea, as elsewhere throughout the Empire, by the middle and upper classes. The labouring classes and the poor had different styles of costume according to region, type of work and income, but these have little bearing on the early development of ecclesiastical dress.

The Tunic

The tunic or shirt was the indoor garment of the Roman, generally worn short by men, especially soldiers and labourers, and always worn long by women and old men, or those in a senior position. The simplest style was the short tunic worn by slaves and young labourers and worn by the Good Shepherd in many early depictions; it was known as the *tunica exomis* (εξωμίς). The length of fabric was fastened, at first by pins or brooches, only on the left shoulder and under the left arm, leaving the right arm and shoulder free. This arrangement could be fastened equally suitably on both shoulders by pins or stitches, and the resulting garment was fairly loose and comfortable. Both styles required a girdle to keep the tunic in place and for decency's sake, to prevent the side from opening. The tunic could be adapted to any shape and length, and in the nature of many clothes, was more elaborate or complicated for the wealthier person.

In Rome the tunic was generally made of wool with an undershirt of linen, although the number of shirts and tunics worn, and the material used varied according to the climate. St Augustine, Bishop of Hippo (395–430) wore a woollen undershirt, and Augustus (63 BC–AD 14) clothed himself in winter with a heavy toga, four tunics, an undershirt, a woollen chestcloth, short hose and leggings.[4] The Christian tradition of making the *tunica alba* from linen as opposed to wool was quite possibly from expediency. The clothes worn at worship were required to be clean and white, indicating purity and continuing, quite naturally, both the Roman and Jewish custom of wearing white at ceremonies. The more linen is washed the whiter it becomes, whereas wool fades to yellow and would soon cease to look 'pure'.

In the wall paintings of the catacombs, second to fourth centuries, the sacred male figures are always represented in white. Other figures are shown in tunics usually painted a yellowish or reddish brown. Wool and cotton were easier to dye than linen, and garments found in Egypt from this period are normally yellow or brown, light enough in tone to form a strong contrast with the *clavi* (decorative bands) which are usually in one of the many shades of purple. A clavus is a woven or embroidered band which crosses over the shoulder and hangs down vertically front and back to the hem of the garment, and is the characteristic decoration of the tunic and later of the dalmatic. Although for the Roman the narrow clavus was reserved for the military man and the broad clavus for the senator, in the Christian period this distinction was apparently not observed. In the catacomb paintings and on tunics found in Egypt narrow clavi are frequently found, and after the fourth century women frequently wear broad clavi when represented in the catacomb paintings. The clavi are usually darker than the garment that they embellish, and generally vary in colour from red-brown to purple. The clavi served no practical purpose but were a simple and effective way of embellishing a plain garment.

When the tunic had sleeves at the height of the Roman Empire, they were loose and covered only the upper arm; tight long sleeves were an oriental fashion and considered effeminate. Nevertheless, long sleeves came into common use by the third century, usually corresponding with the long tunic (*tunica talaris*) which reached to the ankles. Despite the fact that it was originally female dress, the long tunic came to represent the garment of gods and heroes, and under the Empire it seems to have been regarded as a dress of special dignity, and as such was adopted by the Church.

The Pallium

Clement of Rome says that St Peter wore a *pallium* with his tunic. This early garment, like the toga, was made of woollen cloth and was usually white without decoration except where small tapestry or embroidered designs were applied on each of its four corners. It was a rectangle three times as long as it was broad, wrapped round the body in a

2 Tapestry woven panel of the Graeco-Roman period, third-fourth centuries. Tapestry woven panels were the main form of decoration in early ecclesiastical garments and were taken from the everyday dress of the Roman Empire. These embroideries and tapestries were used to embellish otherwise plain garments, and when these wore out they were cut out and applied on to new garments.

simple and natural manner. One-third hung in front from the left shoulder to the knee and enveloped the upper arm; the remaining two-thirds were drawn across the back, under the right arm, across the front and again thrown over the left shoulder where it was either fastened with a pin, or simply draped over the left forearm.

This simple garment was favoured by the early Christians, and the toga was never adopted (in the paintings in the catacombs there is only one figure wearing the toga). The pallium represented the cosmopolitan aspect of the Empire and had been worn by Christ and his apostles as well as the philosophers and thinkers of the Greek civilized world. The toga was associated with the senators and politicians of Rome. The convenience and utility of the pallium was even recognized in Rome itself and it had partly superseded the toga, before both garments gave way to the even greater convenience of the dalmatic and the paenula. The pallium was retained by the Christians, transformed into an ornament or insignia.

The Paenula

The *paenula* (the direct forerunner of the chasuble) was originally an outer protective garment, expressly a storm-cloak, made of heavy woollen cloth and more rarely of leather. It need not have

been a foreign importation, but may have developed from some common garment of the labouring classes or perhaps from the military, who must have acquired a protective garment, especially when working out on the northern frontiers of the Empire. Seneca (born 61 BC) describes a riding tour which he had taken with a friend and the manner in which they camped out. (*Epist.* LXXXVII):[5] 'Culcita in terra jacet, ego in culcita. Ex duabus paenulis altera stragulem, altera opertorium facta ext.' – 'The mattress lay on the ground, and I lay on the mattress. One paenula served the purpose of a blanket underneath; the other that of a coverlet to throw over.'

St Paul probably wore a paenula in his travels and when writing to Timothy he asks 'When you come, bring the cloak that I left with Carpus at Troas, also the books, and above all the parchments' (2 Timothy 4:13). The paenula came in a variety of shapes but the basic principle was a large piece of cloth broad enough to cover the shoulders and long enough to reach below the knees at front and back with a hole in the centre for the head. The paenulas in the catacombs are shaped at the hem to give a more stylish and dignified appearance and there is also an unusual style depicted which is long at the back but in the front is only a small triangle which covers the breast. (Incidentally, this style recurs in the eleventh century.)

Roman monuments show that the paenula was provided with a hood (*cucullus*) and from mosaics, wall paintings and literary references it can be seen that originally it was dark in colour, usually a chestnut brown, the natural colour of some caucasian wools, or dyed a solid colour in one of the shades of 'purple'; it was rarely decorated. From *De Oratoribus*[6] we learn that in the middle of the first century it was an innovation for it to be worn by advocates in the forum, but by 382 a sumptuary law permitted its use even by senators, although the official toga was still to be worn in the conduct of all public business. The full round paenula worn by Christians was not yet a specifically Eucharistic vestment, and certainly St Paul had not indicated that he had any special regard for the cloak he left behind at the house of Carpus. However, we know that Christians wore the paenula during worship in the second century from the reaction of Tertullian (died *c.* 230) when he learnt that some Christians were taking it off at prayer. From his account (*De Oratione*, Cap. 12: tom. iv) we learn that the heathen worshippers thought it indecorous to wear paenulas when engaged in public prayer and that on such occasions they removed them. We learn too that many Christians had adopted the same custom, and that such scruples were regarded by Tertullian as savouring of superstition rather than of religion.[7]

Although the paenula can be established as a garment worn during the Eucharist, it continued to be worn not only by women but also in general as a travelling cloak. Sulpicius Severus (*Dialog* 2:1)[8] tells the story of St Martin of Tours (died 397) who gave his shirt to the beggar. He also informs us that St Martin was accustomed to celebrate the Eucharist in a tunic and *amphibalus* (the broad round paenula): 'The saint, without the poor man seeing it, drew out his tunic from under his amphibalus and sent him away clothed.' Such a feat could have been accomplished secretly only under a mantle of this sort and probably only

3 The Good Shepherd from the Catacomb of Domitilla. This early picture of Christ as the Good Shepherd shows the tunic in its most simple form, a rectangle of cloth fastened on the left shoulder and held in place at the waist with a girdle. This simple garment was worn as underwear and could just as easily be pinned up or stitched on the right shoulder as well, and could, of course, be longer.

if the tunic was fastened above the shoulders with pins or brooches (*fibulae*) according to the fashion described. This version of the paenula is the style of garment which becomes the chasuble in the centuries that follow, although there were also other styles of cloaks: the *byrrus*, the *chlamys* and the *cappa* or *pluviale*. It is appropriate to record the story of St Alban here. Tertullian, *c.* 200, in a tract against the Jews, says that there were parts of Britain inaccessible to the Romans yet subject to Christ. Forty years later Origen refers in two passages to the British people having come under the influence of Christianity.[9] The first Christian in Britain whose name is recorded was Alban whose history is given by Bede (*E.H.*i:7).; this story also records a specifically Christian garment for the first time in Britain.

Alban, a Romanized Briton, living in the Roman city of Verulamium (St Albans), gave shelter to a Christian priest fleeing from his persecutors. While he hid the priest Alban became converted, and when the soldiers came, he dressed in the priest's cloak, gave himself up in his place and was executed on the hill where St Albans Abbey now stands. The date assigned to this event varies enormously and so little can be precisely inferred from this slight but important evidence for the distinction of early clerical dress.[10]

Distinctive Dress in the Third Century

The third century was a time of great advance for the Church despite the persecution by Decius who became emperor in 249 and by Valerian who suceeded him in 257. In 212 the Constitutio Antoniana conferred Roman Citizenship on nearly all the free men in the Empire, and there were long periods of security and toleration for the Church under the Emperors Alexander Severus, the Gordians and Philip in the first half of the century. The Church was no longer on the defensive and Origen (died *c.* 253) had shown that Christianity and the philosophy of the Greco-Roman world could be harmonized; he even felt secure enough to allow his sermons to be recorded by shorthand writers. When and how the offices of bishop, priest and deacon were created is by no means clear, but by the third century they had emerged as established distinctions and with this development specifically religious clothes become identifiable. In the middle of the third century Pope Steven I forbade the use of liturgical dress for workaday purposes, thereby indicating that it already existed. St Jerome in his commentary on Ezekial 44 (end of the fourth century) says 'Moreover the worship that is of God has one habit in Holy Ministry and another for the usage of common life' and further 'from all these things we learn that we ought not to enter the Holy of Holies clad in our everyday garments and in whatever clothes we will, defiled as they are by the usage of common life: but with pure conscience and in pure garments we ought to hold the sacraments of the Lord.'[11]

The words 'clean' and 'pure' in connection with clothes are easy to understand; St Clement of Rome's use of 'shining' has caused more problems. There is a rubric in the liturgy of Clement that directs a priest to begin the service 'girded with a shining vesture.' Most authorities have decided that by this he meant white, as both literary references and mosaics show that the tunic and pallium or paenula worn in the ministration of the Church – whether linen or wool – were commonly white. (Hence *tunica alba*; it was only later in the Middle Ages that the adjective superseded the noun and gave us the alb.) White was a colour appropriate to the dress of the ministry and was also in keeping with both the Roman and Biblical tradition. Plato wrote, 'White colours will be most seemly for gods; as in other things, so also in this of woven garments offered to them. Dyed garments should not be offered, save only as ornaments of war.'[12] At the beginning of the third century Tertullian thought dyed colours were displeasing to God,[13] and Clement of Alexandria (died 220) wrote 'I honour the ancient Lacedaemonian people, who allowed none but harlots to wear garments wrought like unto flowers, and ornaments of gold.'[14]

However, this evidence is by no means conclusive. Although unquestionably the *tunica alba* was white, and probably nearly always of linen, the other vestments were not always so consistent. There is another problem perhaps with the 'shining' of Clement – could it have meant gold? There is not enough evidence of gold threads in the early clothes but there is one story of an ill-fated robe that can be told here. It was narrated by

Theodoret (*c.* 393–457) who became Bishop of Syria in 420, and is an account of the charge preferred against Cyril, Bishop of Jerusalem, before the Emperor Constantius:

The Emperor Constantine, of famous memory, as a mark of honour to the Church of Jerusalem, had sent to Macarius, then bishop of that city, a sacred robe, made of threads of gold, which he should put upon him when performing the office of Holy Baptism. This robe, Acacius declared, had been sold by Cyril, and that a stage dancer had bought it and put it on, but that, in dancing, he fell and received injuries which proved fatal.[15]

The Dalmatic
By the end of the second century the dalmatic had come into use in Rome; it was substantially nothing more than a particular variety of the ungirdled tunic, although, as its name suggests (*tunica dalmatica*) it was probably originally of foreign importation, from Dalmatia which was

4 Painting from the catacomb of St Priscilla, from third-century Rome. This portrait of an early Christian shows the dalmatic with the two clavi running parallel from the shoulders. In the early period the dalmatic was worn by men and women and by ecclesiastics and laity. The dalmatic came to be special to deacons, a very early position in the Church with Biblical precedents for both men and women.

famous for the rich and skilful decoration of its garments. From the beginning it was richly ornamented, frequently decorated over its whole surface with a diapered pattern, or else plain but dyed to a rich colour. In the wall paintings of the catacombs we see that the dalmatic adopts the clavi of the tunic, running from the shoulder to the hem, and adds clavi to its wide sleeves. Women could wear it, although theirs were longer, to the ankles, and often with bigger sleeves. The dalmatic might be of linen or wool and was essentially an outer garment. As such it was worn over the tunic, but was not a storm-coat and so when it was later adopted as episcopal dress it was worn under the chasuble, the descendant of the paenula.

The *Liber Pontificalis* ascribed to Sylvester, Bishop of Rome (253–7), the regulation that deacons should wear the dalmatic in church. In the life of St Caesarius of Arles it is related that on the occasion of the visit of the saint to Rome Pope Symmachus (498–514) granted him the privilege of wearing the pallium, and to his deacons that of wearing the dalmatic, 'as was the custom in the Roman Church'.

The earliest depictions of the dalmatic as the dress of deacons are in the mosaics of Ravenna in the mid-sixth century, where the dalmatics are white. It was also worn by bishops and so general was its use that St Isador of Seville (*c.* 560–636) actually calls it the 'priestly tunic', 'tunica sacerdotalis candida cum clavis ex purpura'.[16] In the mid-third century St Cyprian wore a *tunica dalmatica* over which was a byrrus or cloak, when he was led to his martyrdom.[17] It must be stressed that this does not indicate that the clothing itself was in any way considered sacred; rather it appears to be an everyday garment which has been accepted and adopted by a Christian bishop.

As well as clavi there were small patches of embroidery or tapestry which were used as decoration on the tunic and dalmatic. These were usually of the richest and brightest of colours in silks and fine wools and were called *segmenta*, *gammadia* or *paraganda*; they showed up like gems against the plainer fabrics of the tunic or dalmatic which they decorated. The tapestry was usually worked in wool with a linen backing upon an upright frame from behind, and was generally appliqué, even for a linen tunic. These segmenta lasted longer than the cloth which they ornamented, and they could be readily transferred to a new garment. Before the fourth century these tapestry segments (usually square or round) were nearly always made in a single colour in one of the numerous shades classed as purple – dark carmine, red, reddish brown, violet to dark blue or black. When the dalmatic was worn over the tunic it adopted the characteristic clavi and segmenta and covered and hid the decoration on the tunic. As a result these decorations disappeared from their former positions on the tunic and moved to the remaining areas still visible – the hem, the wrists and the neckline. The shorter tunic could be dyed and occasionally would be figured all over with a small design regularly repeated, but from the third century on can be looked on as a garment distinct and separate from the long-sleeved long *tunica talaris* or *tunica alba*, which was to become the distinctive dress of the clergy.

The Byrrus

The *byrrus* was a heavy winter cloak with a central opening, almost certainly provided with a hood, and fastened at the throat by a button, pin or brooch. It was always undecorated and probably drab and dark in colour. This cloak retained its function as an outdoor garment, and although in the first thousand years it remained a purely practical garment with no special function in the church it is mentioned here as the precursor of the cappa or pluviale. This came into use as an ecclesiastical garment when the paenula, or chasuble, ceased to furnish sufficient protection against the cold and inclement weather which was encountered during processions and other functions held in the open air.

Christianity in the Fourth Century

The passing of the Edict of Milan in February 313 when Constantine removed the ban on Christianity and the Church could grow without fear of persecution, was a momentous event and the Church entered upon a new phase in its history, no longer classed as an 'illicit' religion. Constantine had become the sole ruler of the Roman World when he defeated Licinius at Chrysopolis in September 324 and in 330 had moved his court to Byzantium and renamed it Constantinople (now Istanbul).

From the small amount of surviving evidence in Britain it is apparent that from the fourth century Christianity became 'established'. Churches were built with a cemetery and a parish after the pattern of the Christian society in Rome in the second and third centuries. Art and artefacts refer to Christianity with symbols such as the chi-rho ☧ and alpha and omega, and the adopted Roman dress gradually became the dress reserved specifically for ordained priests and deacons at worship.

Monastic Dress

The monastic movement was born in the third century in North Africa. Origen's way of life as an ascetic teacher, sleeping on the ground, going about barefoot, contenting himself with one garment only and drinking no wine, were regarded as an inspiration to the monastic movement.[18] Anthony (251–356), the Coptic son of a well-to-do farmer, was brought up in a large village on the Upper Nile in a Christian family. The story of his life is told by Athanasius who may have met him as early as 318 and held him in deepest respect: 'It happened that the gospel was being read, and he heard the Lord saying to the rich man "If thou wouldst be perfect, go and sell that thou hast and give to the poor, and come follow me and thou shalt have treasure in heaven"'.[19] Anthony sold his farm and went into the desert and by the time of the Great Persecution the 'desert was becoming full of monks'. His affection for Athanasius never wavered. On his deathbed in January 356 at the ripe old age of 105, he bequeathed to him his most prized possessions – his old sheepskin tunic and the mantle on which he slept. In the writings of Pachomius (290–345) it is possible to discern the beginning of more ordered community life subject to definite discipline. Each novice would find himself living in one house within the monastery as a member of a group of about twenty monks probably working at the same trade. He would be clothed in uniform dress, which included a hood, a mantle of goatskin, a girdle and a stick, and he would be under the discipline of his seniors.[20]

It was also possible to practise asceticism within the home. Eusebius of Emesa, writing in the mid-fourth century, tells of the dedicated virgin who would live at home, read the Bible, observe daily hours of prayer, keep to a Lenten diet and wear a distinctive dress. The Rev. Edward L. Cutts[21] has found another example in the story of Pammachius the Senator and friend of Jerome.

When his wife Paulina died in 397 he caused it to be proclaimed by sound of trumpet throughout Rome that on the occasion of the funeral, a funeral feast, followed by a distribution of money, would be made to the poor in the Church of St Peter. As they left the feast Pammachius gave to each a new robe and considerable alms. After this Pammachius became a monk and it is a valuable illustration of the times which is placed before us when we are told that he took his place in the Senate in his brown monk's tunic amidst the laughter of his pagan colleagues.

The Celtic Church in the Fifth Century

In the fifth century in Britain the Celtic Church was being established by people such as St Ninian who founded the monastery at Whithorn in Galloway, and who had come to Britain after studying the monasticism of St Martin at Marmoutier, possibly as early as the year 397. While Ninian was at work in Galloway, Patrick was growing up in the west of England, the son of a local administrator called Calpornius who was a deacon, and the grandson of a priest. He received his training, possibly in Gaul, where he came in contact with the monastic movement, and in the year 432 was consecrated as a bishop for work in Ireland. He founded many monasteries with no one particular rule and from them the missionaries went out with the message of Christ. While in Ireland Christianity was advancing, in England it was forced to retreat. Early in the fifth century the Romans abandoned their hold on England, and the country was rapidly overrun by the invading armies of the Jutes, Angles and Saxons, with Christian strongholds only surviving in the west (Wales) and the north. The most famous British saint was St David (*c.* 520–88), a native of Wales, who was a typical Celtic abbot-bishop, an evangelist and founder of monasteries. He was ably supported by other saints – St Illtyd, his teacher, St Deiniol and others.

We can assume, on the basis of what is known about the life of the ascetic and the travelling

5 Mosaic from the church of St Apollinare, Ravenna. St Apollinare is wearing the paenula, or chasuble folded back over the arms. It is patterned regularly all over and has a wide neckline. Immediately underneath is a white dalmatic with two clavi and the narrow sleeves of the tunic are visible at the wrists and are also decorated with narrow strips. The pallium is a folded strip of white wool worn around the shoulders and hanging front and back from the left shoulder, terminating with an embroidered emblem and stripes.

missionary, that the clothes they would have adopted would have been simple, inexpensive and very hardwearing. The *planeta* first appears in the fifth century and we can assume from the fact that it is mentioned in connection with nobles and senators, that it was a richly embellished cloak.

(This garment is also associated with the early chasuble.) Cassanius mentions it as a dress whose price prevents its use as a monastic habit,[22] and St Isidore expressly forbids members of religious orders to wear it.

There continued to be a resistance to the idea of clothes assuming any importance in ritual. Pope Celestine, Bishop of Rome (422–32) in a letter addressed to the bishops of the provinces of Vienna and Narbonne says:

By dressing in a pallium [amicto pallio] and wearing a girdle round their loins [et lumbus praecinti] they think to fulfil the truth of Scripture, not in the spirit but in the letter. . . . We should be distinguished from the common folk, and from the rest, by our learning, not by our garments; by our mode of life not by what we wear; by purity of thought not by peculiarities of dress. . . .

At the same time, St Isidore of Pelusium found significance in the type of textiles worn by clergy. Writing to Count Herminus[23] he says:

The linen vestment with which the deacons minister in the Holy Place is a memorial to the humility of our Lord, in washing, and wiping dry, the feet of the disciples. But that which the Bishop weareth on his shoulders made not of linen, but of wool, signifieth the fleece of the sheep, for which, when it had wandered away, the Lord sought and took it up on his own shoulders.

The mosaics in the church of St Vitale at Ravenna depict the pattern of clothing worn at the close of this formative period. By the end of the fifth century under the influence of the Byzantine spirit of minute classification, which prescribed a uniform for almost all classes of the Empire, clerical dress became distinctly and permanently fixed in its chief lines, marking the distinctions between the different orders of clergy as well as between clergy and people. It cannot, however, be assumed that a distinctive sacred dress, exclusively appropriate to priestly ministrations, was created at this time. As the garments ceased to serve the practical purpose of protection against the rain and cold, their shape in some degree was altered, and their fabrics and the character of the adornment were adapted to their new function.

The most dramatic change occurred in the pallium. The original form has already been described (see above, p. 13) and although no visual evidence for this transformation survives, the pallium worn by the Pope and Roman Catholic archbishops today is probably descended from the original large piece of cloth worn draped around the body in the first few centuries.[24] From the catacomb paintings it is apparent that the archaic pallium was held in great respect and almost sacred estimation. All important figures are represented wearing the pallium and Moses is depicted wearing a pallium decorated with a cross on its corners (Catacomb of Thrason, fourth century). Thus, when the paenula took over, the pallium could not be lightly discarded, even though from a practical point of view it had been rendered superfluous by the introduction of the wide paenula.

The garment worn by St Peter[25] and possibly by Christ himself could only have been retained by the practical expedient of folding the cloth lengthwise into a narrow scarf as we find in the sixth century usage. As the broad paenula did not permit the *pallium contabulatum* (the new narrow development) to be passed under the right arm, it now lay across both shoulders with one end hanging in front and the other hanging down the back. It continued to be made of white wool as before, and retained the simple embroidered crosses that correspond with the conventional decoration in tapestry which had adorned the four corners of the archaic pallium. In order to hold it in place it was fastened to the paenula by three pins or fibulae, at the centre front, the centre back and on the left shoulder where the fabric was thrown over front and back. As time passed the length of material became narrower until instead of a folded piece of cloth it was a narrow strip; it was called an omophorion (ὠμοφορίον) and must not be confused with the stole or orarion (ὠραρίον). The Roman Catholic pallium retains one other link with its ancient predecessor, for despite subsequent changes in the design it is still made with a double thickness above the left shoulder, over which the original mantle was twice thrown.

The Stole and Maniple
Two vestments with an equally complicated and obscure history appeared by the sixth century;

6 Mosaic from the Basilica of St Vitale, Ravenna. On either side of the figure of Christ enthroned are two angels. The narrow sleeves of Christ's tunic are visible at the wrist but the rest of the garment is hidden by the dalmatic which is decorated by clavi. Over the dalmatic is draped the pallium which is worn over the left shoulder, leaving the right arm free. The corner is decorated with a simple motif but otherwise the garments are quite plain. The ecclesiastic on the right is wearing the paenula, the forerunner of the chasuble, a large bell-shaped garment which envelopes the figure and covers the arms and the hands. Underneath the paenula the dalmatic can be seen with its clavi, and a patterned border around the hem. The dalmatic is traditionally a highly decorated garment, and the plain *tunica alba* is revealed underneath it, much fuller and with no added embellishment. The fringed ends of the stole hang down pendant beneath the dalmatic. The later version of the pallium is clearly illustrated here, folded to form a narrow band hung around the shoulders, with the decorated corner showing uppermost. The pallium no longer has any practical use and cannot go under the left arm because of the paenula. St Vitale on the left is in civic dress, wearing the chlamys, the cloak that fastens on the right shoulder. This form of cloak was worn by the military and high officials but never adopted by the Church.

these are what we now know as the stole and maniple. The fashion of contabulation again furnishes the explanation of their development into ornamental insignia of office, from the towel or napkin which was the natural adjunct of the practical service characterizing the office of deacon. There are numerous pagan monuments illustrating a similar towel carried on the left shoulder of *camilli* (youths who ministered at the sacrifices) and *delicati* (table servants).

The name stole is not used during this period. The proper title *orarium* is first mentioned by St Isidore of Pelusium (*Ep.*1:136). In connection with deacons he gives it the name *linteum* (which was a form of towelling made from linen) and likens it to the towel with which Christ washed the disciples' feet; the deacon wore the orarium over his left shoulder. The orarium worn by priests and bishops had a separate origin which explains the different way in which it was worn. It could be made of white wool or coloured silk and took the form of a scarf, originally worn, as it is to this day, around the neck and under the chasuble, for it was properly a neck scarf. Both the paenula and the dalmatic had apertures too broad to afford any protection to the neck, and even the tunic was collarless, and so this scarf was introduced to protect the neck from cold, or at least to preserve a sense of decency and dignity. When the deacon's orarium became ornamental, and no longer served the purpose of a towel, it differed from that of a priest only in the manner in which it was worn.

As well as on the left shoulder the towel can also be seen carried on the left arm. The original maniple was at first worn exclusively by Roman deacons, and was needed for their practical ministry as the dalmatic was considered sufficient to distinguish the office of deacon. The *Liber Pontificalis* recounts that Sylvester (314–35) prescribed that the deacons in the Church must cover the left hand, or forearm, with the *pallium linostinum*, evidently a napkin or a towel. A similar order is ascribed to Zosimus (417–18) and it would appear that this was specific to Roman deacons, and was worn or carried instead of wearing the orarium on the left shoulder as other deacons did. (The deacons depicted in the mosaics at St Vitale, Ravenna, wear the orarium on their left shoulder.)

The other source of the maniple is the *mappa*, a ceremonial handkerchief. This should not be confused with the towel of the deacons mentioned above. The *pallium linostinum* had nothing in common, either in use or in the way it was worn, with the mappa with which the emperor and higher officials signified the commencement of the games. Called a *mappula* or *sestace* by the older Roman ordines, it was carried in the left hand, possibly because togas had no pockets. Once it was accepted in the Church it came into use with the orders of clergy superior to the deacons, but this development did not take place until the ninth century.

It is certain that the orarium, whatever form it took, was considered a sacred vestment by 327, when in the Council of Laodicea it was forbidden to anyone below the rank of deacon. It is also known that in the Second Council of Braga in 563 the deacons are requested to show their oraria: 'Since in some churches of this province the deacons wear their oraria hidden under their tunic, so that they cannot be distinguished from the subdeacons, for the future they must be placed over their shoulders'.[26]

Although the orarium was adopted by all clergy it was forbidden to monks in 511; the Council Aurelian in canon 20 forbids the handkerchief (*orario*) and a kind of boot of barbarian origin (*tzangas*) for use in monasteries: 'Monacho uti orario in monasterio, vel tzangas hebere non liceat.'[27]

The Alba
The long *tunica alba* became a specifically Christian garment in the fifth century and, at the fourth Council of Carthage *c.* 400, one of the earliest regulations to govern the ritual usage of vestments in connection with the alba was passed.[28] In 589 at the first Council of Narbonne it was ruled that 'neither deacon, nor subdeacon, nor yet the lector, shall presume to put off his "alba" till after mass is over.'

The Chlamys
The Ravenna mosaics show that the *tunica alba*, dalmatic and paenula were all white, and decorated with clavi and segmenta. The silk embroidery had come into common use in the fifth century under Byzantine influence. Also to be seen in the mosaics is the *chlamys* (χλαμύς, *sagum*, *paludamentum*) which is included in this analysis as it is frequently represented in Christian monuments of this time, although it never became adopted as ecclesiastical dress. It differs from the ancient pallium only in size and the way it was worn, which was by bringing together two corners of an oblong piece of cloth over the right shoulder and fastening them there by means of a clasp pin. It is a military cloak and Christ himself was clad in a scarlet chlamys by the soldiers who mocked him (Matthew 27:28). By the sixth century the chlamys had become accepted as Byzantine court dress. Also called the *paludamentum*, it was worn long by courtiers as well as the emperor who was clad in the imperial purple; no woman except the empress was allowed to wear it.

Sandals and Shoes
The sandal that was commonly worn with the pallium was accepted by all the ranks of clergy and was adopted by the monastic orders who retain them to this day. The shoe (*calceus*) was worn at this time, especially with the toga, and denoted the dignity of the Roman citizen, but it does not appear to have been adopted by the

Church, even by the senior ranks, until much later.

The Breechcloth

The breechcloth (*cinctus*, περιζωμα) or the loin-cloth (*ventrale*, κοιλιόδεσμος) was worn under the tunic and indeed without such a garment a law forbade any appearance in public. When it is reported that certain martyrs were thrown naked to the wild beasts, it is presumed that this garment was still retained. The *ventrale* was a broad band of cloth adjusted so that the two ends hung down in front.

Trousers

The Romans associated trousers (*braccae*) with the costume of barbarians and in works of art they are often used to depict 'foreigners'. Notwithstanding the prejudice against this article of dress it became common in Rome in the third century, and it was the precursor of modern male attire. However, it has no relation to the development of ecclesiastical dress, as even in the northern climes it never appeared in either church or monastery. The one item of barbarian dress which was adopted at the end of this period, and which will be dealt with in more detail in later chapters, is the *vestis talaris* which became the cassock or soutane. This long robe of sturdier fabric was maintained by the clergy while in the fashions of the laity it became shorter; in 572 the Council of Braga ordered the use of the cassock, which has continued to be worn by the clergy to the present time without a break.

Headwear

In both Greek and Roman custom, men commonly wore no hats. In the act of sacrifice they would cover their heads with the border of their pallium or toga, and in the same way, perhaps, they would protect themselves from the rain. When travelling or exposed to the elements their cloaks, whether the paenula or the byrrus, were usually provided with hoods. Only those especially exposed to the sun – fishermen, farm-labourers or messengers – wore a broad-brimmed hat (*petasus*) such as that often shown in representations of Mercury. A headdress of some sort was worn by most of the barbarian people to the north and the east of the Empire, and it seems to have been usually the *pileus* (πîλος), a close-fitting brimless cap, made of fur, leather or wool and generally worn to protect the head from cold weather. St Jerome, fourth century, in thanking Paulinus of Antioch for a gift of such a cap, speaks of it as intended to warm his aged head.[29]

No form of headwear appears in ecclesiastical dress within this period and the monk's hood (and eventually the academic gown and hood) would develop from the hood on the cloak, or byrrus, which continued in use as a lay garment and became church dress in the tenth century. The papal tiara, the episcopal mitre and the doge's hat apparently came from a type similar to the Phrygian cap, conventionally used in the first centuries to represent the costume of the extreme orient, especially worn by the Magi, or by Jews.

Before leaving the first few centuries it is also worth noticing that certainly in the time of St Jerome, priests did not shave their heads: 'Their heads they shall not shave, and their hair they shall not closely poll, but a covering shall they have upon their heads', thus indicating that in the fourth century, in Rome, at any rate, the 'tonsure' was unknown as a mark of a Christian priest. The tonsure apparently started in the Eastern Church and eventually became a distinctive outward indication of both priest and monk in the Western Church by the sixth century.

CHAPTER TWO

The Church in England
586–1066

ST GREGORY, when he was the abbot of a Benedictine monastery which he himself had founded, first saw some Northumbrian boys on sale as slaves in Rome in about 586. He sought permission to leave Rome and devote himself to missionary work amongst the heathen English, but was refused, and never managed to get to Britain himself. When he was made Pope he sent Augustine, his friend and prior of the monastery, with forty other evangelists from the same place, to England, to convert to saxon inhabitants. After a false start they arrived in Kent in the spring of 597 and met the king, Aethelbert. He was a man of culture as well as a warrior and his contacts with Christian Gaul as well as the beliefs of his Christian wife Bertha undoubtedly influenced him; he offered himself for baptism by the summer of that same year. With no coercion but led by the King's example his courtiers and subjects followed his lead and the rapid increase of converts meant that it was necessary for the growing Church to have the rule of a bishop. Augustine accordingly applied to the Church of Gaul for episcopal orders, and on 16 November he was consecrated Archbishop of the English by Vergilias, Archbishop and Metropolitan of Arles.

Aethelbert had allotted the missionaries on their arrival a house to live in near the stable gate at Canterbury, and the church of St Martin for their public offices. Now they built a cathedral and a monastery with a cemetery in Canterbury, on land given to them by the king, and thus arose the Cathedral Church of Christ at Canterbury, then as now the mother church of English Christianity. Augustine needed to increase his mission staff and Gregory, undoubtedly delighted with his success, sent four more priests, among whom were Mellitus, Justus and Paulinus; they reached Kent in 601. They brought with them altar cloths and vestments, relics and books, letters from the Pope, and, most importantly, the pallium.

The Pallium

The pallium is still sometimes confusingly referred to as the pall in this period of history. The pallium was the narrow strip of white woollen material which encircled the neck loosely and hung down at the front and the back. It was given to an archbishop (more rarely a bishop, and never to an English bishop) by the Pope himself, to signify his authority. By the seventh and eighth centuries a symbolical meaning became attached to it, and a doctrine in the interests of the papacy grew up around it. In 866 Pope Nicholas I declared that no archbishop might be enthroned or might consecrate the Eucharist till he had received the pallium at the hands of the Pope. To add to the confusion the Roman Missal has called altar cloths both pallium and pall, and although church furnishings are not the subject of this book it is worth mentioning briefly the appearance of the pall in this period so that the two quite separate articles are easily distinguished. In the sixth century Gregory of Tours speaks of a silk pall as a covering for an altar, but it was in the eighth century, under Pope Leo III, that altar cloths came into general use. In the English coronation service the gift of a pall is prescribed as part of the oblation to be made by the sovereign, and Queen Victoria made an offering of a pall of cloth of gold. Pall has now become the name for a small square of white linen used on the altar, or the cloth used to cover a coffin or a body before burial.

The pallium developed from the folded piece of cloth worn like a scarf, as seen in the Ravenna mosaics. As it had to be arranged each time it was put on it must have given what was considered unnecessary trouble to the wearer and so a simplified shape was developed. The early form in this period was cut and sewn in place, although it was still made of white wool with the cross embroidered on it. The ends hung down the centre front and back and the branches were almost horizontal, passing around the body just below the shoulders and above the elbows. This in turn must have been considered inconvenient, as it would restrict arm movements and the pallium developed again into a different shape with the strip of cloth passing over each shoulder from centre front to centre back, resembling a Y shape.

The pallium at first still needed the three brooches or fibulae to hold it in place, and as the vestments were made of simple fabrics the pins could be run through pallium and chasuble without damaging the fabric. As the vestments came to be made of richer stuff and embroidered, small loops were sewn on to protect them. By the tenth century the pallium no longer needed to be held in place, as it kept its shape and although the loops were abandoned quite naturally, the pins or brooches were retained as ornaments because they were made of gold and set with precious stones. These three jewelled pins can still be seen on the pallium worn by the present Roman Catholic Archbishop of Westminster.

The Celtic Church

Augustine was consecrated in France either because he did not know of the existence of Christian bishops in the north of England or because he was already aware of the impending controversy between the Celtic Church and the Roman and preferred to go to a bishop who acknowledged the rule of Rome. Since 410, when the Emperor Honorius had ordered the Roman withdrawal from England, leaving the country unprotected from the Saxons, Angles and Picts, the Church had retreated to Northumbria, Scotland, Ireland, Wales, Cornwall and Devon. For 150 years communication with Rome had been cut off and as a consequence there were some major differences between the new missionaries who came over with Augustine and the existing Church. The Celtic Christians celebrated the festival of Easter according to the calculations of a calendar which had long ago been proved to be erroneous, and had been superseded over most of Europe by a more accurate one; they neglected to use certain parts of the Rite of Holy Baptism upon which Roman theologians in recent years had come to lay great stress, and they still cut the tonsure of the clergy after a fashion which had been obsolete in Western Christendom for a century.

To Augustine these appeared as mere relics of barbarism and ignorance, which must at once be swept away before the enlightenment of Rome and the authority of the Pope. Pope Gregory, writing from Rome, also appeared to have little consideration for the Celtic Church, and in the letters which came in 601 he suggested to Augustine that the government of the Church should be under two Metropolitans, one in London and one in York (both chief Roman cities and centres of administration). Neither archbishopric was set up in Augustine's time, London because it remained stubbornly pagan and York because the British bishops resented this enforced authority.

The tonsure, an outward sign of allegiance, had developed in the fifth century for all ranks of clergy as a sign of ordination and continued to be used by the clergy and clerks until the sixteenth century. From the sixth century the tonsure was conferred as a preparation for the divine service and was therefore worn by monks and clerks. In the seventh century it became the custom that monks should proceed to holy orders and this led to corruption within the orders, with servants employed to do the jobs previously done by the monks themselves.

The custom had originated in the East where it was already associated with affliction and suffering. The Eastern tonsure had the front part of the head completely shaven, leaving the hair on the back untouched. The Celtic or Scotic tonsure was similar to this with a crescent shape shaved away at the front, a style often seen in depictions of St Paul; and the Romans shaved their heads according to what they called the tonsure of St Peter, leaving a circle of hair round the shorn head, supposed to represent the crown of thorns, and therefore also called the coronal tonsure. The tonsure peculiar to each party became its badge.

Canon 61 in the Acts of the 4th Council of Toledo, held under the presidency of St Isidore of Seville in 633 shows that there were problems even with the Roman tonsure.

All clerks, or readers, as well as levites and priests, are to cut off the hair from the whole of the upper part of the head, and leave only a circular band of hair beneath; not as hitherto in parts of Gallicea appears to have been done by readers, who wearing their hair long like laymen, cut a scanty circle away at the top of the head. For in Spain this fashion has been confined hitherto to heretics.[1]

Monastic Dress

The monasteries of the Celtic Church kept the basic rules set down by St Benedict of poverty, chastity and obedience, but they were not as rigorously ordered as those on the Continent. Like Lindisfarne, they were centres of scholasticism and sent out many missionaries, within Britain and to northern Europe and Germany.

St Aldhelm (or Ealdhelm) possibly received a Celtic tonsure when he went to study in the school of the Irish monk and hermit Mealduib.[2] Tradition states that this was in 661 when Aldhelm was fifteen. However, he later went to Rome and as an adult tried to convert the Britons in the west of England from their persistent error regarding the tonsure and the date of keeping Easter. After a synod of Saxon bishops held in 705 in Wessex had asked Aldhelm to write a letter of rebuke and exhortation to Geraint, the British king of Devon and Cornwall, he wrote:

Secondly, it is widely said that in Devon and Cornwall priests and clerics wear a tonsure of Celtic ordering, refusing that of Holy Peter – a celtic tonsure that follows the example of Simon Magus, the magician who himself attempted black art against this apostle. But the Roman tonsure worn in the Church of Christ by Peter and his successor is of the shape of the crown of thorns, the crown of true priesthood.[3]

William of Malmesbury said that these words bore fruit.

St Wilfred of York originally wore the Celtic tonsure when he studied at Lindisfarne under St Aidan. In 652, the year after the death of St Aidan,

Wilfred went to Kent where he studied with monks of the Roman tradition before setting off for Rome in 653 with Benedict Biscop. He adopted the Roman tonsure to indicate his change of allegiance, but although he diligently worked for Rome, he did not always meet with success. He attended the synod at Whitby held in the monastery of St Hilda in 664 expressly to resolve the date of Easter and in a convincing argument against Colman, the Bishop of Lindisfarne, probably did much to secure the conclusive authority of St Peter and Rome. This was not a complete victory and when he went to the monastery at Ripon, his Roman tonsure and Italian affectations were not in accordance with the simple habits of the Scottish monks who soon quitted their home.[4] He also got into trouble through too much opulence in his bishopric at York and

7 Twelfth-century illustration of the tonsuring of St Guthlac. St Guthlac, as an outward sign of his acceptance of holy orders, is losing the hair from the crown of his head. The bishop's tonsure is hidden by his mitre but the clerk standing behind him has the coronal tonsure. The abbess and the nuns have probably shaved their heads as a symbol of throwing off earthly vanity but their heads are here, as always, covered by a veil. Guthlac and the clerk wear a long tunic with some form of drapery which is not easily identified, but the bishop is vested in alb and chasuble, with one end of the stole visible (this is not the pallium, the vestment of the archbishop, which is generally decorated with crosses and worn over the chasuble).

despite backing from the Pope suffered exile and imprisonment during his career.

St Cuthbert, who went into the monastery at Old Melrose at about the time St Wilfred was leaving Lindisfarne, received the Celtic tonsure. He went with a party of monks to Ripon where, coming under the influence of St Wilfred, they changed their tonsures to the Roman tradition. In 661 he was made Prior of Old Melrose and in 664 Abbot of Lindisfarne.

There is no reason to believe that Celtic monks changed their tonsure when they accepted the Roman date for Easter, and indeed, it must be noted that when St Theodore was sent by the Pope expressly to guide, organize and administrate the Church in England according to the laws of Rome, he had to wait four months while his hair grew out of the Eastern tonsure (the bald head attributed to St Paul) so that he could arrive in a proper coronal tonsure.[5] However, he made it perfectly clear in his Penitential, 'Those who are ordained by Scotch or British Bishops, and do not conform to the Catholic practice about Easter and the tonsure, are not deemed to be in communion with the church, and should be confirmed by a fresh imposition of hands by a Catholic Bishop'. In the Great National Council held in 705 which St Aldhelm tells us was attended by an innumerable crowd of priests from nearly every part of Britain, there were still certain priests and clerics who obstinately refused the tonsure of St Peter, and Adamnan, Abbot of Iona was expelled by his monks who could not tolerate his acceptance of the Roman tonsure.[6]

Monasteries were in a confused state at this time, although all could be considered as coming under the general rule of St Benedict. The habit was generally of plain wool. When St Wilfred first went to Lindisfarne he was dressed in coarse woollen stuff, girdled by a rope and barefoot.[7] Bede wore the same dress night and day – a long tunic of coarse woollen stuff, fastened by a girdle. Early monasticism in the East, founded by St Anthony and St Basil, adopted black or dark-brown woollen habits with cowls, and a girdle of leather or cord. In illuminations of Anglo-Saxon manuscripts of the ninth and tenth centuries the habits of Saxon monks are represented in different colours – white, black, browns and greys. This does not mean that they used dyes; the custom at Lindisfarne was that 'none should wear varied or costly colours in their garments but only use the natural colour of the wool.' The Celtic Church encouraged children and adolescents to join monasteries and with the emphasis on teaching and missionary work and the unavoidable contact with the outside world, monks and nuns tended to be tempted by lay dress. It is easier to find detailed references to what was worn which should not have been, than descriptions of what should have been worn but apparently was not. St Cuthbert, the Venerable Bede and many others wrote and complained about this laxity in dress and a typical illustration of the problem is from a letter written by Aldhelm to Hildalid, abbess, and her community at Barking:

Really I am ashamed to tell of the bold and shameless pride, the stupid and arrogant display, seen nowadays among both women and men. Not only monks and nuns living under monastic discipline in community, but even ordained clergy, subject to episcopal command, are found breaking the canons of the church and the precepts of the regular life, that they may deck their carnal bodies here, there and everywhere, with forbidden ornaments and trappings. Satin underclothing, forsooth, blue and violet, scarlet tunics and hoods, sleeves with silk stripes, shoes edged with red fur, hair carefully arrayed on forehead and temples with the curling iron – this is the modern habit. Dark veils yield to headdresses, white and coloured, sewn with long ribbons and hanging to the ground; fingernails are sharpened like the talons of hawks or owls seeking their prey.[8]

It should be noted that this very long letter, which was treasured and preserved by the nuns of Barking to edify future generations of nuns, was written in a difficult and elaborate Latin and indicates the respect in which the women of the cloister were held in Anglo-Saxon Britain – for their education if not, perhaps, for their fashions.

In the absence of direct written or illustrated material from the sixth, seventh and eighth centuries it is not possible to analyse monastic habits in detail but we know from evidence in later centuries that the basic woollen gown, girded at the waist and with a hood either attached to the cape or the gown itself must have continued with only a few modifications throughout this period. Cloaks made of skins and furs are not often mentioned or illustrated, but with the Spartan lifestyle which existed in the monasteries it would not be surprising if these were found in most monastic orders. It has already been mentioned that the uniform dress of the monk under Pachomius (290–345) included a mantle of goatskin, and that St Antony had a sheepskin tunic. When St Boniface wrote to Pope Zacharias in 742 he sent gifts to accompany the letter including a 'stout shaggy cloak'.[9] These would have been purely practical garments and as a general rule no decoration was applied to the dress of monks or nuns, although, as ever, there are exceptions.

Church Vestments

Vestments of the clergy, on the other hand, were gradually becoming more elaborate and costly and acquiring more mystical associations and sacred connotations. Despite a great tradition of learning and scholarship in the seventh and eighth centuries and later, there was no apparent interest in Classical Greece and Rome or in the society in which the early Church grew up. The vestments were accepted as sacred objects inherited from past generations and not surprisingly the general assumption was that they had developed from the robes of the Levitical priests of the Old Testament. As rules and regulations were made the vestments themselves became more sacred and symbolical. Occasionally they were revered as relics of the saints and given mystical qualities.

From the early days the Church was endowed: Ethelburt gave Augustine a church and house in Canterbury, and land outside the city for a site for his monastery, and estates at Reculver and elsewhere for maintenance; Oswald gave Aiden the Isle of Lindisfarne; Ethelwalch gave Wilfred 87 hides at Selsey; Cynegils, on his baptism, gave Birinus lands around Winchester, and his son Coinwalch endowed the church there with three manors. It would appear that with these gifts of land there would also be donations to enable the church to be furnished, and thus provide vestments for the clergy. Certainly gifts of vestments were often made to or by the Pope and his bishops when they sent letters. By 1009 the moneys acquired from fines for sins against God were to be spent according to the discretion of the bishop

on the relief of the poor, the repair of the churches and ecclesiastical vestments (amongst other things) but never on any worldly vanities; so it follows that even though vestments were becoming elaborate they were not considered 'worldly vanities'. The 4th Council of Toledo, held in 633, states in canon 28:

If a bishop, presbyter or deacon, be unjustly disposed, and in a subsequent synod be found innocent he cannot be what he had previously been, unless he receive again the rank he had lost, from the hand of a bishop, before an altar. If he has been a bishop he must receive orarium, ring and staff, if a presbyter orarium and planeta, if a deacon orarium and alb, if a subdeacon patten and chalice, and so the other minor orders are to receive, with a view to their restoration, what at the time of ordination they originally received.[10]

The Stole and Maniple

The orarium or stole was common to all ranks of clergy and in this council that of the deacon is described as being still fairly close to its original form. Canon 60 explains that under no circumstances could anyone wear two oraria: 'The deacon therefore, must wear one orarium, as befits his office, and that on the left shoulder. But the right side should remain free, so that he may hasten to and fro in duties of sacerdotal services. . . . He should wear but one, and that plain not decked out with any colours, nor with gold.'

From this we can infer that the stole of the deacon still retained a hint of its original function which was as a towel or napkin, plain and carried on the left shoulder, leaving the right arm free; and also that the stoles of bishops and priests had already begun to be embroidered – decked out with colours and with gold.[11]

The stole is now undoubtedly a Mass vestment and had been ordained as such since the 2nd Council of Bracara, 572, when it was prescribed that no priest should celebrate Mass without an orarium. Originally a strip of cloth to denote rank or merely an ornament to cover the neck of the priest left bare by the large neck openings of the tunic and paenula, it took on a very special significance during this period. In the 4th Council of Braga in 675 the manner of wearing the stole was prescribed, and the style of the stole when worn with the alb has remained constant to this day. The vestment was to be passed round the neck over each shoulder, crossed in front and secured thus under the girdle of the alb.[12]

A venerated priest or bishop would be buried in his vestments, including the stole and maniple. The body of St Birinius was found vested in a red chasuble and two stoles, with a metal cross and a chalice.[13] A particularly famous stole is that found on the body of St Cuthbert with the corresponding maniple, both of which are preserved in Durham Cathedral. The wife of Edward the Elder (901–25), Queen Aelfleda, ordered the making of the stole and maniple, the earliest extant examples of English embroidery. At one end of each vestment is an embroidered panel 'AELFLAED FIERI PRECEPIT' and 'PIO EPISCOPO FRIÐESTANO' meaning 'Aelflaed commanded the vestments to be made for the pious bishop Fridestan'; as the queen died before 916 and Fridestan was consecrated Bishop in 909 we have a clear indication of when they were made.

King Athelstan visited the shrine of St Cuthbert at Chester-le-Street two years after the death of Fridestan in 931, and presented two chasubles, one alb, one stole with a maniple, one girdle (*cingulum*), three altar cloths, chalice etc., and two bracelets of gold. As items answering to this description have been found in the tomb, it can be assumed that this is when and how they came to be placed there.

These vestments have been dealt with fully in other publications,[14] and with no comparative material on which to draw, definitive judgements must be avoided; however they are too important to be passed without some consideration. The next chapter, dealing with the great period of Opus Anglicanum, covers the flowering of the art of embroidery in England; here we see an early manifestation of that skill. The vestments also represent one of the signs of the full and direct impact of the Carolingian Renaissance on English art.

In 820 Amalarius, sometime Bishop of Trier, maintained in *De Ecclesiasticis Officiis* that the stole symbolized the 'light yoke of Christ', and the maniple 'the pure and pious thoughts wherewith we wipe away the disorders of the mind which arise from the body.' Bishop Fridestan's stole is strangely embroidered, not with saints or martyrs but with prophets from the Old Testament, which, as Christopher Hohler points out, is wildly inappropriate as they are rather symbols of the heavy yoke of the law.[15] On the end panels of the stole are the two half figures of St James and St Thomas (again an unlikely subject as 'Doubting Thomas' was never a popular saint). On the maniple are Popes Gregory and Sixtus with their deacons Laurence and Petrus and on the end panels are John the Baptist and John the Evangelist. The Popes and deacons are shown in Mass vestments without additional ornament. With the possible exception of St Laurence, all wear the stole over the dalmatic and St Peter the deacon is wearing his stole in the correct manner, over the left shoulder and under the right arm. Interestingly, although in accordance with the older usage Bishop Fridestan's stole and maniple are of a uniform width throughout their length, those worn by the ecclesiastics shown on the maniple have the broad ends which we generally associate with the heavily embroidered vestments after 1000. The maniples are carried by the figures, not fixed to the wrist, and in two cases they are carried in the right hand. This we can attribute to artistic licence for the sake of symmetry, as St Gregory has to bless with the wrong hand because he is holding the maniple in his right hand. (The fixing of the maniple to the wrist only becomes the rule in the eleventh century and in the Bayeux Tapestry, Archbishop Odo still carries his maniple.)

Although these vestments are a unique relic of this period it it known that it was not unusual to present vestments to tombs and that it was normal practice from very early times to bury kings in

8 St Dunstan, from a twelfth-century copy of a ninth-century commentary on the Rule of St Benedict. St Dunstan wears the white alb, undecorated, which falls to the feet and is narrow at the wrists. His amice has the stiffened apparel which gives it a collar-like appearance at the neck. Above these he wears the dalmatic with wide sleeves which is decorated by an embroidered band at the hem. The split at the side which is a feature of the dalmatic is just indicated at the sides. The chasuble is loose and flowing with a small all-over pattern and an embroidered band around the edge. The pallium is here a formal narrow band which encircles the upper arm and hangs down pendant from the centre front. Small crosses are interspersed with another cruciform pattern. The mitre with a broad orphrey has two lappets or infulae, which end in fringes.

their robes and ecclesiastics in their vestments. We also have evidence that the skill of embroidery was practised by men and women for both the Church and the king. William of Malmesbury tells us that Edith, the queen of Edward the Confessor, herself embroidered the rich robes worn by the king at festivals, and Archbishop Dunstan, for example, himself a skilled craftsman as well as a great reforming influence on monastic life in the tenth century, is known to have designed for embroideries.[16] Secular robes were given to the Church to be made into vestments. It was not unusual for kings and persons of rank to present their coronation robes or mantles for this purpose. A mantle, presented to the monks of Ely by King Edgar (956–78) was transformed into a cope, and this same king presented his coronation robe to the abbey of Glastonbury, to form a decoration for the altar. The coronation mantle presented by Witlaf, King of Mercia, in the year 833 to the monastery of Croyland was probably used in the same manner, and this monastery also owned two precious vestments given by King Harold. Matilda, queen of William the Conqueror, made a will in the year of her death, 1083, (now in the Bibliothèque Nationale, Paris): 'I give to the abbey of the Holy Trinity [at Caen, founded by herself] my tunic worked at Winchester by Alderet's wife and the mantle embroidered with gold, which is in my chamber, to make a cope. Of my two golden girdles, I give that which is ornamented with emblems for the purpose of suspending the lamp before the great altar . . .'.[17]

The Chasuble

When the tomb of St Cuthbert was first opened in 698 (eleven years after the saint had died) the chasuble was taken from the body to show to the bishop as proof of the freshness and lack of corruption that had been found. The bishop kissed it, ordered it to be kept as a relic and a new chasuble to be provided for the body. The original was kept in an ivory casket and many miracles were attributed to it. A legend about a miracle, which grew up after St Aldhelm's death, will serve to emphasize the special reverence in which some vestments were already held. One morning at the end of his Mass in the Lateran, St Aldhelm was so rapt in contemplation that in taking off his chasuble he let it fall behind him, as his server was usually there to receive it. This time, however, the server was not there. But the Lord, records William of Malmesbury, 'who never slumbers nor wanders in thought,' was at hand to protect the sacred vestment. He sent through the window a sunbeam, on which the chasuble rested until it could be reverently borne away. When St Aldhelm was in Rome at the end of the seventh century, the chasuble he wore at Mass was said to be his own and to have been preserved for centuries afterwards at Malmesbury. It was made of deep red silk, figured in black with designs of peacocks 'evidently of foreign and probably Eastern workmanship.'[18] In 735 St Boniface sent to Pecthelm, once a monk and deacon under Aldhelm and a friend of Bede, now the first Bishop of Whithorn, a chasuble embroidered with a design in white, and a towel to dry the feet of priests after the ceremonial washing on Maundy Thursday.[19]

The chasuble had developed from the paenula, the travelling cloak and also the planeta, the heavily ornamented cloak which was always regarded as rather costly. In this transitional period, for which there is such an unfortunate dearth of visual evidence, there appear to have been two kinds of chasuble in use, the Eucharistic and the processional. The distinction was utilitarian rather than ritualistic and consisted mainly of a hood sewn on to the back of the latter. The processional chasuble gave way to the cope; and a hooded chasuble does not appear to be extant in representations of a date later than the tenth century. The cut of the vestment varies as does the decoration on it, probably as a result of financial expedience. Although the chasuble began as a plain garment with embroidered panels sewn on, it was already becoming more elaborate, as has been seen, and all variations on cut were essentially dependent on the seamstress, the embroideress or the person who had to pay for it. Liturgical writers of the time had their own interpretations. Rabanus Maurus, writing in about 820, submits that 'the chasuble surmounts and safeguards all the other vestments; hence the chasuble signifies love, which surmounts all the other virtues, and safeguards and illumines their beauty with its protection.' From this it can be seen that at no time, even in the Dark Ages, did the chasuble cease to be the uppermost garment. Amalarius of Metz (820) asserts that as the chasuble is common to all clerics, so it 'ought to set forth the works which are common to all: fasting, thirsting, watching, poverty, reading, singing, praying and the rest'. Pope Innocent III (1198–1216) holds it to signify the virtue of Apostolic succession 'for this is the Vestment of Aaron, to the skirt of which the oil ran down; but it ran down from his head to his beard and from his beard to his skirt. Forasmuch as we all receive of this Spirit, first the apostles afterwards the rest ...'. Thus the chasuble is supposed to represent the historical link with the Old Testament.

The Alb

The long white alb (as the name was now settled) continued to be worn with little change. It was still a pure white garment; Rabanus Maurus believes it to inculcate purity of life. Amalarius of Metz, contrasting Jerome's description of the tight-fitting Jewish tunic with the flowing alb of his own day, considers that it denotes the liberty of the New Testament as contrasted with the servitude of the Old Testament. Its ample cut contracted until the vestment fitted with comparative tightness to the body and arms by the ninth century. Although the embroidered panels known as apparels did not come in until a later date, some decoration was added in the form of calliculae, metal or embroidered ornaments. Letters, monograms or letter-like signs – OOOOOO or SSSSSS for example, were used without any apparent significance.

The Cassock

The cassock became popular on the Continent before it reached England; although adopted by the Council of Braga in 572, it was probably in 705 that Wilfred brought with him from Rome a letter from the Pope, bidding the English clergy to change their 'full gathered lay habit' for the long straight cassock worn by the Roman priests, as the English clerics in Rome had lately done.[20] (He also brought with him costly purple vestments for his priests and altars.)

The Amice

The amice appeared for the first time in the ninth or tenth century. St Cuthbert was wearing one when his body was buried, but the figures on his maniple are not. The probable reason for this is the small scale of the embroideries, and, as the amice until it acquired its apparel in the twelfth century was a very humble garment, it is often not represented. Basically a square of white linen worn around the neck, it developed into a hood to protect the expensive vestments from grease and hair oil. The amice is put on first, then all the other vestments are put on over the head, and when everything is in place the amice is pulled down where it settles round the neck in folds.

The Dalmatic

The dalmatic, which had always been decorated in some form, continued to be ornate, and was sometimes grander than the chasuble. Its main distinguishing features were the splits up the sides and the fringe decoration. The bishop would wear a dalmatic that was fringed all around the sleeves, the hem and the slits. The dalmatic of the deacon was only fringed on the left sleeve and the left side slit for reasons of convenience when serving at the altar, the fringe being both heavy and a fire risk. We are informed by medieval writers on vestments that as the left side typifies this present life and the right that which is to come, so the fringes on the left indicate those cares through which we must pass in this world, while their absence on the right symbolizes freedom from care in the world to come. Why the bishop was not regarded as exempt from care in the future world is not explained.[21]

The dalmatic and tunicle in which St Cuthbert was buried were described by Reginald of Durham. They were made of costly purple stuff tinged with red and ornamented on the loom. The dalmatic 'crackled in the fingers of those who handled it on account of the solidarity of the work and the stiffness of the thread. In it were interwoven figures as well as of birds and of small animals, extremely minute in their workmanship and subdivision.' The robe was 'variegated with frequent dashes of citron colour, as it were in drops. The edges were embroidered in thread-of-gold', and a similar border was found on the cuff of each sleeve, with a broader one around the neck covering both shoulders as well as hanging in front.[22]

Footwear

Clergy were still wearing sandals, although in the northern climate shoes were obviously more popular. Many monastic orders retained the original simple sandals as part of the ascetic life they had chosen to lead. As vestments became more elaborate, the tendency was to decorate the footwear to match and the fashion of fenestrated shoes (with decorative holes cut in the uppers to reveal the foot), became irresistible. Rabanus Maurus first mentions sandals (and the amice), not previously listed as clerical attire, in 820 and he likens the open or fenestrated variety, in a mystical sense, to the partly revealed gospel.[23] Stockings are not mentioned until the twelfth century when they are referred to by Ivo of Chartres and Honorius of Autun.

Headwear

The two popes embroidered on Fridestan's maniple are not wearing mitres. The mitre is not really considered a Eucharistic vestment until the eleventh century, although St Cuthbert was buried wearing one. By the eighth century the Pope, being normally an elderly man whose head needed protection from the cold, had adopted for outdoor processions and other purposes the head-gear of respectable men of the period, which was a linen conical hat or skull-cap. The *Liber Pontificalis* states that Pope Constantine I (708–15) wore this kind of cap when making his solemn entrance into Jerusalem, but the word 'mitre' does not occur until the end of the ninth century. It is in the eleventh century that the first reliable statement occurs (and the word is not common in England until well into the twelfth century). When

Eberhard, Archbishop of Treves (Trier) was in Rome in 1049, Pope Leo IX (1048–54) placed on his head, in St Peter's on Passion Sunday, the Roman mitre. The Pope's words in the charter are: 'We adorn your head with a Roman Mitre, which both you and your successors will always use in the ecclesiastical office after the Roman manner, in order to remind you that you are a disciple of the Roman See'.[24]

Roman Vestments

When Charlemagne was crowned Emperor by the Pope in Rome in 800 he adopted many Roman customs and introduced the Roman Rite into the Gallican Church. Roman vestments replaced unorthodox Gallican clothing. Writers, especially those in the northern provinces, not only composed lists of vestments for the first time, but also endowed each of them with mystical meanings. Rabanus Maurus writing in 820, is an especially useful source.[25] This reforming influence spread into England but the Great Danish Invasion (867–70) which virtually extinguished monastic life north of the Humber took its toll. Monastic life had been easily corrupted with inherited orders – a convent passing from a woman to her daughter for example – and the remaining monasteries in Wessex and south Mercia had either become extinct during the wars or degenerated into houses where any number of priests and monks lived together without any common rule.

St Dunstan, Abbot of Glastonbury and Archbishop of Canterbury, was an important reformer, and while he was archbishop the canons of Edgar (AD 959–75) ruled that everyone should come to the synod yearly, attended by his clerk and an orderly man as his servant; and that he bring his books and vestments (so that it might be seen that they were complete and in good order).[26]

CHAPTER THREE

The Growth of Monasticism and the Beginnings of Opus Anglicanum 1066–1250

Monastic Dress

THE STUDY OF monastic dress as an identifying uniform must start with the rule of St Benedict, which sets down general precepts which were followed, more or less, by all the orders created in the eleventh and twelfth centuries. The Benedictines had become known as the 'nigri monachi' or 'black monks' by the eleventh century because they wore black, but the original habit, being made of undyed wool, was either white or grey, and over this was worn a black gown and a black hood or cowl. When working or travelling they would don a black scapular and so they gave the appearance of being black monks. The principal elements of the monastic costume are a simple frock or habit, girded with a leather strap; a scapular, a long strip of cloth with a hole for the head, which fell front and back, and was not caught in place by the belt or girdle; a cowl or hood (also called a *caputium*) and a mantle or cloak, which is also generally provided with a hood. This outfit would be worn alike by novice, monk and abbot; the harsh class distinction of the outside world was softened by the fusion within the cloister where princes became monks and monks such as Dunstan (924–88) and Anselm (1033–1109) became archbishops with enormous political power. Some abbots were allowed by special privilege to use the mitre, pastoral staff (*cambucca*) and other parts of episcopal costume, but ordinarily their dress exactly resembled that of the other brethren.

The period of preparation, the novitiate, was made in lay clothes; and the habit and the tonsure were taken after the probation period (in 817 the Council of Aix-la-Chapelle insisted 'Nor let the novice be tonsured, nor change his former ves-

ture, until he promises obedience').[1] In the early centuries lay fashions did not differ much from monastic dress but by the eleventh century at Cluny it was decided to put the novice in a habit at the beginning of the year's novitiate; this was adopted by the Cistercians and also spread among nuns.

St Benedict's rule 'of the clothes and shoes of the brethren'[2] suggests that monks should be clothed variously according to differences of latitude and conditions of climate. It starts not with the principle of poverty but with a precept of discretion, precluding excess, fancifulness or confusion. St Benedict himself asked and received from St Romanus a special habit: 'He asked for the habit of a Holy Life'.[3] His own rule is simple: 'We think, however, that in temperate climates a cowl and a tunic should suffice for each monk: the cowl to be of thick stuff in winter, but in summer something worn and thin: likewise a scapular for work, and shoes and stockings to cover their feet.' The cowl here means more than just the hood; it is a garment fitted with a hood (*vestis cucullata*) and could be one of many garments – the casula, paenula, mantle or cloak. All of these would have to be taken off and the scapular put on when the hands and arms needed to be free for work. (One of the most important features of the rule of St Benedict was that after the three vows of poverty, chastity and obedience, he introduced the idea of seven hours of manual labour a day, not only for self-support but as a duty to God and Man.) In the ninth to twelfth centuries the casula was slit along the sides and the two portions fastened together at intervals by bands or straps called 'St Benedict's stitches', although from the tenth century there were also cowls with sleeves.

THE HOOD

The hood itself, the simplest and most efficient way of keeping the head warm, underwent a series of transformations in different orders, presumably as it became part of the identifying uniform of the monk. Under the influence of Cistercian and Franciscan custom it grew long and tapering; in some places it became very full, falling over the shoulders like a veil or cape.

THE SCAPULAR

The scapular was also sometimes provided with a hood; it seems certain that originally it was protection for the head and shoulders, and became the working dress of monks because it left the arms free and protected the tunic underneath. The sides were left open and sometimes the two parts were secured together by strips of fabric. There is no mention of a garment of this name before St Benedict and it has always been a distinctive feature of monastic dress (although not adopted by the Cluniacs in the eleventh century).

THE TUNIC

The tunic (*colobium*) was made of wool, coarse and common rather than refined and expensive, and the more fervent religiouses such as anchorites wore a tunic made of goat's or camel's hair. Monks would wear the tunic all day and also sleep in it, still with the belt or girdle. 'Let them sleep clothed, and girded with belts or cords – but not with knives at their sides, lest perchance they wound themselves in their sleep – and thus be always ready, so that when the signal is given they rise without delay, and hasten each to forestall the other in going to the work of God, yet with all gravity and modesty.'[4]

The bracile was the belt or girdle used during the day, large enough to serve as a receptacle, instead of pockets. From it hung the knife (*cultellus*) which was used in the refectory and elsewhere; in it was kept the handkerchief (*mappula*).

FOOTWEAR

St Benedict also specifies 'pedules et caligas' which are difficult to identify: *pedules* could mean stockings, socks or light indoor footwear and *caligae* were probably sandals such as soldiers wore. St Gregory the Great speaks of 'caligae clavatae' (nailed boots) which were worn during work in the monasteries of St Equitius. In footwear, as in all other things, the most important thing was to be practical and unostentatious.

COLOUR, FABRIC AND POSSESSION OF CLOTHES

The rule of St Benedict states 'Of all things and their colour or coarseness let not the monks complain, but let them be such as can be got in the region where they live, or can be bought most cheaply. Let the abbot be careful about their size, that these garments be not short for those who wear them, that they fit well.'

There is no decision made about colour in the rule of St Benedict, but an austere and inconspicuous colour was required and the cloth was generally undyed, resulting in greys, creams and browns. Black became the prevailing colour of the Benedictines which was adopted by the Cluniacs, while the Cistercians preferred white.

When they receive new clothes let them always give back the old ones at once, to be put by in the clothes-room for the poor. For it is sufficient for a monk to have two tunics and two cowls, as well for nightwear as for convenience of washing. Anything beyond this is superfluous and ought to be cut off. In the same way let them give up their stockings, and whatever else is worn out, when they receive new ones.

Monks did their own washing and took care of their clothes, although all their garments came from the common store. 'And in order that this vice of private ownership may be cut off by the roots let the abbot supply all things that are necessary: this is cowl, tunic, stockings, shoes, girdle, knife, style, needle, handkerchief and tablets.'[5] Special clothes were issued for monks when travelling abroad or when receiving important visitors to the monastery. 'Let their cowls and tunics also be a little better than those they usually wear; they must receive these from the clothes-room when setting out on their journey, and restore them on their return.' This was regarded as an act of consideration towards visitors and the outside world and while they were to avoid the defect of 'excessive care and nicety' they had also to dress so as 'not [to] attract notice by affected negligence.'

9 Six Bishops, *c.* 1140–60, from the Psalter of Henry of Blois. The three bishops on the right wear the very early form of mitre which is a decorated band around the head ending in two lappets and containing a soft cap which forms two peaks either side of the head. They wear no amice (or it is invisible under the neckline of the chasuble) and the alb sleeve can only be seen at the wrists of the figure on the right. The chasuble, which is shorter in the front, is in all three cases made of plain fabric with an orphrey round the neck, down the centre front and forming a border. The figure on the right has crosses on the neck and front orphrey but this does not mean that he is wearing a pallium. The dalmatics are all of the same cut, more formal and less flowing than the chasuble and tunicle with the slits at the sides having been cut in a notched shape and outlined in the border orphrey. The stole ends hang pendant below the dalmatic and are unadorned except for a fringe. The lowest garment is probably the alb although it is unusual for this vestment to have a border design. However, the habits of the bishops on the left have decorated borders, which is also unusual and technically wrong and so this could be artistic licence or a contemporary erroneous fashion.

The three figures on the left are monks and at least two of them are bishops as they carry the crozier, a sign of their office. 'Mitred abbots' could adopt the full set of Mass vestments but some preferred to retain their monastic habits. The hood is falling back from their heads to reveal their tonsures, and they are clean shaven whereas the secular bishops have the fashionable beards. The long hanging sleeves of this group are not easy to understand: the second figure has one visible long sleeve, the right one, and the third figure has an extra long left sleeve. The decorated borders on the habits and hoods are not allowed by the rules of St Benedict, and it is possible that this is an example of an individual and temporary change in monastic fashion.

Breeches or drawers are rarely mentioned except in the following instance: 'Let those who are sent on a journey receive drawers [femoralia] from the clothes room, and on their return restore them washed'. The Cluniacs adopted the use of drawers but the Cistercians did not. Peter the Venerable had to defend the practice[6] and Thomas Becket wore hair drawers in violation of the Cistercian rule.[7]

THE CLUNIACS

In the tenth and eleventh centuries, as their wealth and power increased, so the Benedictine monasteries fell into disrepute and there was a series of endeavours to revive the primitive discipline and return to the original intention of monastic life. Reform consisted of a series of new orders, all of whom took a modified version of the Benedictine rule. The Cluniac was the first of these orders, so called because it was founded in Cluny in Burgundy in the tenth century. The first Cluniac order introduced into England was established at Lewes in Sussex in 1077 but never became popular in Britain. They adopted the Benedictine dress and some aspects of harsh rigour, such as rising at midnight for the night office. They were mocked by a contemporary satirist, Nigel (a Benedictine monk of Christ Church, Canterbury) for their generosity of diet and for the luxury of their fur-lined clothes.[8] It was also Cluniac practice that all monks should wear copes on the greatest feasts (and they were numerous – the Assumption, SS Peter and Paul, All Saints, etc.).

THE CISTERCIANS

The Cistercians were a reformed order of the Cluniacs and were very much more austere, abstaining from a flesh diet, wearing only white woollen clothing and insisting on hard work. The Chronicler Gerald de Barri (1146–1223), said, 'they seem to bring back to one's eyes the primitive life and ancient discipline of the monastic religion, its poverty, its parsimony in food, the roughness and meanness of its dress, its abstinence and austerities.' The order spread rapidly – they were founded in 1098 and first came to England in 1122. They set up their abbeys in remote places in the fens and wolds and became great sheep farmers, making England famous for fine wool.

William of Malmesbury, writing in the early twelfth century of the foundation and regulations of the Cistercians says, 'they wear nothing made with furs or linen, not even that finely spun linen which we call staminium [shirt]; neither breeches, unless when sent on a journey which at their return they wash and restore. They have two tunics with cowls but no additional garments in winter, though if they see fit, in summer they may lighten their garb. They sleep clad and girded . . .'.[10] This indicates how close they were to St Benedict's rule in everything but the colour of their clothes.

Thomas Becket resided at a Cistercian abbey at Pontigny during his exile (1165–70), and donned the habit of 'thick and coarse woollen cloth' which the Pope had personally blessed and sent to him. Underneath his habit he took to wearing a hair shirt from his neck to his knees and it has been suggested that Becket, who was over-sensitive to cold, might have been grateful for the extra layer for warmth in the penitential life of the abbey.[11] He was still wearing the hair shirt underneath his vestments at his martyrdom in 1170. The Archbishop Robert of Merton lifted the outer garments and showed the monks that underneath his splendid robe Thomas was wearing a hair shirt as well as his monastic habit, and 'all ran up to see him in haircloth whom they had seen as Chancellor in purple and byssus.'[12]

CONVENT DRESS

The Benedictines, Cluniacs and Cistercians all had female houses of the same order who adapted a feminine version of the dress, with a wimple and veil to cover the head completely. So a Benedictine nun would wear a white undertunic, a black gown and a black veil with a white wimple around face and neck, and the Cluniac nun wore the same; the Cistercians were dressed entirely in white and were called 'the white ladies of the Cistercians'. The Carthusians, the most severe of all the reformed Benedictine orders, were alone in not having a house for women.

THE CARTHUSIANS

The Carthusians (an order founded in 1086 by St Bruno at the Grand Chartreuse near Grenoble) wore a white habit with a leather girdle and a great cowl. Either the head was entirely shaved or just a narrow strip of hair was left around the head. The white scapular worn over the tunic and cowl was joined at the sides by a broad band of the same fabric about six inches wide. The austere asceticism of the order encouraged scanty clothing and coarse hair shirts.

CANONS

The orders of canons founded at this time also wore a form of monastic dress. The Praemonstratensian canons (founded in 1120 by St Norbert at Prémontré and brought to England in 1143) were known as 'white canons' because their habit was of white material with a white cincture or girdle. The order of Grandmontines founded in 1045 originally wore a rough brown tunic with scapular and hood, but later the colour of the tunic was changed to black, and the hood and the scapular were replaced by a biretta and rochet. The Gilbertines ('white monks and nuns') were an order peculiar to Great Britain. St Gilbert of Sempringham (1083–1189) founded an order of nuns based on the rule of the Cistercians. When

10 St Radegund, who established a nunnery at Poitiers in the sixth century under the rule of St Caesarius is shown in the habit of the Benedictines, the earliest established order. She wears a white veil or bindae close to her head and covers it with a black veil. Her black habit is covered by a black mantle and she holds a pastoral staff as she is an abbess.

the Cistercians refused to take on the responsibility for this, St Gilbert provided the nuns with a small body of canons, who acted as chaplains and spiritual ministers. The habit of the canons consisted of a long black tunic or cassock, with a scapular and a white cloak and hood and they wore beards; the nuns wore white.

CRUSADING ORDERS

With the Crusades other orders grew up associated with the military life, such as the Knights of St John the Hospitaller (1100) and the Knights Templar (1123). The Hospitallers dedicated to St John the Almsgiver were originally under Benedictine orders and had a simple function as guides and feeders of pilgrims; they threw this aside in 1118 to become a military force, offering allegiance only to the Pope. They wore a white cross on their tunics and took as their patron St John the Evangelist. The Knights Templar were also originally Benedictine but later became independent. They were divided into three groups: knights, often of noble birth, who wore a red cross on a white tunic; sargeants, middle class who wore a red cross on black tunics; and clerics whose functions were religious and medical rather than military.

MENDICANT OR PREACHING ORDERS

Friars were a further type of religious order again set up in an attempt to reform. The monasteries with wealth and power had become remote and exclusive and the ignorant secular clergy could not combat the strange heresies brought back from the East by the returning army of crusaders.

The Dominicans or black friars were strictly a preaching order founded in Spain by St Dominic (born 1170). They wore a white woollen habit with a black cloak and distinctive pointed hood and came over to England from France in 1221. The place name Blackfriars in London still survives as a reminder of them, but they were also called 'frates de picâ' or 'magpie brethren' because they wore black and white.

'Grey friars' was the early name for the Franciscans but the brown habit soon became predominant. The simple woollen tunic, scapular and hood and the distinctive knotted cord around the waist (from which arose the nickname cordeliers

or cordigeri) have made them possibly the easiest order to identify. They still wore grey when Matthew Paris told the following story. Henry III of England was constantly in serious financial difficulty; although he was at times generous in his gifts, they were sometimes at least suspected of being acquired from some third party. On one occasion, about the year 1252, the Franciscans received as alms from the King a two-horse load of grey woollen cloth suitable for their habits. The friars, however, at the same time heard that Henry had all but taken the material from the merchants without payment. They consequently sent back the cloth at once in the cart to the king, declaring that it was unlawful for them to receive as alms what had been taken from the poor.

The second order of Francis, the Poor Clares, was founded by Clare, a daughter of a wealthy Assisi house, during St Francis' lifetime, and they first came to England in 1224.

In the course of time the Franciscan friars split up into various sub-divisions. The brown habit was worn by the Friars Minor and the Friars Minor Capuchins. The Friars Minor Conventual wore black, the other distinctions being that they

11 Dominican Gradual, letter G. Saints from the Dominican order greeting St Peter and St Paul. The tonsured men wear a black mantle and cowl with the hood down, over a white habit. The nun in the background wears a white veil over the black veil and has a white bindae around the throat.

had shoes instead of sandals and also wore the biretta.

All friars wore sandals if they had any footwear at all. The Carmelite order (both friars and nuns) were either discalced (barefoot) or calced (with sandals). They were also known as the 'white friars' because of the white mantle which was worn over their brown tunic.

The body known as the canons regular of St Augustine or black canons were founded in the mid-eleventh century but became the fourth mendicant order in 1256. They are also known as Austin canons and Austin friars and were divided into a number of groups such as the Williamites; Hermits of the Holy Trinity; Bonites; and Brittianians. Their habit was black with large sleeves, a black leather girdle, and a long pointed cowl that reached to the waist. Certain peculiarities of their costume led to their being confused with the Friars Minor and many disagreements resulted because of this.[14] The simplicity of monastic dress was bound to cause a certain amount of confusion between various groups and descriptions are often so general that it is difficult for the costume historian to be specific. A typical description, which in this case describes the Augustinian canons, reads: 'Their habit is neither splendid nor abject, so they avoid both pride and the affectation of holiness. They do not need a great variety of gear, and they are content with a moderate expenditure.'[15]

The order of Servites, or the Servants of Mary, were the fifth of the mendicant orders, founded by a group of young men from wealthy Florentine families (originally laymen) in 1240.

The hermits, anchorites and anchoresses, were those who chose to lead a religious but solitary life and they had no habit as such, but the nature of their life meant that they wore coarse and rough clothes. The *Ancren Riwle*, a book of rules for hermits, enjoins them to 'wear no iron, nor haircloth, nor hedgehog skins'[16] and there is evidence of gifts of furs; Dame Lucy, who was enclosed in the churchyard of Bury St Edmunds, received a supertunic of bifle, and a member of the Scrope family left to an anchorite of Holy Trinity, Lincoln, twenty shillings, a tunic furred with calaber with a double hood, and a cloak furred with gris.[17]

Liturgical Dress

Despite the simplicity of the monastic dress, it was during this period that greater elaboration of ecclesiastical vestments became apparent, and monks and abbots played no small part in the development. Lanfranc, the Archbishop of Canterbury (1070–89) was a monk but was also well versed in liturgical practice and daily routine. He adorned Christ Church, Canterbury with gold and silver plate for the liturgy and vestments heavy with gold thread and embroidered with dragons and strange birds. He could match the expertise of Archbishop John of Rouen on the use of the chasuble or the vestments of the sub-deacon.[18] He could also be pragmatic and ruled in favour of copes which, although they had no intrinsic liturgical significance, gave splendour and magnificence to the great feasts that he felt appropriate in a primatial see. He presented Christ Church with several copes that survived for three centuries and were so heavily woven or embroidered with gold that it was found worthwhile, when they were worn out, to reduce them to ashes in order to recover the precious metal.[19]

When Pope Innocent IV noticed the embroidered and gold-worked orphreys of the copes worn by the English ecclesiastics at the Council of Lyons in 1246, he sent to the Cistercian abbots in England with the papal command to send him the well-worked orphreys to ornament his copes and chasubles: 'Just as if', says the chronicler, Matthew Paris, 'they could be got for nothing'.[20]

THE COPE

Copes became established during the eleventh and twelfth centuries and although they never reached any liturgical status they were used on important festive occasions by all ranks of clergy, including monks. In 970 the Concordia Regularis of English monks shows that copes only appeared rarely, and were worn by only a few: firstly, the abbot at the blessing of the candles on the feast of the purification; and secondly, at the quasi-dramatic office of the Resurrection on Easter morning, and then only for the three or four people engaged in that ceremony.[21] However, by the end of the tenth century the practice was for all the monks to wear copes on the greatest feasts at Cluny, and this spread to other orders. Abbot Faricius (1100–17) gave twenty-nine copes as against three chasubles to Abingdon,[22] and inventories show an increase in the number of copes owned by the churches, abbeys and cathedrals.

The cope came to be seen as the proper vestment for the cantor. Pope Innocent III (1198–1216) includes the cantor in his six orders of clergy (the others being bishops, priests, deacons, sub-deacons and acolytes).[23] Honorius of Autun, writing before 1125, included cantors as a particular order for the first time in *Gemma Animae*. They had assumed the cope, a rich silk variety, as special to them. 'The cope is the proper vestment of Cantors' says Honorius. 'It has a hood at the top, it reaches down to the heels, it is open in front and fringed at the bottom.'[24] Rupert of Deutz (died *c.* 1130) said that the cantors took from the sacristy precious vesture. 'We put on copes also on greater feasts, that we may praise God ... which copes are open in front, and except the necessary fastening or clasp are without any sewing ... they are also adorned with fringe below.'[25] The cope was considered a vestment proper for any member of the clergy and choir and Sicardus, Bishop of Cremona, (1185–1215) shows that although it was the special attribute of the cantor, it was not an identifying garment as it could be worn by anybody. 'Then let the cantor put on his vestment, that is the cope, which adapts itself also to every order, *so it is of no account to what order he belong!* [sic].'[26]

The canon's cope was a large flowing cope closed along the centre seam at the breast, the head having to be put through an opening. This cope was ordered to be black, according to the Sarum Rite (late twelfth century) and it was most likely to have been made of some thin woollen cloth.[27] Black was a popular colour for processional copes and travelling copes, and although usually plain they could be used for the more elaborate ecclesiastical vestments. In the inventory of Christ Church, Canterbury of 1315–16 there are two copes from Lanfranc (died 1089) which were black and adorned with gold and gems and each had around the edge 51 silver-gilt bells; the morse of one was set with a great topaz and four enamels.[28] From this inventory we find at least four more large copes from the period. There are two more from Lanfranc, embroidered with gold

and with gold 'tassels'. There is also a 'profession' cope of red cloth diapered, with round black 'tassels' embroidered, probably the gift of Thomas of Bayeux who held the see of York from 1070 to 1100.

The 'profession' copes were those given to the church of Canterbury by every suffragan bishop in the southern diocese at his profession of canonical obedience. Abbots also gave copes but there are only five in the list, all from abbots within the diocese of Canterbury.[29] The other cope in the 1315 list which belongs to this section is that of Ralph, Bishop of Hereford (1234–9) – of red samite with 'tassels' and enamels in the middle.

'Tassels' were probably ornamental plates or buttons sewn on to the orphrey, to which were attached the bands or morses that held the cope together in front. They were not morses, as one cope 'cum tassellis aureis' had also a morse of ivory, and two other morses of gems. They could not have been hoods as they are always mentioned in the plural. They are also found on chasubles, dalmatics, and tunicles. St Paul's inventory of 1245 mentions tassels on copes and chasubles but not on dalmatics and tunicles, and from descriptions it is clear that the word does not mean the pendant tassels made of silk thread found on later dalmatics and tunicles, which hung at the end of the laces that drew together the neck opening and which are recognizable to the twentieth-century reader as tassels.

Before we leave the cope two other features must be noted. The hood was common to all people, but the clergy and the monks had the special feature of the hood being sewn on to the garment. Chaucer guessed that a man was 'some chanoune' (that is to say, a religious) because his hood was sewn to the gown.[30] All copes had hoods and after they ceased to be practical they were not discarded but retained in the form of a vestigial flap, an ornament.

The *cappa clausa* (closed cape) came in two forms and was ordained as regular wear of the clergy. The constitutions of the provincial synod held by Stephen Langton in 1222 re-affirmed this. The first form was an all-round cape reaching to the ankles with a slit in the front for the hands to come through, although it was generally worn

12 Cardinal. The figure is wearing a *cappa clausa* with slits at the sides for the arms to come through. The garment is lined with white fur as is the cowl with the hood, which covers the breast and shoulders. He wears a skull cap, covering a tonsure.

lifted over the arms. The second form had two slits at either side for the arms, and this was the origin of the chimere.

THE MITRE

By the end of the eleventh century the mitre was worn by all western bishops and granted to many abbots. At first it was only a simple white cap with lappets or infulae, and white was maintained as the ground colour until the nineteenth century with a few exceptions. Leoffin, an abbot of Ely who lived at the end of the tenth century, gave to his church 'a red mitre of wonderful workmanship, which is broidered underside and on the top with flowers, continued on the back, liked as something stoned with gems and gold.'[31] The mitre, with the gloves, was adopted as part of the processional insignia of the bishops and was a sign

of temporal power rather than assuming any liturgical significance. Ivo of Chartres, who died in 1115, mentions the 'mitre' of the Levitical priest, but is silent as to any similar ornament among the Christian vestments.[32] Honorius of Autun (writing *c.* 1122–5) includes the mitre among the seven vestments of the bishops,[33] and St Bruno, Bishop of Segni (died 1123) says 'the mitre, because it is of linen, signifies purity and chastity'.[34] Innocent III (1198–1216) mentions its two horns, two infulae and a golden band or orphrey enriching it.

At the same time, the papal tiara was coming into existence; it is mentioned by Bruno of Segni (1108), and Pope Innocent III (1198–1216) wore it. Like the mitre it would appear to have been looked on as a symbol of temporal and regal sway, not of spiritual and priestly power. Boniface VIII (1294–1303) added the second crown and Urban V (1362–70) completed its decoration with the final coronal.[35] Archbishop Stigand is not wearing a mitre when he is depicted standing next to the enthroned Harold in the Bayeux Tapestry, but this is not necessarily because he did not have one, but rather that he would not have worn one in those circumstances. The mitre, then as now, would be worn with the processional cope on solemn occasions. The lappets hanging from the back of the mitre are often elaborately embroidered and decorated and are called infulae. Confusingly the word 'infula' first occurs in the twelfth century, meaning chasuble.[36]

THE CHASUBLE

The chasuble still came in many forms and was still proper to the lower orders on occasion. The deacon and the sub-deacon wore a chasuble during the penitential season of Lent and on the Ember days. The deacon rolled his up over his shoulder (the broad stole) and the sub-deacon took it off at a particular time. By the end of the thirteenth century the practice had fallen into disuse and the chasuble was reserved for priests and bishops. Vestments became more elaborate in their decoration, although they were usually plain wool or silk with added bands of woven or embroidered textiles called orphreys. From the old inventories we can see that they were some-

1

2

3

4

5

6

7

8

13 Eight bishops' seals:

1 Geoffrey, Bishop of Durham, c. 1133
2 Alexander, Bishop of Lincoln, c. 1140–5
3 Simon, Bishop of Worcester, c. 1125
4 Roger, Bishop of Worcester, c. 1164
5 Richard, Bishop of Winchester, c. 1180–5
6 Richard, Archbishop of Canterbury, c. 1174
7 Hugh, Bishop of Durham, c. 1153
8 Richard Poore, Bishop of Durham, c. 1229

Geoffrey, Bishop of Durham, has a soft early form of mitre which is a white cap held in place with a band around the head. As the cap grew larger it formed two horns either side of the head which can be seen clearly in the seal of Alexander, Bishop of Lincoln. Richard, Archbishop of Canterbury, in the last quarter of the twelfth century, wears the last form of the mitre with the horns on the side of the head, which has become formalized. For obvious reasons horns had associations that were not compatible with the higher offices of the Church and the mitre was swung round

with horns back and front, the lappets remaining at the back. Simon, Bishop of Worcester, has a domed mitre, rare in Britain and so has the later Bishop of Worcester, Roger. The mitre developed very fast and in 1153 Hugh of Durham is shown with the first gabled mitre on a seal in England. These seals provide useful information as they are unselfconscious representations of the clothes of the bishops as they were. Geoffrey of Durham, the earliest, does not appear to have an amice and subsequently the amice becomes clearer and more distinct. All the chasubles have orphreys except those of Richard of Winchester and Richard, Archbishop of Canterbury, who wears a pallium. Most of them are wearing maniples which are always hanging from the left wrist. In these small objects there is not much scope for decoration but there is a fine dalmatic on the seal of Alexander of Lincoln, and the flower and orphrey on the chasuble of Richard of Durham are clearly decorative.

times distinguished into three parts: front – pectoral, back – dorsal, over shoulders – humerals, and they could be decorated with gems

and pearls, enamels and semi-precious stones as well as embroidery. In the 1315–16 inventory of Christ Church, Canterbury there is a large black

chasuble that formerly belonged to Archbishop Lanfranc. This chasuble, together with two others given by him and a fourth ascribed to Henry (probably Lanfranc's first prior) were noted for their great magnificence, with orphreys enriched with gems and pearls.[37] When chasubles are decorated all over it is generally by a woven pattern in the fabric and so they can still retain their full and large shapes. The chasuble found in the tomb of Archbishop Hubert Walter (died 1205) was a splendid silk, possibly of Spanish origin, with a medallion pattern and a 'pseudo Kufiq' ornamental band woven into the design at intervals. The orphreys are tablet-woven bands in the Y shape. The chasuble appears to have been semi-circular in shape – the so-called 'bell chasuble'.[38] D. Rock identifies a separate piece of decoration found on Anglo-Saxon chasubles and

14 French Pope, thirteenth century. This seated figure is fully vested with the 'Y' shape pallium over a full chasuble, dalmatic and alb, all undecorated. Even the apparel of the amice, the stiffened band of embroidery that gives this vestment a collar-like appearance, shows no sign of decoration. The maniple hanging down from the left wrist has a fringe, but it is otherwise plain as is the conical cap which is the early form of the papal tiara, and not the mitre. This sculpture shows the shape of the vestments, but the fact that these early pieces show plain vestments does not necessarily mean that they were undecorated. All written sources indicate that the vestments were made of richly patterned fabrics and embroidery was used extensively.

15 The Clare chasuble 1272–94. This chasuble is made of blue silk embroidered all over. Blue is always a popular colour for vestments although it is not strictly a liturgical colour, and where it is included in the colour sequence it is part of the black section. The main part of the chasuble is foliate scrolls with lions and gryphons, but this has been cut away at a later date. The broad orphrey embroidered directly on to the vestment shows four scenes; at the top the crucified Christ with Mary and the beloved disciple John, a scene that comes to be favoured for the orphrey on the chasuble; below that is the Virgin and Child; below is St Peter on the left carrying the key to the Kingdom and with the bald pate that was the model for the coronal tonsure adopted by the Roman Church; St Paul on the right has the receding hair line which was the Greek and the Celtic tonsure, i.e. shaved back from the forehead. All the Biblical figures wear the long tunic and the pallium (the Virgin Mary wearing a palla) a tradition of dress that has continued unbroken from the earliest depictions of the second-century catacombs in Rome. The lowest scene is the martyrdom of St Thomas, who is wearing the chasuble, the amice and the maniple, and has a tonsure.

in the early Norman period. This was a heavily embroidered part round the neck and the shoulders, quite distinct from the chasuble, put on over it and called the 'flower'. As well as embroidery it could have costly jewels and precious stones or even a broad band of gold studded with gems. William the Conqueror, 'that royal robber', took from Ely Minster eight chasubles and their corresponding 'flowers'.[39]

THE DALMATIC AND TUNICLE

The dalmatic and tunicle were special to the deacon and sub-deacon and were also worn by bishops. They are listed in inventories as pairs but it does not necessarily mean they were matched in decoration or colour. The pair which formerly belonged to Lanfranc in the 1315–16 inventory of Canterbury are different in both respects. The dalmatic is dark blue (*inde*) fretted with gold, and the tunicle is black, embroidered with stars and golden beasts in circles.[40] (Liturgically black and blue were considered the same colour.) The fragment of silk which W. H. St John Hope,

16 An archbishop, from the Westminster Psalter, *c.* 1200. Here the archbishop is wearing full pontificals. His status can be identified by the cross staff he is carrying and the narrow pallium decorated with small crosses which he wears above all his vestments around his shoulders and hanging pendant down the centre front (a bishop carries a pastoral staff and does not wear the pallium). All the other vestments are common to bishops as well. He wears a mitre with orphreys and two lappets or infulae hanging down behind. He has gloves and a ring (*annulus*) on the fourth finger of the right hand, and a pair of buskins, the embroidered stockings which were like soft cloth boots. The stole is hidden by the tunicle, but the maniple can be seen suspended from the left wrist decorated in the same manner as the border of the dalmatic and the apparel of the amice, and finishing off with a fringe. The alb and the amice are both embellished with apparels, although in different designs, the apparel of the alb being stitched in a long panel at the hem. Both the tunicle and the dalmatic are split up the sides for ease of movement, the tunicle being here trimmed with a fringe and the dalmatic not (although the fringe is generally proper to the latter vestment). The dalmatic is made of the most elaborate fabric, which is also traditional, and in this example the chasuble is completely plain. Oddly, the sleeve of the dalmatic loses the pattern – this can be seen on the left arm, and the sleeve of the tunicle (only visible on the right-hand blessing) has a dark border or apparel. The pallium, which is extraordinarily narrow, has been added to the figure as an afterthought, sketched in over the drapery of the chasuble and unfinished at the bottom.

probably correctly, identifies as the dalmatic,[41] is in the same sort of silk as the chasuble but more elaborate in design. This would make sense, as traditionally the dalmatic is a highly decorated garment. Silk was used extensively for these garments in the twelfth and thirteenth centuries. Dalmatics had traditionally been slit at the sides, but in the twelfth century were often notched and a feature was made of this with a border of a different colour or textile. Remnants of the fringe are found on the clavi and fringing remains a special feature of the dalmatic.

THE AMICE AND ALB

It was in these centuries that the custom of decorating the white linen alb and amice with embroidered patches called apparels became widespread, if not universal. Archbishop Stigand in the Bayeux Tapestry wears a plain alb with no amice but Pugin notes an amice decorated with gold from 915, and Leoffin, Abbot of Ely at the end of the tenth century 'brought most valuable ornaments to his church, forsooth, a renowned alb, with the amice and its apparel together . . .'.[42] Albs listed in inventories before 1200 tend to be of linen rather than silk and in the tomb of Hubert Walter where all the linen perished, it is only the apparels of the alb and amice in which he was buried that have survived. (In fact, the absence of gloves and a maniple suggests that they too were of linen; only the silk embroidery is left of the stole.)[43] In this case the apparels of the alb are made of pieces of the same silk as the chasuble and dalmatic, neatly hemmed and lined and are the large patch placed just above the hem, and two smaller pieces from the wrists. The apparel of the amice is embroidered and probably English work from the end of the twelfth century, with medallions containing the archangels Michael and Gabriel, and the four gospel writers, and with a central medallion showing the seated Christ.

THE SURPLICE

The surplice had now developed from the alb, but was not decorated with apparels. The council held at Treves in 1238 ordered that when priests carried the blessed sacrament to the sick, they should be habited with an alb, or surplice. The name comes from 'super-pellicea' as it replaced the alb which was too slim a garment to fit over the fur-lined cassock which had come to be used in the colder climates of the north.

THE ALMUCE

The almuce was widely worn in England and northern Europe and was a hood of fur, worn by canons and other dignitaries in the choir as a defence against the cold. The usual colour of the fur was grey, but white ermine was worn in cathedral chapter and in the few cases where the bishop was a temporal prince, spotted ermine with the tails around the hem was permitted.[44] Cold was a problem but the Church adapted clothes and adopted headgear to compensate. In 1243 the Roman Pontiff Innocent IV (1243–54), on being asked, gave leave to the Benedictines of St Austin's Abbey, Canterbury, to wear caps in the choir during divine service.[45]

THE STOLE AND MANIPLE

St Cuthbert's stole and maniple, tenth century, provide evidence for the use of embroidery on these vestments from an early date. Leoffin's gift to his church included a stole and maniple 'made out of gold and precious stones woven together'.[46] The word 'fanon' is used for maniple in inventories of this time, and it was during these centuries that the maniple ceased to be carried in the left hand and was fixed to the left wrist.

LITURGICAL COLOURS

It was in the twelfth century that liturgical colours were first set down as special to a season. These do not seem to have been taken up by every church; many tended to use the vestments in the best condition, or of the richest fabrics for special festivals. Colours used in the Levitical priesthood, i.e. gold, white, red, blue and purple, had been accepted by the Latin Church, reserving green

and black for processional copes. Abbot Egelric (c. 984) 'gave also to the choir twenty-four copes, viz: six white ones, six red, six green and six black.'[47] The Sarum Rite (c. 1210) only mentions red and white. Ivo of Chartres (died 1115) only refers to gold, blue, purple, white and red; Sicardus, Bishop of Cremona (twelfth century) says that the colour is changed according to the season: 'white is used at Easter, because the angels appeared in white; red at Pentecost because the Holy Ghost descended upon the apostles in the form of fiery tongues.'[48]

The colour sequence set down by the black canons of the Latin Church of the Holy Sepulchre at Jerusalem, from the early twelfth century, gave the list as black, red, white, blue with the best frontal for Christmas day; Lichfield in 1240 reserves the 'most precious' for Christmas day. Inventories and lists seem to indicate that a great variety of colours and textiles were in use in churches, and as so many vestments were gifts the emphasis was on the richness of the fabric and the embroidery rather than the colour.

EPISCOPAL DRESS

The episcopal suit was settled with gloves and mitre, and the extra layer of the tunicle, completed by buskins and sandals. Sicardus, speaking of the mystical meaning of the sacred vestments, says 'the buskin was all of silk, to signify purity'.[49] Buskins and sandals of silk were found in the tomb of Herbert Walter and were in good condition, of green silk lined with amber silk. The sandals or shoes were embroidered in silver gilt thread probably of English work.[50]

The suit had now become complete and although in colour, decoration and cut there were changes in future centuries, the basic items of dress remained the same in the Roman Church until the middle of the twentieth century.

CHAPTER FOUR

The Great Age of Opus Anglicanum until the End of the Middle Ages 1250–1509

As THE CHURCH in Europe became prosperous and powerful within society there was a growth in the elaboration of vestments, there were changes in cut and new textiles were used, but there were no new clothes introduced for those officiating at the altar. Liturgical vestments, their use and purpose, were by this time established and such changes as occurred were relatively minor. In the thirteenth century the chasuble became reserved for the celebration of Mass and the cope replaced it for processional and other occasions; the surplice replaced the alb except for the celebration of Mass, and the mitre settled into its shape with the two horns front and back, but remained the processional dress of bishops and some abbots, with no liturgical significance. The great period of Opus Anglicanum, the famous English medieval style of embroidery, now reached its maturity and vestments became ornaments rather than costume, and as such the shapes underwent certain transformations; but essentially the suit was preserved. We can draw information from some comprehensive inventories of church goods that were drawn up;[1] and because of their great value some vestments have been preserved and are available to the twentieth-century student.

In the lay dress of the clergy and the costume of those in holy orders we are again faced with a lack of information as to what they were *supposed* to wear, although we have many examples of excesses in dress and the rebukes that followed. This problem is illustrated clearly in Chaucer's description in the Prologue to the *Canterbury Tales*, (c. 1387) of various men and women who have accepted religious orders. With those he does not respect, items of dress are clearly described,

but for the honest parson who travels with his brother, a ploughman, no garments are mentioned, just a simple description of his Christianity:

But Christes loove and his apostles twelve
he taught, but first he followed it himselve.

Various councils and synods continued to attempt to regulate the outdoor dress of the clergy and severe penalties were prescribed for disobedience, apparently with little effect. In 1237, a national council, under the Legate Otto, insisted on the *vestis talaris*, a long gown or cassock, for all clerks of the bishop's household, and in 1268 the papal Legate Othobon held another national council which renewed these provisions in a constitution which has ever since been regarded as the English rule and was closely followed in the canons of 1571 and 1604. The obligation of a habit, formerly imposed only on those in holy orders, was now extended to the whole clergy, without distinction of time and place, and all priests were to wear the *cappa clausa*, except when travelling.[2] The provincial synod, under Archbishop Pecham of Canterbury in 1281, deplored the neglect of the rule and imposed further penalties. The strictness of Othobon's definition, however, was somewhat relaxed and the clerical habit was merely required to be distinguishable. From this we can assume that clerical dress was a form of cassock and gown or cloak, but the precise details are lost and it cannot be identified as the 'uniform' that the clergy adopted in the eighteenth and nineteenth centuries. In 1342 a constitution of Stratford directed against certain minor abuses of dress, such as excessive brightness of colour and looseness in the sleeves,[3] but in 1368 a description of the wardrobe of Hughes de Chataignier of Rouen

17 Lady confessing to a priest, from *Romant de la Rose*. An example of a priest in completely secular dress with a hood or chaperon and a very large purse suspended from his belt. There are countless references to clergy wearing secular dress throughout the history of the Church; it is by no means a post-Reformation phenomenon, although before it was undoubtedly associated with spiritual laxity.

shows 'a fair but not undue supply of clothing of the usual bright colours affected by the clergy at that date, green and red well lined with fur.'[4] Lyndwode, Bishop of St David's in 1429 observes that the constitutions were never put into force and 'although certain colours [such as red and green] and certain shapes are forbidden, yet in this country clergy have no fixed habit assigned to them, either in shape or colour, and therefore may wear any kind of dress which is suitable to their

state, provided it is not expressly forbidden.'

Chaucer's description of the prioress and her affectation of exposing her forehead in the contemporary lay fashion is easily proved to be a common abuse in the fourteenth and fifteenth centuries.

And she was cleped Madame Eglatine
full semyly her wympul pinched was;
But sikerly she hadde a fair foreheed;
it was almoost a spanne brood, I trowe;
ful fetys was hir cloke, as I was war.

In 1441 Prioress Clemence Medford (Ankerwyke, Buckinghamshire) is censured for wearing golden rings and silken veils and for carrying her veil too high above her forehead, which, being entirely uncovered, could be seen by all.[5] In 1394 Margaret Fairfax, Prioress of Nun Monkton, is reported to have worn expensive fur and silken veils and from Moxby Priory, Joan 'Blaunkfront's' nickname means 'white front or forehead'. Sacheverell Sitwell quotes from a letter to Elstow, a Benedictine nunnery in Buckinghamshire, in which the bishop writes: 'We ordain and by way of injunction command under pain of disobedience from henceforth that no lady nor any religious sister within the said monastery presume to wear their apparel upon their heads under such lay fashion as they have of late done, with cornered crests, neither under such manner of height showing their foreheads more like lay people than religious.' The bishop goes on to condemn their fashionable shoes, and orders: 'Their gowns and myrtles be closse afore and not so depe voyded at the breste and noo more to use rede stomachers but other sadder colers in the same.'[6]

Liturgical vestments were included with the chalice, the Mass book, or missal, and all the other items proper to the Church and the liturgy and were to be provided by the parishioners. In 1250 the Archbishop of York, Walter Grey, published a series of constitutions 'to the honour of God and the present information of the Church of York', that all churches should be decently provided for with 'the principal vestment of the church, the chasuble, alb, amice, stole, maniple, girdle, with three towels and corporals, and other decent vestments for the deacon and subdeacon, according to the condition of the parishioners and the church, with a silk cope for the principal festivals and two others for presiding in choir at the festivals aforesaid ... three surplices ...' etc. About thirty years later, Archbishop Pecham of Canterbury published a similar constitution, and the vestments named were 'the principal vestment of the church, the chasuble, clean alb, amice, maniple, girdle' etc., all belonging to the parishioners. In 1305 Archbishop Winchelsea expands the list: 'that the parishioners of every church in the province of Canterbury may for the future certainly know what repairs belong to them, and they may have no disputes with their rectors, we enjoin that for the future they be bound to find all the things underwritten ... the principal vestment with the chasuble, a dalmatic, a tunic, a choral cope and all its appendages ...'. Lyndwode, Bishop of St David's, commenting on this constitution in 1429 declares that by the term 'appendages' used here is to be understood the alb, amice, girdle, stole and maniple. Archbishop Winchelsea goes on to include three surplices and a rochet.[7]

From the constitutions we can see that the principal vestment, which can be understood as a cope, the chasuble and the alb, amice and girdle, are common to all three. The stole is only mentioned in the York province although the maniple is listed in all three, and in another constitution of Canterbury the stole is prescribed for ministering the Eucharist to the sick.[8] 'Three surplices' are mentioned in both the northern (York 1250) and the southern (Canterbury *c.* 1280 and 1305) provinces, but are not intended to be worn simultaneously with the garments named, but in turn at less solemn functions.

The Surplice
The surplice was an ample garment which never received any embroidered decoration. 'Twenty yards of fine linen to make a surplice' is mentioned in a bequest to an English parish church pre-Reformation[9] and it had very large sleeves. Towards the end of the fourteenth century priests belonging to collegiate churches are represented in processional vestments on monumental brasses, and in these figures (as in the figures at the beginning of the fifteenth century) the surplice is usually long, completely covering the cassock.

18 The John Huntingdon brass, 1458, Manchester Cathedral. John Huntingdon is in choir dress – a full-length surplice with an almuce, a fur cape with hood, which has two 'tails' hanging down the front not to be confused with the stole.

There is some written evidence that the surplice was worn under the alb and amice confirmed by Lyndewode (1429). In 1286 Durandus, Bishop of Mende, mentions it as the practice of some to wear the surplice under the amice, and this appears to be the case in a service of defrocking a priest; as each garment was removed, so he was deprived of a rank or order.[10] As the chasuble was taken off the words used were 'we deprive thee of sacerdotal [priestly] rank'; the stole was connected with diaconal rank; the maniple with subdiaconal; the alb and amice with collet; and the words on removal of the surplice were 'we deprive thee of the rank of singer'. This does imply that the surplice was worn underneath the amice, but for obvious reasons there is no visual evidence of this custom.

The surplice was usually worn by all ranks of clergy and also acolytes and those in the choir, in place of the alb on less solemn occasions. In his *Instructions for Parish priests* John Myrk, canon of Lilleshall in Shropshire writes:

When thou shalt to sick gone,
A clean surplice cast thee on,
and thy stole with thee right,
and pull thy hood over thy sight[11]

The weepers around the tomb in St Paul's Cathedral of Henry de Lacy, Earl of Lincoln, who died in 1310, are surpliced canons of the church to whom he had been a great benefactor.[12]

Possibly because surplices were not embroidered and therefore not valuable, they are rarely mentioned in inventories. In 1368 William of Swynflete, Archdeacon of Norwich, made a record of the furnishings of over 350 Norfolk churches.[13] St Olave, Norwich, Postwick and West Lexham had surplices for boys 'pro pueris' and at St George, Tombland, and at St Michael at Plea, Norwich, were thirteen surplices of which six and three respectively were set apart 'pro pueris'. Four surplices were newly made for a visitation of July 1365 at St Mary Magdalen, Wiggenhall, and one surplice from St Peter, Hungate, Norwich had the letter G on the breast (from the name of the donor).[14] Although each church was ordered to have three surplices there were twenty-three churches which had no surplices and fifty-five had only one or two. However, All Saints, Great Massingham and All Saints, Tilney, had twenty-four surplices; St George Tombland, Norwich and Griston had fifteen, and Harpley had fourteen.

One rochet, the vestment of the bishop, was prescribed by Winchelsea in 1305 but in 1368 in the diocese of Norwich 231 churches had no rochet although at Burgh next Aylsham there were no less than five! Thirty-six churches had two, and seven had three.

Opus Anglicanum

Opus Anglicanum is the term used for the English medieval embroidery that was internationally famous. In 1246, Matthew Paris records

the Lord Pope, having observed that the ecclesiastical ornaments of some Englishmen, such as the choir copes and mitres, were embroidered in gold thread after a very desirable fashion, asked where these works were made, and received an answer, in England. 'Then' said the Pope, 'England is surely a garden of delights for us. It is truly a never failing spring; and there where many things abound, may much be extorted.'

He sent to the Cistercians for orphreys and there is evidence that many embroideries came from monasteries and nunneries, and that a great deal was given to the Pope; in the Vatican inventory of 1295 Opus Anglicanum is mentioned 113 times.

Christina of Huntingdon, the first prioress of the St Albans cell at Monkyate, was famed as an embroideress. Three mitres and sandals of wonderful workmanship which she made were the only gifts Pope Adrian IV (1154–9) chose to accept of all the costly offerings made by Abbot Robert de Goreham (1151–66).[16] Pope Clement V (1305–14) had at least three English embroidered copes that were probably gifts, and in turn gave two English copes to the Cathedral of St Bernard-de-Comminges in 1309.[17]

Like illumination, Opus Anglicanum probably began in the cloister but later passed into the hands of lay craftsmen. Edward II (reigned 1307–27) paid 100 marks to Rose, wife of John de Bureford, a citizen and mercer of London, for a choir cope of her embroidery, which was sent to Rome as an offering to Pope John XII from Queen Isabella. This Pope also received copes from the Bishop of Ely, John Hotham, and from the Archbishop of Canterbury.[18]

In 1360 Cardinal Talairand, Bishop of Albano, makes mention in his will of some white vestments elaborately ornamented with English embroideries[19] and there are many other examples of Opus Anglicanum on the Continent.

There is a cope very similar to the Butler-Bowden cope in the Victoria and Albert Museum, London, which was listed among the possessions of Jean, Duc de Berri in 1403,[20] and a description in an inventory of St Albans, compiled during the reign of Henry IV (1399–1413) also conforms with the Butler-Bowden cope, if 'camaca' is taken to mean silk velvet: 'Item, a cope of red camaca with a fretwork of gold, with woodbine on the border; on which are different canopied niches with the likeness of various saints, and on the back towards the foot is the salutation of the blessed virgin, and in the next canopied niche ... which is the gift of John Kelselle, formerly a monk of this assembly.'[21]

At Langley, a Leicestershire nunnery of Benedictines, there are indications in an inventory of 1485 of a whole sacristy full of embroideries including altar frontals and suits of vestments. There was a vestment of black damask embroidered with roses and stars and a complete vestment of white worked with 'rede trewlyps'. These are true lovers' knots, not tulips (which had not yet been brought to England from Turkey).[22] The monk in Chaucer's Prologue is described as fastening his hood with a pin fashioned in the form of a love knot,

And, for to festrie his hood under his chyn
He hadde of gold ywrought a ful curious pyn;
a love-knotte in the gretter ende there was.

An inspection of inventories shows that the embroidered decoration was by no means always of religious subjects. It must be remembered that many vestments were made of fabrics originally of secular origin bequeathed or given to the churches by benefactors, in a spirit of practical Christianity; and it was the quality of the textiles and quantity of rich silks or silver and gold threads that made up the rich vestment worn to the glory of God which were important.

Queen Philippa bestowed upon Simon, Bishop of Ely, the gown she wore at her churching after the birth of the Black Prince. The robe was murray-coloured velvet, powdered with golden squirrels, and so ample that it was made into three copes for choir use.[23] In 1491 Sir Gervase Clifton directs 'all the altar cloths of silk, a bed of gold

Bawdkyne and another bed of russet satin which belonged to [Archbishop Boothe of York] to be delivered to make vestments' for use in various chantries in Southwell Minster.[24] In the inventory of Christ Church, Canterbury of 1315–16 there is a rich suit (of vestments) of blue cloth with golden fleurs-de-lys given by Philip, King of France who also bestowed on the church another suit of red samite with orphreys of France, that is blue with gold fleurs-de-lys. A suit means a set of vestments, and can also include the altar-frontal, in the same way as the term vestment can mean a set of vestments and not just the chasuble alone. A suit that had belonged to Archbishop Robert of Winchelsea (1294–1313) of red samite embroidered with golden trees or branches with orphreys worked with pearls, included a chasuble, a cope, a tunicle, a dalmatic for the Archbishop and a second tunicle and dalmatic for the sub-deacon and deacon.[25]

Among the objects found decorating various vestments in the 1368 inventory in Norfolk[26] some had no religious significance, for example castles, gold crowns, lily-pots, stars of silver and of gold, a great variety of flowers (especially roses), birds, beasts both real and mythological and letters (probably the initials of the donors). Coats of arms were also a very popular form of decoration, almost always those of the donor and his or her family. The 1295 inventory of St Paul's Cathedral includes two copes embroidered with knights fighting.[27]

There still exists a pattern book which was used by a group of artists who designed for vestments.[28] Its use appears to have begun soon after 1280, and to have continued until at least the end of the fourteenth century, which indicates the continuity of the workshop tradition. The pattern book includes some excellent sketches of birds and beasts, some of which are identified in embroideries; there is the landrail and the tabby cat of the Comminges cope, the long-tailed parakeet of the Butler-Bowden cope, the pelican in piety of the Lateran and Toledo copes, and many other birds and beasts found in like form on vestments. The pattern book might equally well have been used for certain fourteenth-century manuscripts and there was a combined tradition of artistic skills in illumination and embroidery design throughout this period. A dragon which appears in Bodleian Ms 614 has been pricked out for copying.[29] The first and only initial to a Lanfranc book at Trinity College, Dublin (Ms.B.35,f3.) consists of a small two-headed bird in green outline, and in the Canterbury inventory of 1315 there is described a red samite dalmatic embroidered with two-headed eagles.[30] The Byzantine silks had introduced griffins, winged lions and especially pairs of birds or animals facing (or facing away from) each other enclosed in a circle; C. R. Dodwell shows that these designs influenced the designs in the Canterbury School of Illumination.[31]

A lady's girdle that was used in William of Wykeham's mitre (1367–1404) is set with enamels showing hares, stags and dogs and monkeys walking on all fours and blowing horns; the same types of animals are found in contemporary manuscripts. Queen Isabella had cushions worked with monkeys and butterflies in her chapel.[32]

Woven Textiles

The prolific art of embroidery did not outweigh the interest in a variety of woven textiles imported into England and used for vestments. Silk was the most commonly used material for vestments and came in a variety of forms, some of which are not now very easy to identify. Cloth of gold is usually silk interwoven with threads of gold and occurs frequently; the colour of the silk shows through, hence entries in inventories can be 'red cloth of gold'. In Norfolk in 1368, there are eighteen examples of plain cloth of gold and twenty-eight red, six black, five white, one green, one red and white, one red and blue, one blue and black and one black and green cloth of gold. Baudkin is closely allied to cloth of gold and is a rich stuff of silk woven with gold thread and manufactured originally in Baghdad. Other names for silks of different qualities are sarsinett, cendal, sindon, samite and tartryn; carde is a material of rougher character woven from coarse silk and sometimes from linen; camaca is another form of silk, a costly and strong fabric; it is also associated with camel's hair; taffeta is a plain thick woven silk imported from Persia. Velvet, another popular fabric for vestments, is also generally made of silk, but like damask the name describes the technique of weaving rather than the fibre it is composed of. Fustian, a coarse twilled material of linen, is chiefly used for the white (sack-cloth colour) ferial vestments for Lent, and worsted (a woollen cloth of long staple and smooth finish) is found in five vestments in the Norfolk inventory – not altogether surprising as it was a local material.[33]

Liturgical Colours

Liturgical colours can be divided into four principal groups – red, white, green and black. Red is the most popular colour and is also called *rubeus*; *purpureus* or red purple; *sub rubeus* or murray; crimson; sanguine; rose; carnation; pink and probably 'horseflesh colour'. White (*albus or candidus*) includes the cream colours and ivory tones in its group. Green (*viridis*) is identified liturgically with saffron or yellow (*croceus*), and therefore includes not only the light bluish-grey *glaucus*, but popinjay green and popinjay yellow and also the deeper shades of yellow, such as tawny and orange. Black included *niger* and *quasi-niger* and all the various secondary shades of blue and brown. Among the former are black purple (*de nigra purpura*) *purpureus* or full purple, *violaceus* or blue-purple of the violet, *indicus bluetus*, *blauus* or dark blue, and *indius blodius* and *caeruleus* which were probably bright blue. The browns include *brunus*, burnet or dark brown, russet, *cinereus* or ashen, crane-colour, grey, dun and dove colour and even the Lenten white.[34]

Christmas day required the 'most precious' (Lichfield statute 1240) or 'embroidered' (Westminster 1258 and 1283) vestment whatever the colour; most churches did not have enough suits to cover the liturgical seasons, and so would not have been able to follow the directions fully. As vestments were often made up of gifts of cloth, it would be difficult to choose a colour. With a few exceptions, different countries and different ages disagree in the interpretations put upon the various colours, and different authors have ascribed different symbolisms, so for a greater part these 'meanings' are a local convention and purely arbitrary. Mixed colours were very common, either in stripes or panes or as a check of two or more colours, or with a mixture in the fabric itself, as in the cloth called melley or medley. What is now called a shot-fabric is often found in inventories as 'changeable', and in fact any and every colour or mixture of colours that was available at the time was pressed into the service of the Church. The guiding principle, definitely expressed in the rules, was that vestments which were specially valuable and handsome, such as those with elaborate embroidery, should be employed on the most important feasts.[35]

The Cope

The cope, the principal vestment of the Church, continued its dual role development. Some churches had large numbers of elaborate copes for festivals; William of Wykeham (died 1404) left to the Cathedral Church of Winchester his new vestment of blue cloth wrought with gold lions, with thirty copes of the same suit orphreyed with the story of Jesse. Assuming that vestment means the whole suit, this must have made a splendid array;[36] at about the same time at Christ Church, Canterbury there was 'a great suit of copes of green colour, namely 96 copes with five chasubles six tunicles, two dalmatics, seventy-six albes with stoles and fanons'. Canterbury also had another set of thirty-nine white copes of cloth of gold.[37]

Copes were worn by the principal officer at the Mass and in the constitutions set out in the thirteenth century (see p. 48). Archbishop Walter Grey of York (1250) and Archbishops Pecham

(*c*. 1280) and Winchelsea (1305) of Canterbury state that the church should be provided with the principal vestment of the Church (the chasuble) and also in the cases of Grey and Winchelsey a choir cope. However in the inventory taken in 1368 of the Norwich diocese, out of 358 churches 127 do not specifically record the cope, and a large number mention only one (St Peter, Mancroft, has the most, with seventeen). It may be assumed that 'par vestimentorum' could include the cope but this is not necessarily so, the cope not being in the strictest sense a vestment. The whole suit of vestments is described in the inventory of 1407 at Warwick College (St Mary's) and there is no mention of the cope: 'An hole vestiment of white tartaryn for Lenten that is to say iij aubes, iij amyts wyth the parures (apparels) a chesible, iij stoles iiij fanons (maniples) iij girdelis, ij auter clothis wyth a frontel and a towail. iij curtyns, a lectron cloth and a veyle of lynnen cloth'.[38]

19 The Syon cope, 1300–20. This cope is unusual and has undergone alterations which are visible around the edge where figures are cut off or pieced in. It was possibly originally a chasuble and certainly the orphrey, morse and border are later additions. The background of couched silk in green and pink is also later and was probably done to preserve the much older figures of angels, saints and Biblical figures, which are good work from a period when much excellent work was being produced.

The general rule for wearing copes was that they were worn by the priests when presiding at much of the office in choir, when incensing the altar at Lauds and Evensong, and also during processions, bidding prayers, weddings and all ceremonial not directly connected with the offering of Mass. They were also worn by the assistant clergy during the celebration of Mass on more solemn days, by the cantors and occasionally by the choir. Copes followed the rules set down as to liturgical colours, when the church could afford it. In Lincoln (*c.* 1260) there is a brief direction as to the colour of the copes: 'Let [the sacrist] see that the copes be as the feast required. If martyr, whether apostle, evangelist or virgin let the silken copes be red for the most part; if confessor green or brown; if a matron or betrothed of saffron colour'.[39] Several brown copes (*brunus, fuscus, russet, brunet*) are mentioned in St Paul's Cathedral inventory in 1245. In Norfolk (1368) the most common colour was red[23] followed by nine green, eight blue, and six gold. They were most commonly made of silk but in the Norfolk inventories already cited there were three of white fustian, one of green linen, one of black worsted and one of spinet.

The fabrics would be as elaborate as the donors could afford, but the orphreys contained the most valuable decoration and the morse or clasp could be of great expense and beauty. The original hood, essential to the cope when it was a practical garment, never disappears completely. Until the fourteenth century the hood sometimes retained enough of its original shape to receive the amice which fitted into it as one hood into another. This practice eventually disappeared but the hood was recalled as a shield-shape ornament on the back of the cope. The reluctance to lose the hood altogether has two reasons: firstly, the hood had become one of the identifying aspects of the religious costume and could not be discarded

unthinkingly; secondly, for a large proportion of the congregation the back of the cope was on view most of the time and it provided an area to enrich and decorate on a large garment which might otherwise be very plain.

The orphreys were getting broader and could accommodate more elaborate embroidery, including figures. The orphreys of the chasuble had also grown quite wide and became a vital part of the vestment (they were an ornament decorated and enriched for the glory of God and the Church, rather than important for the garment). The orphrey was originally a decorated strip to hide the central seam front and back, as, until the invention of the flying shuttle, it was difficult to produce a fabric wider than 27–30 inches (the notable exception was broad cloth, but it needed two operators). From the fourteenth century the orphreys became more ornamental, growing increasingly broad and serving as a background for images of saints and armorial bearings. The psi-cross-shaped orphreys of the chasuble gradually became identified with the emblem of Redemption and from the fourteenth century it became common for the chasuble to be decorated with the figure of Christ on the Cross.

The Chasuble

The chasuble was the vestment which changed its shape most with the use of Opus Anglicanum. This was the vestment of the priest officiating at the Mass and one of the most important parts of the liturgy is the elevation of the host, when the priest holds the bread and wine high above his head for all the congregation to see. When the chasuble became heavy and stiff with embroidery it was obviously impossible to roll it back along the arms as had previously been done. It had to be curtailed at the sides and there are various shapes as a result (shield-shape, violin-shape, etc.); however the garment was still essentially without fastening, worn loose and never girded. Deacons and sub-deacons still wore the chasuble during penitential seasons, Advent and from Septuagesima to Easter. At Reedham, Norfolk, in 1368 there was a chasuble 'for the gospel' and extra chasubles, doubtless for the deacon and sub-deacon, are frequently mentioned.

Although often only cathedrals could afford

20 An orphrey: a detail showing the fine embroidery of the great age of English needlework, Opus Anglicanum. The seated King wears a mantle lined with minerva (the fur from the bellies of squirrels); the small, shield-shape forms are visible behind his right arm and where the garment falls away. The folds in the drapery and the hair are formally executed in the style of illustration of the day, not because of limitations in the needlecraft.

vestments in all the liturgical colours, ordinary churches seem to have had three suits and this suggests a division into: festal or principal; dominical or Sunday; ferial or workaday. In an inventory of churches and chapels in Cambridge-shire in 1277, 65 out of 150 churches had three suits,[40] and many had more. In Norfolk in 1368 nearly every church had three or more vestments. These, as has already been suggested, were not chosen for their colour but rather because of their good condition. At the beginning of this period, as with copes, there were many brown chasubles. Brown is part of the black sequence of colours and was ordered for Advent, Septuagesima and Lent up to Passion Sunday; also on Christmas Eve at Lauds, Mass and Evensong; on the Circumscision, by the Black Canons of the Latin Church of the Holy Sepulchre at Jerusalem and for all feasts of Our Lady. Innocent III (before he became Pope in 1198) wore black for most of the above seasons but also chose black for Passiontide and reserved white for the feasts of Our Lady.[41]

In the early part of the thirteenth century Wokingham, in the diocese of Salisbury, had three chasubles, of red sendal, of sendal newly lined, and of canvas; (they also had a fourth 'de fusco tincto – old and worn'). Hurst possessed a silk chasuble, new and decent, and another old and torn. Knook in 1226 had a new silk chasuble ('infula') another of brown colour old and worn and two old suits. Hill Deverell possessed a silk chasuble old and worn, and another of reddish brown ('de fusco tincto rubeo'), likewise old and worn.[42] Of the seven brown chasubles men-tioned, six were old and worn; this could indicate that the original colours of the silk or brocade had faded to brown or that as they were not used for festivals they were not replaced as frequently as the festal vestments.

The Dalmatic and Tunicle

The dalmatic and tunicle followed the colours of the chasuble, and by the fourteenth century lost their fullness as they in turn became more ornate. The dalmatic which had always had slits or in some cases a scooped out space at the sides, had to be slit higher and higher up the sides to assist the deacon's movements. By the fifteenth century it had developed a stiff truncated form. The original clavi on the dalmatic had developed into orph-reys, running vertically in parallel lines down the front and the back. To bless and light the Paschal with the new fire was the special prerogative of the deacon, who did so in memory of the women who brought spices and announced the tidings of the Resurrection to the apostles. (Bede said this custom arose because it was the disciples and not the apostles who buried Jesus Christ.) In the event of a priest conducting the ceremony single-handed he would put on the vestment of the deacon, a dalmatic, for the blessing. In 1541, Ludlow inventory includes 'Item, payde to the dekens for the tendynge of the pascalle iii jd'. In 1540 at Westminster Abbey a tunicle of 'diver's colours' was reserved to hallow the Paschal.[43]

The tunicle was a simpler garment in its origins than the dalmatic and when worn by the bishop, under the dalmatic and chasuble, was the least decorated. When it was worn by those in minor orders, from the fourteenth century, there was a growing tendency for it to become identical to the dalmatic, and also to adopt orphreys.

The Stole and Maniple

The stole and maniple (known as fanon or phanon in contemporary sources) were made of the same colour and material as the chasuble or dalmatic, or more frequently as its orphreys. The maniple differed from the stole in size alone and the ends often terminated in a fringe. The maniple was generally fastened on the left wrist; when it appears on monuments or in embroidery as carried on the right, it is generally agreed that this is probably an error on the part of the sculptor, or a desire to achieve symmetry.[44]

Stoles and maniples are frequently mentioned but seldom described, but there is evidence that they were generally at least as luxuriantly de-corated as the orphreys. In the 1315–16 inven-tories of Christ Church Canterbury there are twenty-three pairs of stoles and fanons adorned with gold plate and gems and embroidered with pearls. Stoles were worn by priests and deacons (although not in the same manner) and maniples by priests, deacons and sub-deacons; thus an entry in the Christ Church inventory '1 cope, 2 stoles and 4 fanons for ferial use' implies one priest, one deacon and two sub-deacons.

21 Altarpiece: the Virgin and Child enthroned among angels and saints by Benozzo di Lese (called Gozzoli) *c.* 1461. Saint Zenobius is wearing an alb with apparels, at wrist and hem; he has a girdle and amice with its apparel falling over the cope like a collar. He wears a *mitra pretiosa*, the most elaborate mitre, which is wedged on his head over a close plain cap. His cope, which is made of a rich damask, has orphreys ornamented with eight scenes from the life of the Virgin and Christ. Saint Jerome, kneeling on the left, is in the simple habit of the hermit, but his cardinal's hat with its shallow crown and wide brim and over-large tassels is on the step beside him. St Francis wears the habit of his order with a cowl and knotted cord around his waist. He wears no sandals (discalced). St Dominic wears a white habit and scapular (worn over the girdle), a black mantle and cowl. St Peter wears the tunic and the pallium in which Biblical characters are always depicted. Above these he wears the ecclesiastical pallium in the tau-cross shape with very simple crosses on the white wool. St Peter has always been shown with a bald crown but with a small fringe of hair at the front. This came to be the shape of the Roman tonsure and all the ecclesiastics in this group have this type of hairstyle.

Alb, Amice and Girdle

The alb, together with the amice and the girdle, appear in every inventory and they were worn by all the clergy. Whereas all the vestments mentioned so far were generally made of silk (with some exceptions), the alb and amice were usually made of linen of more or less fine quality. From the thirteenth century both albs and amices were increasingly decorated with apparels (*parures*) and this can cause some confusion in understanding the inventories. In a form of shorthand the albs are described by their apparels and thus we read in the Peterborough inventory for 1539: '30 albes of old cloth of Baudkyn, 27 red albes for Passion Week; 40 blue albs of divers sorts; 7 albes called ferial black.' Macalister[45] takes this to mean that the alb itself was of a coloured fabric but the following entries from the same inventory show perhaps more clearly that the apparels are the means by which the garment can be identified: '6 albes with Peter Keys, 6 albes called the Kydds, 7 albes called Meltons, 6 albes called Doggs'. Although there is proof of coloured albs in 1368 at Rougham in Norfolk – 'three albs of stained or coloured linen' – 'the old cloth of Baudkyn' is far more likely to describe the apparels; it makes sense to use up old fabric or left-over parts of fabric from the chasuble or dalmatic (see page 45) rather than break with the tradition of the white linen alb, which certainly continued throughout the medieval period and to the present day.

The apparels could be of great value and in the Canterbury inventory of 1315–16 amices were of unusual richness. One, formerly belonging to St Thomas, was ornamented with gems, and even the sixty in ordinary use had apparels 'of orphrey work ornamented with gems'. The embroidered amice apparel found in the coffin of Archbishop Hubert Walter (died 1205) had imitation gems upon it.[46] The embroidery itself could be of great artistic importance and value; an alb apparel in the Metropolitan Museum, New York, of English embroidery is silver gilt, silver and silk thread on silk ($7\frac{1}{2}$ by $29\frac{1}{2}$ inches) and shows a Crucifixion scene with four saints with a cinquefoil arched arcade. In the spandrels of the arches are coats of arms; the adjacent arms of Castille and England indicate a date prior to the death of Eleanor of Castille, queen of Edward I, in 1290.[47]

Apparels, like other items of embroidery, were not necessarily of religious subjects. In Norfolk in 1368 the apparels of the alb (and probably the amice, as they usually matched at this time) show a variety of subject matter in the decoration. At St Peter Mancroft, Norwich, there was red velvet powdered with butterflies; at St Peter Hungate, red and white powdered with peacocks; St Andrew had a grey-blue (*glaucus*) fabric powdered with the heads of goats; at St Martin-in-the-Bailey, the apparels were decorated with eagles; Pentrey had fustian decorated with birds and Scoulton, black strewn with red roses. There were five apparels (said to signify the five wounds of Christ on the cross), one on the amice, two at the wrists and two above the hem front and back of the alb. The apparel at the back was sometimes left off, and occasionally the apparels at the wrist go all the way round, forming a cuff. There do not appear to be any rulings on this and it is a detail of dress that probably changed as fashion or the wearer dictated.

In the Norwich inventory, albs are found made of fabric other than the usual fine linen: at Spixworth fustianus, a coarse cloth of linen, is described; at Rougham, tartryn, a rich silk imported from the East; Babingley has one and Great Witchingham three albs of spinet, a textile deriving its name from Spinney in Cambridgeshire.

In 1453 at King's College, Cambridge, there were 'iij dalmatiques of reed with aubes amyts stoles and phanons and iiij aubes for childre with parours according to the same for Lenten'.[48] The alb with its amice, apparels and girdle was also the regular dress of acolytes at Mass, Lauds and Evensong, as well as the regular costume of all ranks of clergy (except when they wore the surplice). Girdles are seldom mentioned and rarely described.

In Norfolk in 1368 there were albs for the boys ('pro pueris') at Alderford and Oxwick. These may have been for choir boys acting as cantors or acolytes or could have been for the ceremonial of the boy-bishop. This curious custom is found throughout England and Europe at this time; a choir boy or scholar of the church school was appointed bishop, or Nicholas-bishop as a reward, after a religious fashion, for good conduct or other deserving merits. The selected boy was

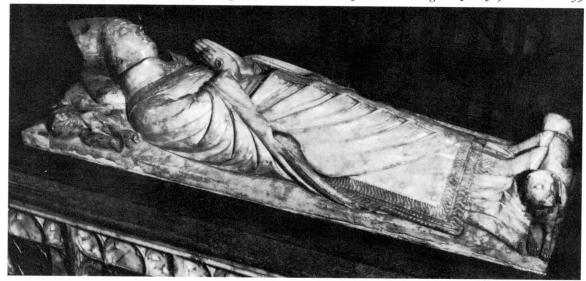

22 Tomb of Cardinal Langham (died 1376), Westminster Abbey. Cardinal Langham, Abbot of Westminster from 1362 and Archbishop of Canterbury from 1366, wears alb and amice (the latter with a broad apparel) a plain chasuble, a fringed dalmatic and tunicle. He wears a pallium, as archbishop, and this is also incorporated in a coat of arms shown on his tomb. The fringes of the stole appear below the tunicle. His gloves are decorated on the back of the hand where a stone was possibly set in, and he wears rings over his gloves.

appointed bishop of St Nicholas Day (6 December) and was vested in special pontificals of a small size during the solemn singing of the Magnificat. He held office until 28 December (Holy Innocents).[49]

In Lichfield in 1345 there were four small choir copes for use of the boys on the feast of Holy Innocents, and in the fifteenth century, a mitre, cope, sandals, gloves and staff for the Nicholas-bishop are named. At St Peter Mancroft, Norwich, in 1368, there was a complete outfit of vestments and altar furnishings for this ceremony, which included a suit of vestments in silk (chasuble, dalmatic and tunicle, cope and three albs), four copes for the boys, a mitre of great value with a crozier and three frontals and altar cloths. Grimson church possessed a cope with tunic, dalmatic and chasuble for a single bishop ('unius episcopi'); St George Tombland, Norwich has 'capae pro pueris' in pairs. The churchwarden's accounts of St Mary Hill, London, 1485–6 show 'item, six copes for children of dyvers sortes, item,

a myter for a bishop at Seinte Nicholas tyde, garnyshed with sylver and anelyd, with perles and counterfeit stones.' Occasional but regular lapses into bad taste verging on blasphemy, especially on the Continent, led to rebukes from the pre-Reformation church. The custom of the Nicholas-bishop was put to an end in England (except for a slight revival in the days of Mary Tudor) by a proclamation of Henry VIII.

Gloves and Footwear

Gloves, buskins and sandals, part of the episcopal outfit, also continued to grow more elaborate. Gloves, which had originally been white linen to signify purity, were now found in colours and embroidered. The gloves left by William of Wykeham (1367–1404) were knitted or woven crimson silk, decorated with gold octofoils in octagonal crimson compartments bordered with gold, with smaller green quatrefoils between them bordered with gold. On the back of the hand 'IHS' is embroidered and the back, and the two-inch cuffs are lined with red silk for protection. There are gold 'rings' on each finger and thumb and one elaborate tassel remains.[50] In the Canterbury inventories of 1315–16 seven pairs of gloves are mentioned. One pair were of linen with silver tassels and embroidered with pearls and five pairs had silver tassels, but it is not known whether this means silver plates or pendant tassels.[51]

Rings were embroidered on gloves, but real rings had grown so large that they were worn over the glove. It was the custom, on the death of the Archbishop of Canterbury, for his best ring to be delivered to the king, but there are rings, albeit inferior, mentioned in the inventories and one was found in the tomb of Hubert Walter, and so the archbishop did have, and wear, more than one. One ring was given to a bishop at his investiture and that would be worn on the third finger to signify his marriage with the Church; however, from the fifteenth to the seventeenth century it became the custom to wear the pontifical ring (*annulus*) on the forefinger.

Buskins and sandals (which were in reality soft slipper-like shoes) did not change much from those found in the tomb of Hubert Walter (page 58). Like those, the three pairs mentioned in Canterbury in 1315–16 were embroidered and they were blue, red and white in colour.

William of Wayneflete, Bishop of Winchester 1447–86, left a pair of buskins, a pair of sandals and an unusual pair of white leather shoes, smooth inside but rough outside, not unlike a ballet pump, fastened with a three-fold lace across the front; from the relative sizes of the buskins and the shoes, it appears that the latter would have been put on first, and from the state of the outside, they were never meant to be seen but always worn under the buskins. The buskins were originally scarlet damask, bearing a repeat pattern of curving branches, a silver eagle with a crown around its neck sitting on a yellow branch of a plant with blue and white cornflowers, and a silver bear encircled by blue columbine flowers sitting on a cloud from which issued green rays. The buskins were lined with coarse linen and fastened below

23 Abbot William Parker (died 1539), Gloucester Cathedral. Here is a mitred abbot who has elected to wear vestments and is shown wearing a *mitra pretiosa*, a mitre decorated with gem stones. The amice is extremely formal and only a small part of the linen is visible folded across at the centre front. The remains of a narrow maniple can be seen on the left arm.

the knee with a button on one side and a lace on the other. The sandals were large, clumsy-looking shoes with no fastening, which were put on slipper fashion; they had leather soles $11\frac{7}{8}$ inches long. They were made of crimson velvet powdered with silver or silver-gilt lily-flowers.

Headwear

Mitres had become stiff and formal with embroidered orphreys (centre front and back); the headband was often of silver or gold and set with gems and pearls. In the Canterbury inventory (1315–16) twelve mitres are listed and the one given by Henry III (reigned 1216–72) was enriched by pearls inside and out and with precious stones. Archbishop Pecham (1279–94) left his best and second-best mitres. The best was made with gold and jewels and the second best was silver with a cross on each horn. Mitres generally had a white ground but that of William of Wykeham (1367–1404) seems from small fragments that survived to have been of red velvet.[52] The vertical band was embroidered with pearls, imitation turquoise and other counterfeit stones, alternating with stellar ornaments. (He also bequeathed to his other college at Winchester a plain mitre with orphreys.) In the list of ornaments and jewels acquired or repaired in the time of Prior Thomas Chillenden of Canterbury (1390–1411) two of the eight mitres mentioned were new ones made of old or broken silver found in the vestry.[53]

There is a mitre made in Ireland in 1418 on which the orphreys have developed so far as to contain niches wherein are found small figures of the Virgin and Child on one side and the donor, a bishop, in the other. The vertical band is silver gilt made with jewel-studded plates hinged together and attached to a leather backing. The front and back central orphreys are surmounted by rock crystal crosses covering inscriptions. Around the headband is an inscription 'me fieri fecit Cornelius O'Deaygh Episcopus', and 'Thomas O carryd Artifex faciens' is written on the bottom of a diagonal orphrey. Assimilation of the Celtic Church of Ireland to the English Church formulated at the Synod of Cashel in 1172, caused Irish fashions in furnishings and ornaments to become almost identical in feeling to those in England.[54]

The low triangular shape of the mitre rose progressively from the fourteenth century and the horns spread and became arched. It is during this period that other forms of headwear became established and the hood (except for those in holy orders) became redundant. Innocent IV conferred the cardinal's hat in 1245 (the red apparel of cardinals hat appeared before this date) and this was a broad-brimmed hat with a low crown. The pilleus or birettum had become the proper adjunct of the ecclesiastical hood, the almuce. The almuce, the hood of fur, was worn by canons regular and secular, by certain rectors of parish churches and by heads of colleges and priests of collegiate churches. The pilleus, a small cap that developed into the square cap of the Reformation church, was also adopted by doctors and was not regarded as of any sacerdotal significance (the Prayer Book of 1549 forbids neither Almuce or cap – it simply ignores them[55]).

The Veil

The veil or sudary was a scarf of silk or linen which was cast about the shoulders and in the ends of which the hands of those who carried certain objects ceremonially were muffled. It was used by the patener or third minister (acolyte) when he brought in the chalice or held up the paten, but in parish churches its chief use was to carry the chrismatory at the solemn processions to the font at Eastertide. The veil is mentioned five times in the Norfolk inventories of 1368; at Hoe it was of green silk, otherwise the colour was unspecified. The Anmer entry is curious as it implies that the paten was held by the deacon, although the custom of the Sarum Rite was for an acolyte to carry out this duty. When not of linen it appears to have been made of some old material of little value: the 1504 inventory of Great St Mary's, Cambridge, refers to 'An olde clothe of silk for berin the chrysmatorye to the ffounte'.

CHAPTER FIVE

The Reformation
1509–1559

Before the Reformation

WRITTEN IN AN EARLY sixteenth-century hand in
the blank leaves before an inventory of 1388 in
Westminster Abbey, there is a note to the 'Westerer', the vester or sacrist, as to how to lay out the
vestments in preparation for dressing the bishop:
'first the Westerer shall lay lowest the chesebell.
Above that the dalmatykes and the dalmatyk with
the longest sleeves uppermost and the other
nethermost then hys stole and his fanane and his
gyrdyll. Opon that his albe theropon his gray
Ames above that his rochett and uppermost hys
kerchur with a vestry gyrdyll to tuck up his
cote'.[1]

The cassock or cote was becoming very full
during this period and there is evidence of girdles
set aside for the priest to tuck up the train of his
cassock or other habit before assuming the vestments. The girdles were kept in the vestry to be
used by seculars as well as regulars and served a
purely practical purpose. At Leverton in 1528
there is in the inventory note: 'for tuckyng
gurdylles to wer at messe ijd.' The Reformation
put a stop to flowing cassocks in the Anglican
Church but in the Roman Catholic Church on the
Continent cassocks developed very full trains in
the sixteenth and seventeenth centuries, and these
continued to be looped or tucked up under
vestments when necessary.

The 'kerchur' referred to in the Westminster
Abbey inventory is probably the amice, traditionally the first vestment to be put on. The rochet
worn under the alb is confusing, but as the surplice
had occasionally been worn with the alb it is
possibly a practice that grew up in some churches
or cathedrals without ever having been officially
ordained, and continued without question. The

rochet could not have had very full sleeves when
worn under the alb and as it was out of sight there
is no visual evidence for the custom. The Prayer
Book of 1549 directs that the priest preparing the
Mass shall put on the vesture appointed for that
ministration, but there is scant evidence for official
lists of vestments before this date and the correct
vesture was probably only known by custom and
practice; but the bishop was clearly ordered to
wear 'beside his rochettes, a surples or albe, and a
cope or vestment [i.e. chasuble].'[2]

The 'gray ames' is the almuce and was originally a fur hood, but by this time the distinguishing
features of this garment were the two strips of fur
hanging down the front, which must not be
confused with the stole. The almuce was not
generally kept in churches, but with its alternative
the tippet, the cassock and the priest's cap, would
be kept by the clergyman as they were part of the
ordinary clerical dress of the time. However, as a
protection against the cold the almuce was universally accepted as part of the choir habit for
many centuries, and thus would find its place in
the vesting of a bishop. (The almuce had also
come to be carried over the left arm as a symbol of
office by canons both regular and secular, and in
this second form took another shape altogether, a
wide length carried over the forearm as a badge of
office.)

The alb is next on the list with the girdle, the
stole and the 'fanane', a word still being used for
the maniple. The alb was also becoming fuller at
the hem which could be seven yards wide, but the
most important development of this garment was
that it lost its apparels which were replaced by
lace. In the inventories of Christ Church Canterbury, taken on 10 April 1540, just after the

suppression of the monastery, there are albs listed with apparels but the majority of the albs are 'garnisshed wt fine nedlework'. Generally these are of white linen, but there is one of white sarcenet and 'Item one other riche albe of fine nedleworke garnisshed with perle, very rich the albe white satein.'[3] There are twelve albs of silk out of a total of 132.

The 'dalmatyks' which were put on next were properly the tunicle and the dalmatic that the bishop wore under the chasuble. These two vestments had become almost indistinguishable and were always listed as a pair; the Canterbury inventory of 1540 does not name them but merely states 'vestment [i.e. chasuble] deacon [i.e. dalmatic] and subdeacon [i.e. tunicle]' followed by the description, for example:

Item one vestment decon and subdeacon of blew damask wt griffons embroudered.
Item vestment decon and subdeacon of black velvet wth floure de lys of golde
Item vestment decon and subdeacon of olde white damaske embroudered wth angelle

The 'vestment' here means the chasuble, the principal vestment for Mass and is not a descriptive word for the dalmatic and tunicle; this is confirmed in the entry: 'Item one vestment decon and subdeacon of stoleworke wt armes whereof the vestment and one deacon very riche'. In all there are thirty suits for priest, deacon and subdeacon and twenty-seven chasubles with their albs. The chasuble remains the topmost vestment and continues to be rich and elaborate, although the life of these embroidered garments could be very long and there are undoubtedly some very old vestments in the inventories taken in the sixteenth century. The great art of English embroidery was ceasing to be the prerogative of the church and secular embroidery was becoming more important, with fine examples to be found from manor houses and mansions (for example the work of Elizabeth, Countess of Shrewsbury, 'Bess of Hardwicke' the most renowned embroideress of the sixteenth century, born in 1518).

Nevertheless, there were still many gifts and bequests of vestments and although the great period of Opus Anglicanum was over, the 'immense treasures in the churches were the joy and boast of every man, woman and child in England who day by day and week by week assembled to worship. ... They looked upon [them] as their own and part of their birthright.'[4] Despite schisms with Rome earlier during the reign of Henry VIII, vestments remained the same as before until his death in 1547, and there were not many signs in the wills, bequests and churchwar-

24 Monument to Stephen Hilliard *c.* 1500, Stevenage, Hertfordshire. This ecclesiastic is also in choir dress – a surplice over a fur-lined cassock (the fur lining is indicated by hatching marks at the cuffs and hem). An almuce is placed over the shoulders with its ends hanging down in front and a choir cope over this is held in place at the breast with the morse. The hood of the almuce comes over the top of the cope at the neck.

dens' accounts of the time of the Puritanism that was to come.

The inventory for Cranbrook parish church in 1509 shows that all benefactors were regularly noted down on a roll of honour that their gifts might be known and remembered. John Hendely gave three copes of purple velvet. 'whereof one was a velvet upon velvet with images broidered' and, adds the inventory, 'for a perpetual memory of this deed of goodness to the common purposes of the parish church, his name is to be read out to the people on festival days.' At Leverton, in the county of Lincoln, the parson Sir John Wright presented the church with a suit of red purple vestments, 'for the which' says the note in the churchwarden's accounts:

you shall all specially pray for the soul of William Wright and Elizabeth his wife [the donor's father and mother] and for the soul of Sir William Wright, their son, and for the soul of Sir John, sometime parson of this place, and for the souls of Richard Wright and Isobel his wife, John Trowting and Helen his wife, and for all benefactors, as well as them that be alive as them that be departed to the mercy of God, for whose lives and souls are given here [these vestments] to the honour of God, his most blessed mother, our Lady Saint Mary, and all his saints in heaven, and the blessed Helen his patron, to be used at such principal feasts and times as it shall please the curates as long as they shall last. For all these souls and for all christian souls you shall say one paternoster.[5]

The Reformation

In 1534 an Act of Parliament consummated the schism for which England had been preparing and the realm was formally separated from the authority of the Pope and from the unity of Christendom. In this year Henry VIII ordered a general survey to be made of all ecclesiastical revenues, the results being recorded in the *Valor Ecclesiasticus*. In 1535 Thomas Cromwell appointed two commissioners to visit and report, and as a result we have a comprehensive record of the vestments of churches, large and small, and of cathedrals and monasteries.[6] Scholars of liturgical history will have seen signs of the Reformation many years before the events that led up to the break with Rome, but costume historians will discover a much slower break with tradition and vestments

25 John Jewel (1522–71) Bishop of Salisbury. Artist unknown. The square cap, which in academic circles developed into the mortar board, is in the transitional stage, the four corners gradually stiffening and flattening. The bishop, author of the *Apology* of 1562, the first official statement of the Anglican Settlement, is wearing professional rather than ecclesiastical dress; specifically religious dress was much hated by some of the reformers.

were the last outward signs of allegiance to disappear.

At Morebath, Devon, in 1528 the vicar gave up his rights to certain wool tithes in order to purchase a complete set of black vestments, which were only finished and paid for, at the cost of £6 5s 0d, in 1547.[7] The royal injunctions of 1548 ordered all the ornaments to be cleared away as superstitions, but the commission of 1553 still found it worthwhile to confiscate more church goods which could be turned into money and paid into the Exchequer. A small village in Berkshire, Boxford, still has vestments which were listed by the commissioners: '. . . one cope of blue velvet embroidered with images of angles, one vestment of the same suit with an albe of Lockeram [a fine linen cloth made in Brittany], two vestments of Dornexe [a rich stuff interwoven with gold and silver, made at Tournay, which was formerly called Doineck, in Flanders] and three other very old, two old and coarse albes of Lockeram, two old copes of Dornexe, ... two surplices and one rochet.' The inventory of 10 April 1540 of the vestments left in the cathedral church of Canterbury after the suppression of the monastery shows a considerable number of vestments for the number of monks – there were only fifty-three monks including the prior. There were 262 copes including sets of 50, 45, 28, 16 and 15, 129 of which were in the inventory of 1315–16. There were thirty suits for the priest, deacon and sub-deacon, and twenty-seven chasubles with their albs, all highly decorated and embroidered in the same manner as in the preceding two centuries, with coats of arms, secular subjects such as flowers or plants (vine branches, columbines, etc.), animals, griffons and birds, all in the traditional colours and fabrics.[8]

The cope was destined to become adopted by the Anglican Church and there were large numbers to be found in all churches. Cardinal Wolsey had forty-four in his chapel.[9] In the Prayer Book of 1549 the rubric directs that the priest ministering the Holy Communion is to wear 'a white albe plaine, with a vestment or cope' and for the ante-communion service, when no celebration followed, the officiant was to wear an alb or surplice, with a cope.

Clergymen continued to be tempted by bright colours and rich fabrics and furs in their private life. A sitting of the Star Chamber on 11 November 1520 decided that whilst it was outside the province of the secular law to determine the cut of a priest's cassock, or the shape of his tonsure, it could clearly determine that no priest should wear cloth made out of the country, or costing above a certain price; and it might fix the amount of salary to be paid to a chaplain or curate.[10] In an inventory of goods and chattels in the Rectory of Allington, Kent, dated April 1534, there is a description of the clothes found in the chamber of the parson's lodgings:

Item one gown of violet cloth lined with red saye
Item a gown of black cloth furred with lamb
Item, two hoods of violet cloth, whereof one is lined with green sarcenet
Item, one jerkin of tawny camlet
Item, one jerkin of cloth furred with white
Item, a jacket of cloth furred ...
Item, one typett of sarcenet[11]

John Sall, the third prior of Butley Priory and precentor of Norwich Cathedral in 1526 had an exquisite taste in footwear. He sported red silk bows on his shoes, sometimes wore dancing boots and sometimes top boots 'and on one occasion did not blush to lift his frock and display his elegant footwear'. Sall's example was not lost on the novices of his house, some of whom are reported to have appeared in 'top-boots' and wearing hats with satin rosettes and lappets.[12] William Thornton, the last abbot of St Mary's York, was also guilty of wearing lay clothes. In 1535 he corresponded with Thomas Cromwell in order to prevent Archbishop Lee coming to inspect his house. The abbot promised to accept the order to wear his habit 'like one of my cloister brethren' unless Cromwell commanded otherwise. His pleas were unsuccessful and the dissolution of this great and wealthy abbey took place in 1539.[13] He had been reproved by the Archbishop of York for wearing 'silken girdles ornamented with gold and silver, and gold and silver rings,' and it was fashionable to wear a great number of rings. The will of William Pakeham 'Yemen', dated 4 August 1504 includes five rings all of which he bequeathes to clerics, (his clothes he leaves to laymen).

... Item to my sayd Lord Edmund [Edmund Lychfield Prior of Butley Aug 1503 – Dec 1504] my rynge of goolde with the grene stone ... item I bequeath to Syr William Woodbregge supprior my brode rynge off gold. Item to Ser John Denston [Canon of Butley] my rynge off goolde with the Sarsyn's hede. Item to Ser John Mendham [Canon of Butley] my broken ryng off gold. Item to Syr Water [Canon Walter Bawdesey] my sygnett off sylver ...[14]

The tonsure disappeared in England among the clergy in the sixteenth century. This had already begun to go in the fifteenth and a synod or council of the province of Canterbury, held in St Paul's in February 1487, condemned the clergy's imitation of the laity in their dress when not officiating, and allowing their hair to grow so long as completely to conceal the tonsure (they were also asked to wear their hair short enough to reveal their ears).[15] As an outward sign of allegiance the tonsure caused much anger in the reformers, and although the practice fell into disuse quite naturally the attempts to revive it were associated with 'popish practices'. Rowland Taylor, the reformer who was condemned to death and burnt in 1558, interrupted an attempt to say the Mass the old way at Hadleigh church. When Taylor heard the bell he found the church door barred but got in at the chancel door and saw 'a popish sacrificer in robes, with a broad new shaven crown, ready to begin his popish sacrifice.'[16]

The correct lay dress of the clergy immediately before the Reformation was the cassock, the priest's cap, the almuce, the tippet and the black cope or cloak. These were not kept in the vestries as they were part of the ordinary clerical dress of the time; the surplice might almost have been included with them, as most clerks wore their own and went to church with them. Priests are represented on brasses in choir dress, that is the almuce and surplice, under which is worn the cassock. The proper adjunct of the almuce, which no longer served the function of a hood, was the pileus or biretum, a simple cap which developed into the square cap so familiar in the portraits of Elizabethan bishops and clergy. As with all headwear the biretta or cap worn in the administration of the Holy Communion was and is unlawful.[17]

As the tippet and hood replaced the almuce the cap was retained. The tippet was a scarf of black silk, sometimes lined with fur, and although associated with the hood took its development at this stage from the almuce. The almuce was worn under the vestments and when worn under the cope could only be identified by the two long strips hanging down the front. Just before the Reformation the custom of turning the fur in, so that only the black cloth lining could be seen, became the rule and eventually the fur disappeared completely. The canonical vestments are very important at this stage of the history since it is these that were adopted as liturgical dress when the vestments of the old order were removed.

In the Prayer Book of 1549 the clergy (not officiating) and choir – at least those in cathedrals and colleges – were ordered to wear surplice and hood and the hood was also recommended to be worn by preachers. Martin Bucer, a German ex-Dominican who was the Regius Professor at Cambridge[18] and an important reformer, noted

26 Reginald Pole (1500–58), Cardinal and Archbishop of Canterbury. Artist unknown. This portrait was undoubtedly painted after 1556 when Cardinal Pole was made archbishop. He is in the hooded cape buttoned down the front which is called the mozetta, and wears a soft square cap, which must not be confused with the biretta of the cardinals in continental Europe. His cardinal's hat is painted on the wall behind, along with his coat of arms.

at the time that, as a concession to the conservatives, the vestments commonly used in the sacrament of the Eucharist were retained. A new Prayer Book and the Second Act of Uniformity followed in 1552 under the influence of Cranmer, the year before the young King Edward VI died. Ceremonies intended to emphasize the priestly functions of the clergy were omitted or modified, which meant that all copes and Eucharist vestments now became illegal and many were destroyed.

The Reign of Queen Mary

In 1554 the staunchly catholic Queen Mary (reigned 1553–8) did her best to reverse the trend and drew up a public set of injunctions which included a purge removing about twenty per cent of the clergy. Vestments which had survived were mended and brought out into use again, and where funds or means permitted new vestments were made. In the City church of St Mary-at-Hill, London, the chuchwarden's accounts for this year record the purchase of many Latin books and the making of a 'bisshopes myter'.[19]

Despite the enormous destruction of vestments there were still many that survived and in Mary's reign 'on the anniversary of St Paul, then a high day in the City, there was a general and solemn procession through London, to give God thanks for their conversion to the Catholic Church. To set out their glorious pomp ... one hundred and sixty priests and clerks, who had everyone of them copes upon their backs, singing loudly.'[20]

Vestments Retained in the Anglican Church

The establishment of the Church of England did not come until the reign of Queen Elizabeth I (1558–1603) who re-introduced in 1559 what was practically the Prayer Book of 1552 in her Act of Uniformity. Here the so-called 'ornaments rubric' was introduced and allowed the vestments in use in the time of Edward VI to be kept, namely the alb and chasuble or cope, and worn at the Eucharist; the puritans' disapproval will be dealt with in the next chapter. The comments in Foxe's *Book of Martyrs* (1563) sum up the changes and the aspects preserved in the liturgy that Elizabeth I considered worth keeping:

In former times, all who officiated were peculiarly habited, and all their garments were blessed, and these were considered as a part of the train of the mass; but, on the other hand, white had been the colour of the priest's vestments under the Mosiac Law, and had early been brought into the Christian churches; it was thought a proper expression of innocence, and it being fit that the worship of God should be in a decent habit, it was continued. Since the sacrifices offered to idols were not thereby according to St. Paul of their own

nature polluted, and every creature of God was good, it was thought, notwithstanding the former abuse, most reasonable to use these garments still.[21]

Dress for Dancers and Performers

Before moving on to the reformed Church we can note here an aspect of the English Church which was very important at the time. Alongside vestments in the inventories are lists of costumes worn by dancers and performers. At the close of the reign of Henry VIII a small parish church, St Dunstan's in Canterbury, possessed a library of some fifty volumes: of these about a dozen were mystery plays, no doubt the Corpus Christi mystery plays, which were carried out with undiminished splendour until the advent of the new ideas in the reign of Edward VI.[22] Morris dancing, brought to England by the returning crusaders, was obviously popular. The churchwarden's accounts of 1537–8 at Kingston upon Thames, Surrey show: 'A fryers cote of russet and a kyrtele welded with red cloth, a mowrens [moor's] cote of buckram, and four morres dauncers cotes of white fustian spangelid, and too gryne satin cotes, and disarrds cote of cotton and six payre of garters with belles.'[23]

Parish plays were a further source of occasional income and were managed for the common profit. For example at Tintinhull, Somerset, in 1541 five parishioners got up a Christmas play for the benefit of the fund required for the erection of the new rood loft.[24] As late as 1556–7 the Church is spending money on its entertainments; the accounts of the churchwarden at St Mary's, Reading, read:

Item payed for the morrys dauncers and the mynstrelles mete and drinke at Whitsuntide   iiis iiijd
Item payed to them the sondy after Mayday   xxd
Pd to the painter for paynting of their cottes   iis viijd
Pd for a peir of showes for the morrys dauncers   iiijs
Pd for iiij dozen belles of the morrys dauncers   ijs
Pd for sewing of the morrys cottes[25]   vijd

CHAPTER SIX

The Elizabethan Settlement and The Birth of Protestantism 1559–1658

THE BOOK OF COMMON PRAYER of Edward VI, 1549, contains the last references to the chasuble and dalmatic in the emergent Anglican Church: for the bishop 'besyde his rochette, a surples or albe, and a cope or vestment, and also his pastoral staff in his hande, or elles borne or holden by his chapeleyne.' The mitre would be worn with the cope for processional wear, and vestment can refer to the chasuble or the set of chasuble, dalmatic and tunicle. As has been already noted, the dalmatic and tunicle had become almost identical by this period and tended to be known as 'tunacles' in the sixteenth century; from this time the rochet became best known as the special garment of the bishop when in choir dress or 'canonicals'; the surplice or the alb was worn when the bishop was celebrating. For the priest ministering the Holy Communion 'a white albe plain, with a vestement, or cope' was required and for the assistant priests and the deacons 'Albes with tunacles'; here again the word 'tunacle' is used instead of dalmatic. In all cathedrals and colleges, graduates might 'use in the quiere, besides their surplesses, such hoodes as pertaineth to their seuerall degrees'.

The Elizabethan Surplice

There is no reference to the dalmatic and tunicle from the reign of Elizabeth I and when a consultative committee met, in December 1558, to discuss the possibilities of restoring the Prayer Book of Edward VI there was no mention of any garment other than the surplice, which was considered sufficient for all the services including the Holy Communion. By the injunction of Elizabeth in 1563 the surplice became the universal vestment of all Anglican clergy at all services.

As the Puritan element grew stronger it was 'a significant sign of the temper of the times that the storm centre of ecclesiastical controversy in the reign of Elizabeth was a piece of linen. In Mary's reign it was the Mass. In Elizabeth's reign it was the surplice. On the whole they did not object to the Prayer Book.'[1]

English advertisements and canons speak of the surplice as 'with sleeves', and the garment came in several forms. On the Continent in the Roman Catholic Church the surplice became very short and in the seventeenth century broad bands of lace became the norm on both surplices and albs. (The apparels of the alb had disappeared in the course of time and the surplice had never been decorated in such a way.) The sleeveless 'chasuble-shaped' surplice, a simple white linen garment with a hole for the head and ample fullness, was generally worn by the lower orders and is found in great numbers in Europe; it can be called a 'fanon' as the cloth of this form of the surplice was used to cover the hands when holding sacred vessels.[2] In 1638 in *Articles to be enquired of within the diocese of Exeter*, printed by Thomas Harper, mention is made of both types of surplice: '2. Item whether you have two faire and fitting surplesses with sleeves for your minuster, and another without sleeves for your clarke.' There is another entry in this document which points out a potential confusion: '63 Item. Is your parish clark of the age of twenty yeeres at the least . . . and doth he usually wear his surplesse or rochet in the time of Divine Service.'[3] The rochet is normally associated with the episcopal linen garment with very full sleeves, but it also could mean a sleeveless version worn by the lower orders.

The surplice in England is generally an ample

white linen garment with large sleeves worn over a gown and put on over the head. With the cap and gown for outdoor wear, the surplice was ordained for all clergy in the reformed Church of England. An unnamed bishop was so uncertain of having to accept gown, cap and surplice that he almost refused the bishopric. In August 1559 he wrote to Peter Martyr, then at Zurich, for his advice and judgement. The reply was to refuse the surplice, which smacked of popery, but not to worry about the cap and gown. This advice was to be the line taken by many Puritans in authority in the future, as the danger of being deprived of the liberty of preaching was too great to risk on mere garments. Peter Martyr repeats this view in another letter: 'for altho' we should not at all approve them, yet we would bear them'.[4]

The surplice survived in the Anglican Church only because those in authority took the line of wearing it, while still preaching and teaching against it, as it was not worth risking being removed from the ministry. On 25 January 1564 Queen Elizabeth I wrote to the Archbishop of Canterbury asking him to stop all diversity among his clergy and 'that he should peremptorily see order in the habits observed by all ecclesiastical persons' and this was followed by a similar letter to the Archbishop of York.[5] 'At which praiers, Mr Deane (when he is here) and every of the Prebendaries are present euery daie once at the Leaste Apperryled in the Quyer and when they preache with surples and silke hoodes. The Preachers beinge at home come to the Common Praier on Sondaies and holie daies wearing surplyses and Hoodes. The pety cannons, the Laye Clerkes and Queristories wear Surplyses in the Quire daylie.' (This also included schoolmasters, 'queries highnes schollers' and ushers.)[6] There were many clergy who refused to accept these 'popish rags' and 'Aaronic habits', often because they had spent some time on the Continent in Protestant communities where such garments had been totally abandoned. In December 1565 the fellows and scholars of St John's College, Cambridge, all with one consent threw off the surplice. The Master of the college, Longworth, was absent (apparently on purpose) and the college company came into the chapel one festival day without surplice and hood. On his return, he

27 William Warham, Archbishop of Canterbury (1503–32). After Hans Holbein, 1527. Archbishop Warham is in choir dress with his mitre, now elaborately tall, and his cross staff behind him. His sleeved rochet is worn over his fur-lined cassock, whose sleeves are folded back to form cuffs. His tippet is also lined with fur, worn around the neck and hanging down the front. As this portrait is set informally, he is not wearing the hood or any other vestments, and he wears a skull cap which is cut low so as to cover his ears.

neither complained nor reported this, although it was discovered by Sir William Cecil, the university's High Chancellor who reported it to the Queen. She was very angry and demanded severe punishment, but disobedience had spread and King's College alone remained quiet and obedient in the wearing of the surplice.

The terms and symbols of the coalition between various Protestant factions were contained in the Act of Uniformity and the Royal Injunctions of 1559. The senior bishops of the time had interpreted these in a number of informal resolutions and had agreed on the minimal requirement of the white linen surplice for all liturgical occasions. In 1565 Matthew Parker (Archbishop of Canterbury, 1559–76), Edmund Grindal (who was to succeed Parker as archbishop) and four other episcopal members of the ecclesiastical commission drafted a collection of articles which codified many details of ceremonial, including vestarian practice. Despite his involvement in these commissions Grindal made no secret of his personal distaste for the prescribed clerical attire and other ceremonies. If he had felt able to exercise a personal preference there is no doubt that Grindal would have had no brief for the disputed vestments. 'You see me wear a cope or a surplice in Pauls' he told some radical Puritans in 1567, 'I had rather minister without these things, but do for orders sake and obedience to the Prince'.[7]

The cope and surplice implied to the uninstructed eye the continuity of the English Church and its past traditions rather than solidarity with the international reformed community. Grindal was free to advise against the surplice to English congregations overseas which came under his jurisdiction as Bishop of London. '. . . neither need you use any surplice, whether they use it or no, for they know that the high Almayne churches use none', Grindal states in a letter to William Cole, preacher to the Merchant Adventurers in Antwerp.[8]

Early in his episcopate Grindal gave dispensation to one of his ordinands, Thomas Upcher, to minister without the surplice to a congregation near Colchester which was deeply prejudiced against 'the popish attire'. Upcher was told to tolerate this situation 'for a time, till it be complained of, yet in the meantime privately to exhort the godly so to frame their judgments that they conceive no offence if it be altered hereafter by authority.' Unfortunately, neighbouring clergy also took advantage of this, which angered Grindal. 'I perceive they intend to make my diocese a place of liberty for every man to break the common orders at his own pleasure. But it may not be so, for as I wish reformation of orders, so the orders standing I will not bear the burden of license in breaking them by private authority.'[9]

Rowley in his *Match at Midnight*, 1633, makes one of his characters say of another 'it has tirn'd his stomach, for all the world like a puritan's at the sight of a surplice'.[10] John Hooper 'the father of non-conformity' refused to wear a surplice and cope which he called 'Aaronic habits', at his consecration as Bishop of Gloucester, declaring

that he would countenance no ceremonies but such as could be justified by the New Testament.[11] The deep dislike of the surplice and cope did not die away. Even before James I (1603–25) arrived at his capital, the leaders of the Puritan party presented him with a petition known as the Millenary Petition, which contained eight points. No. 5 was 'that the surplice should not be compulsory'.[12] At the time of the Prayer Book of Charles II, 1662 (worked out at the Savoy Conference) the King acknowledged the items which were the 'storm centres', such as the surplice, kneeling in the Holy Communion, the sign of the cross in baptism, and bowing at the name of Jesus, and allowed them to be regarded as optional until the Savoy Conference had come to a final decision.[13]

The Cope

The cope had been retained by cathedrals and collegiate churches, and generally less fuss was made about it than about the surplice, possibly because many bishops, like Grindal, felt that it was not worth losing their authority as a preacher over a garment; perhaps also some of the older men felt more comfortable in the vestments with which they had been brought up. However, the old copes that had survived in the cathedral vestries were still being sold for cash and only a few were reserved.

From the inventories at Christ Church, Canterbury, it is apparent that some vestments had survived the confiscations and destruction of Henry VIII. In November 1570 'Item yt is agreid that the vestments and the other vestrye stuffe remaynyng in the vestrye shall be viewed and solde, reservyng some of the coapes, and the money that shall arryse of the same to be bestowed in byeng of necessary armor.' (The church was probably being asked to provide money for armour after the northern rising of 1569.) But in 1584, notwithstanding the order of 'reservyng some of the Coapes' not one was kept of the good stock left by the archbishop in 1563.[14]

In the Public Record Office there is a list of plunder delivered to the Treasurer of Augmentations. Some of the items, including copes, can be identified with items from the Canterbury inventories of 1540. The ten copes of gold no doubt belong to the set of fifty of Cardinal Morton's gift. The 'one coope of golde bawdekyn wt red rooses' is possibly that described in the inventory as 'one cope of red golde bawdekyn wth orpheras embroudered.'

The vast majority of copes were probably sold because they were very valuable, but there were also not many people who clamoured for their preservation. In the Canterbury inventory of 1540 there were nearly a hundred white copes and in 1563 only fifteen remained; in 1540 there were over fifty green copes and in 1563 only eight remained. All the remaining copes can be traced back to the earlier inventory, which shows that no new copes were made. The red and blue copes are not all so easy to identify, so it is possible that some new ones were made; this could well have happened in the reign of Mary, although the descriptions are not always very clear. Interestingly, the greatest proportion of surviving copes are twenty blue copes in 1563 out of thirty seven in 1540 (only five can be positively identified). Blue, as we have seen in earlier chapters, is not strictly speaking a liturgical colour, but has always been greatly favoured in the Church. In the vestments still recorded in the sixteenth century the main liturgical colours are all also represented: white, red, green and black.

Another, albeit minor, threat to the survival of copes was the sudden intrusion of clergy wives who, now living in the previously bachelor precincts and closes of cathedrals, set about making their accommodation more comfortable. In 1563 the dean and chapter of Worcester were accused of breaking up the large organ which had cost £200. Its metal pipes had been melted to make dishes for the wives of prebendaries and its case had been used to make beds for them. Sir John Bourne, who lodged his complaint with the privy council, said the wives would have shared the copes and ornaments if the unmarried men had not prevented them.[15]

In 1634 the only cope remaining in the vestry at Canterbury was 'a scarlett cope lyned with minerver left unto the church by Dr. Clarcke'. This was not the traditional cope but a type of academic cloak which had belonged to Richard Clarke, doctor of divinity, who was living in the precincts (although not a member) of the cathedral church in 1634 (the year he died).[16]

The Cap and Gown

The Puritans wanted to get rid not only of the cope and surplice but also of the cap and gown. The injunctions of Elizabeth I in 1559 stated that the clergy 'shall use and wear such seemly habits, garments and square caps as were most commonly and orderly received in the latter year of the reign of Edward VI'.[17] The massacre of St Bartholomew in 1572 added fuel to the fire of anti-papal feeling in Europe.

When the news reached England that Pope Gregory and his cardinals had walked in procession from church to church to give thanks for this colossal murder, the sensation was profound . . . the popularity of those who advocated the abolition of every shred and tatter of Romanist practice was immensely increased. The puritans within the church who were for reforming her altogether by making a clean sweep of sacerdotal vestments and ritual were provided with new argument.[18]

A series of satirical pamphlets was published by an unknown author in the 1580s known as *Martin Marprelates Tracts*. He brought to light scandals concerning bishops of the time, including Whitgift of Canterbury (1583–1604), Aylmer of London and Cooper of Winchelsea. In one pamphlet he proposes a bargain: 'If they encourage preaching, making only Godly and fit persons preachers . . . punish nobody for refusing to wear popish garments', he on his side would promise 'never to make any more of your knavery known to the world'. The last Martin tract was printed in July 1589.[19]

The long clerical gown and square cap ordered for the clergy in 1559 acquired, as uniforms are apt to do, a special and emotive significance. Although this costume was supposed to be nearly neutral in religious terms and not connected with the Catholic Eucharistic vestments, it became, like the surplice in the ministrations, associated with the old Church and was rejected by the Puritans. From the point of view of Elizabeth and her senior bishops these garments were necessary as merely 'distinct habits' with no special, holy or superstitious meaning.[20]

There were various forms of gowns which came from the everyday dress of professional men and pre-dated Edward VI. In the sumptuary laws

28 Richard Bancroft, Archbishop of Canterbury (1604–10). Artist unknown. Richard Bancroft is in the ecclesiastical dress of the newly emergent Anglican Church. Vestments have been discarded but the black gown or cassock is retained, covered by a white linen rochet, a type of surplice special to bishops. He wears the black scarf or tippet, and possibly the hood though it is not visible here. He wears a square cap and has the fashionable beard and ruff around the neck.

of Henry VIII (set down to regulate the materials used, not the habits themselves) the clergy are described as wearing both the gown and the 'sleeveless cote' and both garments can be found on brasses of the date. Gowns were worn long and the sleeves came in various widths. The preacher's gown with wide sleeves was originally worn at court by clergy who were not doctors, although in this form and made of silk it became the gown of doctors in divinity at Oxford and Cambridge in the early seventeenth century. Another form of gown had wide sleeves gathered in a band at the wrist with a small frill (the pudding-sleeved gown). This was not such a popular style and its general lack of use was possibly due to the inconvenience of the bulky sleeve and the buttons at the wrist. The rochet, made of fine linen, took

over this style and these inconveniences were no drawback to this garment's development.[21]

The 'sleeveless cote' is a development of the *cappa clausa*, open in front with slits at the side through which the arms were put. The *cappa clausa* had been adopted by the universities as the dress of doctors and in the form of a closed cope with a slit at the breast for the arms survived at Cambridge until the twentieth century. Originally it could be of any material, depending on the wealth of the clerk, but the doctor's cope of Cambridge, which was worn on various occasions by doctors in divinity, was of scarlet cloth, 'The hood, which is of the old full form loosely attached and coming round the shoulders, of white fur.' White fur also forms the border of the opening for the hands (The Cambridge form was also slit down the centre front at a later date for convenience.) This style had vanished from Oxford at or before the Reformation. Alexander Barclay seems to imply that it was in his day (1514) peculiar to Cambridge. He says in his first *Eclogue*

And once in Cambridge I heard a scoller say
(one of the same that go in Copes gay)[21]

The Oxford doctors' convocation habit was a scarlet gown with slits at the side through which the sleeves of the master of arts gown, or surplice, were drawn. It was this sleeveless gown that became the bishop's chimere, and the scarlet chimere could not be worn by a bishop who did not happen to be a doctor.[22] In the reign of Elizabeth the colour was changed to black as a compromise. Bishop Hooper was among those who objected strongly to the colour scarlet.[23]

The Puritans wore the Geneva gown, a black preaching gown with wide sleeves and open down the front (adopted by Calvin and most Protestants on the Continent); they also wore the hat, and hated the cap and gown. Nowell and others made a request to the convocation of 1562 'that the ministers be not compelled to wear such gowns and caps as the enemies of Christ's gospel have chosen to be the special array of their priesthood.'[24]

Again the two sides of the argument were taken by those who abhorred the offending garments and those who did not think they were worth the

1 *St Cuthbert's maniple. Detail: Peter Deacon, embroidered between 909 and 916. Peter is wearing the correct dress for a deacon, with his stole over his left shoulder and the maniple carried in the left hand. He wears the dalmatic over the alb*

2 *The Marnhull orphrey, 1315-35. Detail of a cross orphrey showing the Crucifixion, with the Virgin Mary and the beloved disciple John mourning at the foot of the Cross. This scene became very popular for the decoration on the chasuble; the shape of the orphrey lent itself to the symbol of redemption, which was most common subject from the fourteenth century. On the left is the figure of St Peter, and on the right that of St Paul*

3 *Apparel of an alb: scenes from the life of the Virgin, early fourteenth century; an embroidery from the great age of Opus Anglicanum*

argument. Bishop Harding, Jewel's adviser wrote in 1570 'Doo not somme wear side-gownes, havinge large sleeves, which is not wel liked of your secte, some of more perfection [that is Puritans] Turkey Gownes, gaberdines, frocks or night-gownes of the most laye fashion for avoiding of superstition. The thinge is indifferent, and may be yelded unto saithe one secte. They be the Popes ragges, and maie not be worn saithe the other secte!'[25]

It is extraordinary that with such strong feeling against them these styles survived, but they did. In 1566 Grindal proposed a meeting with the bishops of Winchester and Ely on 19 January to try to come to an agreement. They tried to introduce a distinctive but novel form of outdoor dress, with a round instead of a square cap. This did not entirely succeed and a year later Grindal was reporting another 'womanish brabble' on account of the square cap he was still wearing. When he appeared in the church of St Margaret, Fish Street, he was irreverently hooted at with cries of ''ware horns.'[26]

Outdoor dress was regulated by the 74th canon of 1603–4 which is headed 'Decency in Apparel enjoined to Ministers'. This includes 'All Deans, Masters of Colleges, Archdeacons and Prebendaries in Cathedral and Collegiate Churches (being priests or deacons), Doctors in Divinity, Law and Physic, Bachelors in Divinity, Masters of Art, Bachelors of Law having any ecclesiastical living ...'. The prescribed rules for clerical dress were gowns with standing collars and without any falling cape, with sleeves straight to the hand, or wide sleeves such as those used in the universities, with hoods and tippets of silk or sarcenet and square caps. During their journeys parsons are ordered to wear cloaks with sleeves, commonly called priest's cloaks 'without guards, welts, long buttons or cuts ... No ecclesiastical person shall wear any coif or wrought nightcap, but only plain nightcaps of black silk, satin or velvet. In private houses parsons may use any comely and scholar-like apparel, provided it be not cut or pinkt: and in public they go not in doublet and hose, without coats or cassocks; and that they wear not any light coloured stockings.'[27]

Clergy were therefore allowed to use everyday dress as long as it was not fashionably slashed –

'cut or pinkt' – and was suitably scholarly. Bishop Davies of St Asaph in 1561 gave permission for short gowns to be worn; in his injunctions for his diocese he gives the order that 'every parson, vicar, curate and minister shall use and wear decent and seemly apparel, that is to wit, a short gown and a square cap with a tippet, and a hat to ride, and a long gown when they come before their ordinary.'[28] With all the many divergent groups within the reformed Church, and perhaps because of the lack of unified authority from above, clergy did not always conform to these directives, and odd varieties of dress did appear. In 1638 Bishop Montague in his visitation articles for the diocese of Norwich asks: 'Does your Minister officiate Divine Service in one place upon set times, in the habit and apparel of his order, with a surplice, a hood, a gown, a tippet, not in a cloak or sleeveless jacket or horseman's coat? For such I have known.'[29]

The citizens of London in the 'Root and Branch' petition of 1640 demanded that 'the four cornered cap, the cope and surplice, the tippet, the hood, and the canonical coat' should be abolished. The 'canonical coat' means the priest's gown which eventually became the cassock. It has already the slightly confusing dual role of being the topmost garment, a coat, when worn outside the church and yet worn under the surplice in the services. When the surplice was removed for preaching the preacher's gown was revealed underneath, rather than the surplice being exchanged for the gown. This is indicated in the words spoken by the clown in Shakespeare's *All's Well That Ends Well* Act I, Scene 3 (written at the beginning of the seventeenth century): 'Though honesty be no puritan, yet it will do no hurt; it will wear the surplice of humility over the black gown of a big heart.'

Feelings were running so high that some clergy were content to suffer a kind of martyrdom by ejection from their livings. In 1566, a year after the 'Advertisements' of Parker and Grindal, thirty-four London clergymen, refusing to be bound to this standard, were suspended from their ministry.[30] The controversy of the cap, gown and surplice vanished at the Restoration when irreconcilable Puritans left the established Church.

Mention must be made of William Laud,

Of God,   Of Man,   Of the Divell.

29 'Of God, of Man, of the Divell'. The lines that go with this woodcut are:

> Loe, here are three men, ftanding in degree,
> The leafte of thefe, the greateft ought to be.
> The other two, of men and of the Devill.
> Ought to be rooted out for ere as evill.

The reaction against clerical dress was not content with the abolition of vestments. The two clerics, 'of Man' and 'Of the Divell' are dressed identically in square cap, ruff, rochet and chimere. The man 'of God' wears a skull cap, cassock and gown, also with a ruff. The Anglican clergy retained the rochet and chimere, despite many attempts to get rid of them. The Non-conformists rejected these and retained the cassock and gown for preaching and official functions.

Archbishop of Canterbury 1633–60, who went to the Tower for his strength of belief in the Anglican Church. He was a bitter opponent of Calvinism and Puritanism and desired to see the Church of England Catholic and reformed in the spirit of Jewel and Hooker, but with more outward expression in ceremonial and ritual. Born in 1573, he was Fellow of St John's College Oxford in 1593. In 1616 he was made Dean of Gloucester where he offended the Bishop, Miles Smith, a Calvinist, by getting the chapter to remove the altar to the east end of the cathedral. In 1617 he went to Scotland with James I and shocked the Presbyterians by wearing a surplice. He was made Bishop of St David's in 1621; interpreting his favourite phrase 'the beauty of holiness' to mean order and ceremonial in the Church, he set himself to restore most of the ecclesiastical arrangements which had been abolished in the Reformation.

The Tonsure

The tonsure had been neglected before the Reformation but was reintroduced during the reign of Mary as an outward sign of allegiance; this, of course, gave rise to great scorn from the Puritans. Thomas Cole, an archdeacon, compared Popish priests to apes 'for, "saith he", they both be bald alike, but that the priests be bald before, the apes behind.' As the clergy lost the tonsure they began to follow the lay fashions and grew their hair and wore beards. An early example is the double portrait by Holbein, 'The Ambassadors,' painted in 1533, where both the cleric and the layman wear beards. The paintings in the National Portrait Gallery show the early clergy Cranmer (1489–1555), William Warham (*c.* 1450–1532), Wolsey (*c.* 1457–1530) without beards; Richard Bancroft (1544–1610), John Whitgift (*c.* 1530–1604), Reginald Pole (1500–58), Hugh Latymer (*c.* 1485–1555), Nicholas Ridley (*c.* 1500–55), John Donne (*c.* 1572–1631) all have beards. Clergy continued to follow lay fashions and later were to adopt the wig as readily.

The Survival of Catholic Vestments

Catholicism continued in Britain, but was driven underground by the strength of the Puritan movement, and no vestments were retained except in complete secrecy. On the whole such Catholics as there were found it practical to dispense with vestments. 'As late as 1585 we have a pathetic picture of "Uncle James", an old Henrican Priest, travelling with his few trinkets about the countryside administering Catholic rites: his chalice and paten of tin, his girdle of thread, his two little boxes for singing bread and an old mass-book.'[32]

Many vestments were taken abroad; Laurence Vaux, Warden of Manchester College went off to Ireland, taking the plate and vestments with him, hoping to return if the old order was restored. The Syon cope was taken away to the Continent with a religious order which went for safety, and thus was preserved; the Bridgettine Nuns of Syon left England early in the reign of Elizabeth, they carried the vestment with them through Flanders, France and Portugal, and they returned with it to England in 1830.

The Commonwealth

Sixteenth-century Britain saw four different rulers, four major rebellions and three changes of religion. The country became so divided under Charles I that even Presbyterianism became a major threat; as Milton said: 'New Presbyter is but old Priest writ large' and Civil War broke out, culminating in the beheading of the king on 30 January 1649 on a scaffold outside the banqueting hall in Whitehall. Oliver Cromwell then headed the Commonwealth until his death in 1658. The religious life of the country was in a state of great confusion, with no proper organization or control after the abolition of the episcopacy. The death of Charles I came as a great shock to many people and for a while he came as near to canonization as is possible in the Church of England, with special services being held each year on 30 January until 1859. An order was issued in 1650 to say that everyone must attend some place of worship or a place where religious exercises were held; but that meant very little.[33] Church life in England was at a very low ebb; only civil marriage was officially allowed, the observance of Christmas Day was forbidden and all the remaining treasure including vestments was removed from the churches. It is surprising, considering all the waves of iconoclasm which hit Britain during the sixteenth and seventeenth centuries, that any Church treasures have survived until the present day.

It was during this period that various branches of the Protestant Church were forming independent units. The Baptists had broken away from the Brownists early in the seventeenth century and came to England from exile in Holland in 1612 when a number of local churches sprang up. From 1633 onwards they became known as General Baptists to distinguish them from the Particular Baptists who were much more strictly Calvinist. The Congregationalists, the true independents, who regarded the congregation as the unit of Church life and vested much power in the laity, also grew up during the Commonwealth. Not surprisingly, the costume of the ministers of these sects is sober contemporary Puritan dress of the time and is not often illustrated or described.

With the enormous upheaval that followed the break with Rome there was little or no direct contact with Italy and the connection between religion and art had been all but discontinued. The great English tradition of embroidery continued, but was now put to entirely secular use and so cannot be given more space in this book; however, it was strong enough to emerge readily in the nineteenth and twentieth centuries when the Church once more required embroidered vestments.

Roman Catholic Vestments

In continental Europe meanwhile, vestments continued to grow more elaborate, although embroidery ceased to be as important, and rich fabrics in large quantities meant that cassocks, gowns and copes developed cumbersome trains and became the grand ornaments of the particular office. The mitre grew to its largest size in the sixteenth century, and accessories assumed more and more importance.

Ecclesiastical gloves became very elaborate; they were worn during the celebration of Mass by the high officers in the Church – the Pope, cardinals, archbishops, bishops, mitred abbots, precentors and certain other dignitaries who might be granted this privilege. Although all were originally white to denote that the hands of the wearer were pure, chaste, clean and free from all impurity, this colour became confined to the supreme Pontiff. Cardinals wore scarlet, bishops wore violet and abbots wore green. They had been decorated to a certain extent for the past hundred years, but in the sixteenth century the most popular form had a golden nimbus on the back. St Charles Borromeo (1538–84), Archbishop of Milan said, 'they should be woven throughout and adorned with a golden circle on the outside'.[34] To this nimbus encircling the letters IHS were added more or less elaborate flourishes. Horizontal rings appeared upon the glove fingers (even though the real rings were worn over the gloves at this time) and during the

seventeenth century the ornamentation spread over the whole hand. The cuffs followed lay fashions; the earlier gloves of the fifteenth and sixteenth centuries often finished with a tassel, but from about 1620 the cuffs became important and grew very big, large enough to go over the sleeve, and they were heavily decorated.

Although the cassocks and gowns in seventeenth-century Roman Catholic circles developed long trains and were very full, the chasuble and dalmatic continued to be cut down and were reserved as more formal ornaments for the Mass. The violin-shaped and the shield-shaped chasuble were common and continued to be decorated with some embroidery and to be made out of elaborate silks, damasks, brocades, velvets and satins, usually patterned.

An unusual chasuble and dalmatic, both inscribed 1570, are described by Edith Appleton Standen.[35] They are made of wool woven in a tapestry technique, which is unusual for vestments. They probably come from what is now Holland, at Gouda, which fell to the Prince of Orange in 1572. These vestments were probably woven for a private chapel at a time when public suppression of Catholics was just beginning, despite their large numbers. In 1580 the last archbishop died and the Prince of Orange supressed all Roman Catholic public worship in Holland. Edith Appleton Standen describes the decoration: 'On both the chasuble and the dalmatic there are broad orphreys containing bulrushes growing above turbulent waves and tangled by the wind. The plants speak in the Latin motto five times repeated: " flectimur non frangimur undis" – "we are bent, not broken, by the waves".'

The split between the Church of Rome and the Protestant communities was irreversible and in many countries irreconcilable. In Great Britain Catholics had to wait until the nineteenth century until they achieved any freedom and equality: the Catholic Emancipation Bill was passed in 1829.

CHAPTER SEVEN

The Establishment of Protestantism and The Anglican Church 1658–1829

AFTER THE RESTORATION of the Monarchy in Great Britain in 1660 and for the whole of the eighteenth century, the clergy and ministers of all denominations adopted to a greater or lesser degree contemporary fashionable dress. The Roman Catholic priests were effectively stifled and continued their ministry in secret, going about their business 'in disguise' – as tutors, schoolmasters and ordinary citizens. The various Nonconformist sects, who had descended from the more extreme Puritans of the Commonwealth, eschewed clerical dress and wore a sober and conservative version of contemporary professional fashions, adopting and adapting such garments as they considered suitable, and thereby creating a uniform of a sort. The clergy of the new established Church of England wore ordinary dress during the week but did reserve special garments, inherited from the Church of Henry VIII and established into some kind of recognizable form in the reign of Elizabeth I, for services and special occasions; such special dress continued with only natural modifications through to the twentieth century.

Fashionable dress will be only barely indicated here, and if some sects of the Church of England appear to be ignored in this book, it is not because they were not important in the history of the Church, but rather that their contribution to a history of ecclesiastical dress is not great. Churchmen, lawyers and doctors (both medical and academic) all created a type of formal dress, usually dark, if not black (the traditional colour for these professions since at least the sixteenth century) which came to be adopted as the norm for all gentlemen in the nineteenth century. During the eighteenth century there are many similarities in the dress of the three groups including the black academic gown, the white bands and wig, and the dark suit which was everyday wear.

The Suit

By 1670 a new version of the male suit of clothes was established.[1] The doublet was discarded in favour of a knee-length coat and vest (known more familiarly to us as a waistcoat). The vest is mentioned by Samuel Pepys, John Evelyn and other contemporary writers by 1666 and Charles II was responsible for introducing it.[2] Knee-breeches completed this original form of the three-piece suit. Boots continued to come in and out of fashion, but stockings and shoes, worn in the 1660s, were adoped by the clergy, lawyers and doctors. The neckcloth or cravat replaced the lace collar and the outfit was completed by the long periwig, a fashion brought to Britain from France.

At the beginning of this period the coat, vest and knee-breeches of the professional classes differed from those of fashionable men in that they were more sober and conservative in cut and made of black cloth. By the 1740s the colours of the fashionable suit became more subdued and by the 1790s black became a fashionable colour, considered dramatic and romantic, offset by the stark white shirt and neckcloth.[3] Clergy and ministers throughout this time continued to wear this suit, and although it can safely be assumed that it was generally more conservative than fashionable, it was in no way a uniform special to the ordained cleric. Parson Woodforde, who wrote his diary in the second half of the eighteenth century, provides a wealth of information about

30 A Non-conformist minister. Compared to contemporary male fashion this minister is dressed very simply. He wears black which was to become the colour of every minister in every branch of the Church. His wide hat is not cocked and his cloak and gloves are quite plain. The Society of Friends, or Quakers, went one step further and wore no buttons or ribbons. Although Puritans despised wigs and cut their hair very short, longer hair became acceptable even in the most Protestant groups after a while.

31 The Rev. and Mrs Thomas Gisborne by Joseph Wright of Derby, 1786. Rev. Thomas Gisborne is in conservative male dress of the day, distinctive only in that it is dark and that he wears black stockings rather than white. He wears the white stock and frilled shirt that were popular with men of all ranks and professions, but would be retained by clergy for a lot longer. As a young man he has lost his wig with his lay contemporaries; only older clergy and bishops retained the clerical wig into the nineteenth century.

the everyday life of a country clergyman and can serve as an example.[4] James Woodforde often gave away his old clothes to his servants or to the poor of his parish, which clearly indicates that the garments were not particularly clerical: 'I gave my man William a good deal of my old cloathes' (23 March 1774) and 'Gave old Richard Bates an old black coat and waistcoat' (25 December 1776). The simple black coat was worn by all Nonconformists and did not completely distinguish one sect from another (as indeed, it did not always distinguish one profession from another).

George Berkely (1685–1753) was a famous preacher with enormous appeal. Indowick Updike, who, as a boy in Newport, Rhode Island, heard him preach, remarked on his unusual popularity with people of other persuasions: 'All sects rushed to hear him; even the Quakers with their broad brimmed hats, came and stood in the aisles . . .'.[5] Berkely himself attributed this to some extent to his costume. In August 1729 he wrote to Lord Percival describing his relationship with the Quakers: '. . . till then they almost took me for one of their own, to which my everyday dress, being only a straight bodied black coat without plaits on the side, or superfluous buttons, did not a little contribute'.[6]

John Wesley (1703–91), himself a model of neatness and simplicity, wrote to Richard Steele, one of his preachers in Ireland, on 24 April 1769 advising him:

2. Be cleanly. In this let the Methodist take pattern by the Quakers. Avoid all nastiness, dirt, slovenliness, both in your person, clothes, house, and all about you.

3. Whatever clothes you have let them be whole; no rents, no tatters, no rags ... let no-one ever see a ragged Methodist.[7]

John Wesley never left the Church of England and so here we see an Anglican advising his own followers, the Methodists, to dress like Quakers! Parson Woodforde frequently mentions ordering clothes from his mercer or tailor; for example on 24 May 1793 amongst a great deal of other shopping in Norwich, he 'called at my Mercers, Smiths, and bespoke a coat, waistcoat and breeches of him'. And on 11 March 1800 'Taylor

Cary, named Robert, called on me this morn' and measured me for a pair of Breeches of black velverett which he had of me 2 yrds $\frac{1}{2}$.' Unfortunately he does not mention the style in any detail and so again we must draw the conclusion that it was conventional dress of the day.

Wigs

The wig was an item of fashionable dress during the time of Charles II which the clergy adopted and made their own. Ministers and lawyers adopted this fashion very quickly and were reluctant to lose it (the legal profession still retaining it in the latter part of the twentieth century). It is extraordinary how quickly the wig came to be accepted by the clergy, as in its original form it was an extravagant fashion from France worn by fashionable men in court circles. Hair had been worn longer in the time of the Commonwealth: the later portraits of Oliver Cromwell show that even he had begun to grow his hair quite long. At first false hair was added but the full wig came to England from the Continent with the Restoration of the Monarchy in 1660. Samuel Pepys bought his first periwig in 1663 but was at first shy of wearing it.[8] Two years later he was reluctant to wear it for another reason: he notes in his diary of 3 September 1665 '... and it is a

32 The First Methodist Conference, June 25th 1744. John Wesley never set down any rules on clothing for Methodists, and here they are shown as sober professional Non-conformists with dark suits and white bands. The president or chairman is wearing a full-length gown, a preacher's or academic gown.

33 John Wesley, by W. Hamilton, 1788. John Wesley never left the Church of England and he is here seen in cassock and gown with bands, the typical attire of the Anglican clergy. The broad sash at the waist replaced the girdle and Wesley is even wearing a wig, or powdering and dressing his hair to look like one.

34 John Tillotson, Archbishop of Canterbury (1691–94). After Geoffrey Kneller. At the end of the seventeenth century the ruff has completely disappeared even among the professional classes who wore it after it had been discarded by fashion. The falling band has developed into tabs which were to remain part of professional dress until the twentieth century. The sleeves of the archbishop's rochet have become very full, and over the rochet he wears the black chimere, a sleeveless gown. Archbishop Tillotson does not have a wig here although he was one of the first clerics to wear one at this time.

wonder what will be the fashion after the plague is done, as to periwigs who will dare to buy any hair, for fear that it had been cut off the heads of people dead with the plague?'[9]

The fashion did survive and at first the clergy disapproved of wigs and spoke out against them. The early fathers of the Church had always denounced wigs when worn by women, calling them inventions of the devil and telling women who wore them that they were guilty of a mortal sin. However, the fashion soon took a grip and the clergy were all to be found in wigs. 'It was observed that a periwig procured many persons a respect, and even veneration, which they were strangers to before, and to which they had not the least claim from their personal merit. The judges and physicians, who thoroughly understood this magic of the wig, gave it all the advantage of length as well as size.'[10]

John Tillotson (who became Archbishop of

Canterbury in 1691) was the first parson to wear a wig, and refers in one of his sermons to the change of fashion, recalling the time when 'Ministers whatever their text was, did either find or make occasion to reprove the great sin of long hair'.[11] Charles II, who could be considered responsible for this fashion, disliked clergy adopting wigs: 'Nathaniel Vincent D.D. Chaplain in Ordinary to the King, preached before him at Newmarket, in a long periwig and Holland sleeves, according to the then fashion for gentlemen: and that his Majesty was so offended at it, that he commanded the Duke of Monmouth, Chancellor of the University of Cambridge, to see the statutes concerning decency of apparel put in execution, which was done accordingly'.[12]

Despite this, by the end of the seventeenth century the full-bottomed wig was worn by clergy and laity alike, and although the styles changed by the 1730s all bishops, Anglican clergy and most Non-conformists had succumbed to the fashion. A writer in the *Universal Magazine* of 1779 described the more rigid Puritans' dislike of long hair, 'The gloomy emigrants who fled from England and other parts, about that period, to seek in the wilds of America a retreat where they might worship God according to their consciences, among other whimsical tenets carried to their new settlements an antipathy against long hair ...' and he quotes a 'curious article' from their codes of law: '... the express command of God, who declares that it is a shameful practice for any man who has the least care for his soul to wear long hair.'[13]

The clerical wig became generally powdered white or grey and short or bobbed, although it did have variations of style. Jonathan Swift said the clergy had wigs of divers shapes:

We who wear our wigs
With fantail and with snake.[14]

The wig became a badge of respectability even in a society where nearly everybody wore wigs. In 1765 John Chubbe in his *Free Advice to a Young Clergyman* strongly advised the young preacher to wear a wig until age made his hair respectable. James Woodforde always wore wigs even before he was ordained. On 25 May 1759 he paid £1 1s 0d for 'a new Wigg' as a perfectly normal purchase for a young man, when he also bought 'a superfine blue suit of cloathes, very good cloth £4.10s.' and a chocolate suit 'bad' which cost him £3.

During the early part of the eighteenth century it became usual to slit the surplice down the centre front, as it was difficult to take it off over the wig, and the square cap disappeared since it was incompatible with the large amount of hair worn. All gentlemen tended to be clean shaven when wearing wigs and the clergy were no exception.

The parish clerk would wear the second-hand clothes of the parson, receiving them as part payment. On 2 April 1790 (which was Good Friday) Woodforde records in his diary: 'Gave to my clerk, Js Smith, a good black striped Coat and

35 Dr Benjamin Hoadly. After W. Hogarth, 1743. As the Order of the Garter is an order of chivalry it has never been given to those in holy orders. Two of the officers of the Order are ecclesiastics however: the Dean of Windsor is the Register and the Bishop of Winchester is the Prelate of the Order. Hogarth painted Dr Hoadly on many occasions and here he is, as Bishop of Winchester, with the insignia of the Order. The vast sleeves of the rochet, ending in a frill at the wrist, are to remain typical of this garment for another hundred years; and the chimere and the bands are also visible. The wig is normal for a man of his age and position and is not specifically clerical.

Waistcoat, a pr of old velverett Breeches and a Powdered Wig.' (However, we also know Parson Woodforde kept some of his old wigs for pottering about in: on 5 October 1781 'He caught me on the hop, busy in the garden, and dressed in my Cotton Morning gown, Old Wigg and Old Hat.') John, the clerk of Samuel Wesley at Epworth, was inordinately proud of the fact that one of his privileges was to wear the rector's cast-off wigs, even though his head was far too small for them. One Sunday Wesley, determined to teach him a lesson in humility, chose the psalm from Sternhold and Hopkins which begins: 'like to an owl in an ivybush'. Whereupon John, peering out of his large clerical wig, drawled out

36 The Archbishop of Dublin, by George Dance, 1795.
This shows clearly the typical clerical wig of the mid-eighteenth century that lasted until the middle of the
nineteenth century in court circles. The grey powdered wig
was adopted by the clerical and legal professions from the
fashionable dress of the 1730s and '40s.

the second line 'that rueful thing am I', much to
the amusement of the congregation.[15]

By the 1770s it was no longer fashionable to
wear wigs. In 1765 the periwig makers had
petitioned the King, complaining 'that men will
wear their own hair'[16] and some younger clergy
began to wear their own hair long and loose and
unpowdered. In the main, however, bishops and
clergy remained faithful to the white bobbed wig
for at least another fifty years. Older men were
reluctant to lose the wig after wearing it all of
their adult lives, although some did, to the
confusion of their friends: 'I did not know old Mr
Dalton at first as he now wears his Hair' wrote
Parson Woodforde on 29 June 1789. Parson
Woodforde in the 1770s was unaware of or
uninterested in the demise of the wig in fashionable circles; his new-style wig which he got on 14
June 1774 obviously caused him some satisfaction.
'Had a new Wigg brought home this morning
which I put on before I went to dinner, it is a more

fashionable one than my old ones are, a one-
curled wig with two curls at the sides. I like it, and
it was liked by most people at dinner. I gave the
barber's man, Jonathan, 1.1.0' – (from the description it could be almost 40 years out of date
although perhaps fashion was repeating itself in
clerical circles). Parson Woodforde continued to
wear the wig – and to buy more – until the end of
his life in 1802. George Murray, who was not
born until 1827, wore a wig; he was the last
bishop to do so in the House of Lords, and he died
in 1860.

Hats

The square cap of the Elizabethan ecclesiastics,
which had been so unpopular with the Puritans,

37 The Heretical Synod at Salter's Hall, February 1719.
These Non-conformists wear flat-brimmed, high-crowned
hats with no trim. Their coats, breeches and leather shoes
are tied with bows and over these they wear knee-length
gowns.

fell into disuse, not because of their dislike (the surplice and cassock survived) but because of these wigs. The three-cornered hat was the successor of the broad-brimmed hat of the cavaliers, but with the brim evenly cocked to make a neat and smart shape. This was worn, or more often carried, as a mark of rank by most fashionable gentlemen in the first three-quarters of the eighteenth century. An alternative form of hat, with a round crown and a wide, uncocked brim, was favoured by the professions and by gentlemen in the country. A low-crowned hat of this type was accepted by the clergy and by the Quakers from the 1680s and was worn by Parson Woodforde. Although he rarely describes the style of his hat – 24 May 1793 'I also bought a hat of him [one Oxley in the Market Place, Norwich] … paid for it 1.1.0.' – he frequently mentions the black crape or satin hatbands he wore for funerals. These would not be visible on a tricorne, but would be clearly seen around the crown of this hat, which was growing taller in the latter decades of the eighteenth century. On 29 April 1790 Woodforde buried Mr Thorne's nephew, Robert George Walker, aged 23 years: 'I had a black silk hat band and a pair of Beaver Gloves.' As proof that he was not the only cleric who wore these, we find an entry for 25 June 1796 describing six clergy, the pall bearers at the funeral of Mr Bodham who all wear the same:

'We each of us had a rich black Silk Scarf and Hatband, and a pair of Beaver Gloves.'

Umbrellas

The burial service was responsible for introducing the umbrella into the daily life of the clergy, half-a-century before it was accepted by the fashionable gentleman. Umbrellas were originally provided by the church, although occasionally the parson would own one. They were used for practical purposes, to cover the clergyman as he conducted the burial service outside in the graveyard when it rained. Early references can be found in the accounts of St Nicholas, Newcastle-on-Tyne:

1717 Paid for an umbrella for the churche's use £1.5s.0d.
1717 Paid Theo. Melburne for charges about ye umbrella £0.2s.0d.

and there are many references to umbrellas throughout the century. 'One of the earliest umbrellas seen at Taunton was the private property of a clergyman, and when he carried it to church on a Sunday he left it in the porch for the edification and delight of his parishioners'.[17]

Although ladies had been carrying parasols and clergy had undoubtedly made good use of umbrellas for many years, in the 1750s James Hanway, the celebrated traveller and philanthropist, returned to England from Persia bringing the umbrella. Lieutenant-Colonel (afterwards General) Wolfe wrote a letter from Paris saying that he had observed the use of umbrellas, 'I wonder

38 The Drawing Room by Thomas Rowlandson, 1808. The plump bishop on the far left is in wig, rochet and chimere but carries a tricorne, a *chapeau bras*, like all the other men in this drawing-room scene. Here the clerical wig can be seen as completely distinct from all the other wigs.

that a practice so useful is not introduced to England.'

Mourning

Mourning was observed, and even the clergyman who wore black habitually was affected. On 25 January 1761 Parson Woodforde notes that he went into second mourning for King George II who had died on 25 October 1760. When his brother Heighes died, mourning was brought from Norwich for Woodforde 'viz a black Coat and Waistcoat for me' (11 April 1789). It would appear from the following entry that there was not an established protocol for correct wear as he turned up for the funeral of Mrs Howes, a local vicar's wife, in the wrong clothes: 'found all the clergy in gowns and some in cassocks also. I did not carry my gown as I did not know whether or not the clergy appeared in them. I borrowed one, however, of Mr Howes and likewise a band.'

The Cassock and Gown

The majority of Anglican clergymen in the eighteenth century seem to have worn the cassock and gown; even John Wesley wore them as he travelled up and down the country preaching the new Methodism. The black cassock was usually long and was distinguished from the Roman Catholic version (not at this time seen in England) by having no cape and by being double-breasted, without the single row of buttons down the front. It could be short and in that case would be worn with black knee-breeches, stockings, buckled shoes, and white bands. It would be worn under the preaching gown, which was always long, and under the surplice at services. In 1662 Wren enquires 'Doth [your minister] preach in cassock and gown [not in a cloak] with his surplice and hood also, if he be a graduate?'[18] The cassock was the lowliest of the specifically ecclesiastical garments, but could be worn on its own to denote the position of the wearer. Thomas Macaulay in *The Character of the Clergy* noted the poverty among the ordinary country rectors at the close of the seventeenth century: '... holes appeared more and more plainly in the thatch of his parsonage and in his single cassock ....'[19]

An interview between Parson Adams and Parson Trulliber occurs in Henry Fielding's novel *Joseph Andrews*, written in 1742.[20] Adams had fallen in the mire when catching hold of one of Trulliber's pigs and went in to clean himself.

39 The Divine Macaroni, published 1772. This caricature shows a cleric in the short cassock and clerical coat with breeches, stockings and tongue and buckle shoes – all in black. The white necktie and *chapeau bras* are common to other professions and the over-large clerical wig is the only part of the costume which justifies the title.

Adams desired leave to dry his greatcoat, wig and hat by the fire. Parson Adams says to Trulliber who had at first mistaken him for someone come about buying his hogs, 'I fancy sir, you already perceive me to be a clergyman'. 'Ay, ay' cried Trulliber, grinning, 'I perceive you have some cassock; I will not venture to caale it a whole one.' Adams answered 'It was indeed none of the best, but he had the misfortune to tear it about ten years ago in passing over a style.'

This cassock was neither the long version or the intentionally short style, but the only one he had, even though, as Fielding says, 'He presented a figure which would have moved laughter in many, for his cassock had just fallen down below his greatcoat, that is to say, it reached his knees, whereas the skirts of his greatcoat descended no lower than halfway down his thighs.' On another occasion, Parson Adams is described, while taking his ease at the Inn: '[He] had on a night-cap drawn over his wig, and a short coat which half-covered his cassock.'

More usually the cassock was covered by the gown, that is the preaching gown which was more important at this time. As before, we can see the order of the garments best in descriptions of defrocking. The degradation of the Rev. Samuel Johnson, 1686, shows this: 'After which they proceeded to degrade him, by putting a square cap on his head, and then taking it off; by pulling off his gown and girdle . . . Mr Rouse, the Under-Sherriff tore off his cassock in the pillory and put a frize coat upon him.'[22]

Although in the country the cassock could be an inferior garment, when worn in town it could be made of silk and was often very beautiful. In the Roman Catholic Church in Europe the cassock became long and flowing with an impressive train; in England, even when a silk cassock was worn, it was the gown which was the more important part of the outfit, partly because it denoted the political allegiance of the wearer. In 1720 Hearne notes that 'It is a custom now in London for all the Tory Clergy to wear the Masters Gown (if they proceeded in the degree of Master of Arts at either of the Universities) which much displeases the Whigs and the enemies of the Universities, who all go in pudding-sleeved gowns.'[23] These two patterns had been established in the reign of Queen Anne (1702–14) with

40 Cardinal Richelieu, by Philippe de Champaigne. This full length portrait of Richelieu wearing a scarlet cassock, mantle and fur-lined cape or hood shows how in continental Europe the styles became longer and fuller with trains becoming so long that special devices were arranged to hold them up, and some junior clergy were given the office of train-bearers in procession. Cardinal Richelieu wears a small skull cap and carries his biretta. The rochet of the Roman bishop does not develop the large sleeves of the Anglican; it is trimmed with lace, and can be much shorter, as here. He is also wearing the Order of the Holy Ghost around his neck.

the Whig Clergy also wearing morning gowns.[24] These gowns were usually worn long but the pudding-sleeved gown at least could also be short. Rev. Samuel Kerrich is given advice by his uncle, on the occasion of his being ordained deacon: 'I would likewise advise you to get a short gown with the sleeves full and long enough to button above your elbow, and to come so far upon your hands that you may just lay hold upon them.' So here we see a short gown; incidently, Samuel Kerrich was a fellow of Corpus Christi College, Cambridge and could possibly have had an academic gown as well.[25]

Parson Woodforde wore his cassock and gown on Sundays and when he went to visit the bishop. On 9 September 1770 he went with his sister Jane

41 Illustration to *Pamela*, by Joseph Highmore, 1745. Pamela walking in the garden with Mr Williams, the clergyman who is wearing a long cassock and gown, bands and sash at the waist. He wears the black shovel hat which is the broad-brimmed hat cocked at the sides.

42 Illustration to *Pamela*, by Joseph Highmore, 1745. 'The marriage ceremony performed in Mr B's own Chappel by Mr Williams'. The clergyman wears a very full surplice completely covering the cassock. It is an undecorated linen garment but very voluminous.

to drink coffee with Justice Creed, dressed 'in my Gown and Cassock', but we do not know whether this was in deference to the position of his host or because it was a Sunday. He was dressed in a 'Gown and Cassock and Scarf' when Mr and Mrs Custance took him to dine with the bishop on 7 September 1783, and two months later, 7 November, he says he is wearing them expressly because he is meeting the bishop. He and Mr du Quesne went to Weston House 'in our Gowns and Cassocks (as we are to meet the Bishop of Norwich there today).' The bishop himself was 'not dressed in his Gown and Cassock, but in a purple Coat and a short silk Cassock under it.'

The short cassock or 'apron' of the bishop and archdeacon was originally informal dress, convenient for travelling (often on horseback) and was not as dramatic a development as it would appear at first sight. The clergy had followed contemporary fashion and knee-length coats were not only normal wear, but eminently sensible when travelling many miles around the diocese.

The gaiters would have developed at the same time and for the same reasons; boots, although worn, were never considered part of ecclesiastical dress. The bishop and his senior officials still wore the cassock and gown in the services. On 7 October 1794 Parson Woodforde 'attended the bishop to Reepham to Mr Priest's, and when the Bishop had robed himself we attended him to Church in our Gowns, where he confirmed about 200 .... A great Many Clergy attended on the occasion, in their canonicals ....' It was only when this garb fossilized in the nineteenth century and became a mark of rank, that the 'Apron and Gaiters' were considered worth commenting on. The gown was the distinguishing feature of the cleric – Fielding in *Amelia* (Book 9, Chapter 9) speaks of a clergyman who is going to the famous pleasure gardens of Vauxhall for an evening frolic, laying aside his gown so as to avoid a scandal.

A description of Rev. Joshua Brooks, the chaplain of the Old Collegiate Church of Man-

43 Edward Stillingfleet (1635–99), Bishop of Worcester. Artist unknown *c.* 1670. By the 1660s the wig had become popular with men, but this young clergyman is wearing his own hair long and softly curled. He wears the falling band which was to develop into the bands worn by professional men. Over his black cassock he is wearing a black gown with very full sleeves, but as the portrait is cut off it is impossible to see the style.

44 The Rev. Joseph White D.D., Prebend of Gloucester, by Rev. W. Peters, R.A., 1785. Rev. Joseph White is wearing his academic gown over his dark suit. His bands made of fine linen are still fairly wide and set close together like the original falling band. The stronger white edge is the hemmed fabric which, being turned over on itself three times, is opaque.

chester, who died in 1821, serves to sum up the dress of the eighteenth-century cleric of the Church of England.

During the week he wore a large brimmed hat, dusky brown coat and breeches and plain woollen stockings – he looked more like a verger or a mechanic. But on Sunday he shone resplendent with his hair combed and powdered, his handsome black suit and clean ruffled shirt, his black silk stockings and brightly polished shoes. Ere the first bell tolled he appeared at his door attired in his silken robes, a three cornered beaver perched on his head, and beautiful white bands pendant from his cravat.[26]

Bands and Stocks

The pendant bands had developed from the 'falling band' of the seventeenth century; again originally lay wear, they were adopted by the clerical and legal professions who continued to wear them throughout the eighteenth, nineteenth

and most of the twentieth centuries, in the form of two white tabs attached to a band worn around the neck. In the seventeenth century they were larger and fuller, and, surprisingly, caused the Puritans to disapprove:

the zealous of the land,
with white hair, and little or no band[27]

For most of the eighteenth century the neck-band of the shirt was completely concealed by some form of neckcloth, the stock or the cravat, and the bands were simply a variation worn by lawyers or clerics and their clerks, when in their gowns. For everyday wear they followed contemporary fashion, and in so doing they nearly always wore white linen stocks or neckcloths (in 1762 Parson Woodforde listed nine shirts, nine stocks and two cravats).[28] Even when Parson Woodforde celebrated Holy Communion at home (his church not being fit for services at the

time) he saw fit to dress properly; 8 May 1796:
'Billy Gunton and his Mistress Mrs Michael
Andrews, came to my house about 11:O'clock
this Morning and I had them into the parlour and
there administered the H. Sacrament ... I put on
my Gown and Band on the Occasion.'

The Surplice

Parson Woodforde does not mention wearing a
surplice, and in some parts of the country the
surplice was not put on again. The Puritans had
condemned it as 'popish rags', and there were
occasions when they had physically removed
them from the clergy, sometimes causing great
distress: 'Dr Turner was siezed by a party of
horsemen during service at his living of Fetcham
... the surplice was siezed and put on one of the
troopers tied round with an orange scarf....'

Lewis Alcock, rector of North Stoneham,
Hampshire '... could not forbear weeping when
he saw this villain sieze his surplice and put it on,
girding a sword about it and riding off in triumph
through the village.'[29] The gown, worn by all
ministers of the reformed Church, continued in
use even when the surplice was re-introduced in
the reign of Charles II. Samuel Pepys (1633–1703)
recorded the fact of his minister wearing the
surplice for the first time: 'To church, and there
saw the first time Mr Mills in a surplice; but it
seemed absurd for him to pull it over his ears in
the reading pew, after he had done, before all the
church, to go up to the pulpit, to preach without
it.'[21] There is a clear inference that the gown was
worn under the surplice.

In the inventories of Christ Church, Canterbury for 1662, there are no vestments of any kind
mentioned, although we know that material for
surplices was bought that year: 'payd also for 40
ells of Holland bought of Mr Beane at 3s.2d. the
ell for 4 new surplices £6.6.8.'[30] In the inventories of 1745 and 1752[31] there are no garments
mentioned but there are:

four presses for surplices in vestry
six presses for surplices in Minor Canon's vestry
presses for their surplices in singing men's vestry.

The surplice became more acceptable during
the eighteenth century in rural areas but was not
universally worn in the established Church. The

45 Archbishop Moore, by George Romney, 1783. This
formal portrait shows that caricatures did not exaggerate the
size of the rochet sleeves which became so big that they had
to be sewn into the chimere to support the weight.

clergy were certainly expected to own one and
were given 'surplice fees' as part of their remuner-
ation. On 16 November 1795 Parson Woodforde
'engaged Mr Corbould this morning to be my
curate ... at the rate of Thirty Pounds per Annum
with all surplice fees'. These payments could be
quite large; in 1817, John Leroo, the Rector of
Long Melford in Suffolk took £20.00 in surplice
fees.[32]

The surplice had to be taken off when the
minister preached his sermon, at the beginning of
this period. To overcome the problems noted by
Pepys above, as well as to avoid disturbing the
ponderous periwig, it was found convenient to
open it down the front. The traditional form also
continued and both styles existed until the end of
the nineteenth century. The Strangers Hall
Museum, Norwich, has a fine example of the type
with a centre-front opening from Closworth,
Somerset. It is heavily pleated all around the neck
and held in place by three rows of smocking.
There is also a single button on the centre back of
the neckband which could be to hold either the
stole in place or even possibly, but less likely, the
wig bag.

The Hood and Tippet

The hood and tippet or stole completed the outfit and could be worn over the surplice or the gown. The academic hood was only worn by clerics who had passed through Oxford and Cambridge and the tippet was reserved for the others. The tippet is a long wide black scarf, also known as the preacher's stole. This replaced the almuce rather than the stole of the old suit of vestments, which had been totally discarded. 'On Whitsuntide 1549, on which feast the book of Common Prayer was for the first time used, "the cannons and petie [minor] canons in Paul's left of their grey and calabre amises and the canons wore hoodes on the surpleses after the degree of the universities and the petie cannons tipittes like other priestes."'[33]

In Christ Church, Canterbury, the preacher's hood is first mentioned in the inventory of 1735 (where it is the only vestment mentioned) but it had been bought in 1724: 'To Michelbourn for a Preacher's Hood 1.19.0'.[34] In February 1745 this hood, or perhaps another, had to be repaired: 'To Plumley for mending ye preachers Hood 2.6'. Although most graduates would have had their own hood, it seems that there would be one in the vestry for those preachers who had not got one, or had forgotten to bring it with them. Parson Woodforde who had taken his M.A. degree at Oxford on 23 May 1767, used the one in Norwich Cathedral vestry when he preached on 8 February 1784: 'At 10.0 this morning we all went in a coach to the Cathedral. I went full dress and being Preacher sat next to the Sub-Deacon Mr Hammond .... After the sermon was over I walked back to the Vestry, had my hood taken of, and then a Person came to me and gave me for preaching 1.1.0. I gave the Virger for the use of the Hood 0.1.0.'

The Cope

The cope continued to be used, but very rarely, and was never worn outside the grandest ceremonies in cathedrals. A popular song describing the visit of James I to St Paul's in March 1620 sneers at 'The Priests in copes, like so many Popes.' Copes were resumed after the Restoration (1660) and were worn for an Order of the Garter procession, which took place at Windsor on St George's Day in the reign of Charles II. A large number of clergy are depicted as vested in 'rich copes of cloth of Gold, Cloth of Bodkin, or most costly embroideries' and the lay clerks and choristers in cassocks and long ample surplices.[35] In 1680, Thoresby was scandalized by the sight of the exceedingly rich copes and robes and records it in his diary. In 1681 he was amazed at the rich embroidered copes and vestments worn in Durham.[36]

Rich copes were worn by the dean and prebendaries at the funerals of the Duke of Buckingham, 1721; the Duke of Marlborough, 1722; and Queen Caroline, 1737, and have always been worn at all coronations. The mitre, however, seems to have fallen into disuse during this period. At the coronation of James II copes were worn over the rochet, or surplice, and chimere, with the flattened square cap which was already looking somewhat like the mortar board. At the end of the seventeenth century the episcopal mitre and pastoral staff were sometimes suspended over the tombs of bishops (for example Bishop Mosley, Winchester Cathedral, died 1696, and Dr Hall, Bishop of Bristol, in Brownsgrove Church, Worcestershire, died 1710) as a sort of post-Reformation relic. This habit may have come from the Continent, where certainly cardinals' hats have been hung over the tombs, but the custom disappeared in Britain as the mitre and pastoral staff fell into disuse.

Roman Catholicism

The Roman Catholics, although suppressed, continued to exist in Britain and there was little trouble during the eighteenth century. Despite the harsh and intolerant penal laws they were largely left in peace, except in times of crisis like the Jacobite Rebellions of 1715 and 1745. The English clergy turned their attention to the Methodists whom they often feared and hated, as their threat to the established way of life was perhaps more overt. Henry Fielding illustrates this attitude in a passage in *Joseph Andrews* written in 1742. Parson Adams meets a fellow traveller in an alehouse and enters into conversation with him. '"Give me your hand, brother" said Adams, in a rapture "for I suppose you are a clergyman" – "No, truly" answered the other (indeed he was a priest of the Church of Rome, but those who

46 The Rev. Edmund Benson wearing a medieval chasuble, by John Constable, 1821. This informal portrait of a family friend shows the priest-vicar of Salisbury Cathedral wearing a chasuble back to front. This is presumably to show off the beauty of the embroidered orphrey, but it is possible that they were completely ignorant of the nature of the vestment as the inscription names it wrongly: 'very ancient cope in the Cathedral, Salisbury Nov. 1821'. The orphrey is typical of fourteenth-century chasubles with the Crucifixion scene in the centre with God the Father and God the Holy Ghost (a dove) in the space above. The lower figures are more extraordinary, apparently secular men in the spaces usually filled by the Virgin Mary and the beloved disciple John. Under this chasuble Rev. Benson would appear to be wearing a rochet although it may possibly be a full-length surplice.

understand our laws will not wonder he was not over ready to own it).'

That the reformed churches should abandon ecclesiastical dress is not surprising as they were discarding all signs of allegiance to the old Church of Rome. The abandonment of clerical dress by the Catholic priests was more painful but expedient under repression in the Protestant countries. 'Allen had been obliged to defend it from traditionalists and did so with good humour. From the Elizabethan bravery of John Gerard and the country dress of Ambrose Barlow, with his battered hat and a "pair of scurvy old slip-shoes", to the long curls of the Restoration, the brown coat and breeches of the 18th Century, and indeed to the ruffles and short hair of the Regency, the Missionary priests in England dressed as laymen, and moved among them with little sense of segregation.'[37]

The priests who stayed in England got jobs as tutors or schoolmasters in the houses of sympathetic laity, but they often had to put up with very poor conditions. Sargeant's *Dialogue* of 1667 tells the story of a Protestant maid who said she knew he was a priest because he was respectably dressed but slept in a garret.[38]

Shortcomings of the Anglican Cleric

The clergymen of the eighteenth century were not held in much respect generally; George II described the bench of bishops as a 'parcel of black, canting, hypocritical rascals'. After the upheavals of the previous age the English people were at first pleased to leave the Church alone to its own devices, and the corruption of the Church was mainly due to the great divide between the rich bishops and the very poor curates. At the deathbed of Queen Caroline (1737) Walpole suggested that the Archbishop of Canterbury be sent for to forestall impertinent criticism: '"It will do the Queen no hurt, any more than any good; and it will satisfy all the wise and good fools who will call us atheists if we don't pretend to be as great fools as they are." So Dr Potter, who was as near an atheist as an Archbishop can be, came morning and evening . . . .'[39]

The lack of liturgical discipline encouraged eccentrics and there were many in the eighteenth century. However absurd their clothes were, they did not have any impact on the development of church dress but Frederick Hervey, Earl of Bristol and Bishop of Derry, wore some extraordinary outfits that will serve as an example. He travelled widely on the Continent and his dress aroused comment. Lord Cloncurry recalled how he had seen 'the eccentric Earl Bishop ride about the streets of Rome dressed in red plush breeches and a broad brimmed white or straw hat, and was often asked if that was the canonical costume of an Irish prelate'.[40] He favoured purple, red and the puce colour which was the prerogative of a bishop, but it was his style of wearing them and the accessories and trim which made them eccentric. In about 1777 he wrote to his daughter, Elizabeth, asking her to send him enough poplin to make two suits of clothes, one of which was to be of a puce colour. In 1783 he was clad in purple, his knee and shoe buckles blazing with diamonds. His gloves were white with gold tassels hanging from them (an archaism which he would have seen on paintings of saints and priests in Rome). With this he wore a hat of the Colonel of the Volunteers as an indication of his military rank. In his latter years in Italy, in the late 1790s, he wore a white hat edged in purple, a coat of crimson silk in summer or of velvet in the winter, a black sash spangled with silver and purple stockings. Miss Catherine Wilmot, a young Irish girl, who witnessed the curious sight of the Earl of Bristol in Rome in April 1803 wrote: 'On his head he wore a purple velvet night cap with a tassel of gold dangling over his shoulders and a sort of mitre on the front; silk stockings and slippers of the same colour and a short round petticoat, such as Bishops wear, fringed with gold about his knees. A loose dressing-gown of silk was then thrown over his shoulders. In this Merry Andrew trim he rode on Horseback to the never ending amusement of all Beholders!'[41]

CHAPTER EIGHT

The Victorian Church, The Oxford Movement and After 1829–1914

AT THE BEGINNING of the nineteenth century the everyday dress of the parson was conservative but not exclusive to his profession. From Jane Austen we understand that clergymen had begun to congratulate themselves that their dress was no different from 'any gentleman'. To an extent clergy continued to wear ordinary dress for a greater part of the week for the rest of the period covered by this history, but the various factions of the reforming movements necessarily affected the everyday clothes as well. As the Roman Catholics and the Non-conformists achieved equal rights in society, the Church of England awoke to its position and responsibilities, and these were manifested in the powerful Evangelical Movement and in the Oxford Movement and the new Ecclesiologists.

Curates and Parsons

The problem of poverty meant that the ordinary curate or parson could not dress as he would have liked to, the church and parish providing only what they felt was necessary for the services; this was only a surplice and preacher's stole, and not always those in the more evangelical churches. George Eliot, writing of the 1830s, outlines the clergyman's plight:

And now, pray, can you solve me the following problem? Given a man with a wife and six children: Let him be obliged always to exhibit himself when outside his own door in a suit of black broadcloth, such as will not undermine the foundations of the Establishment by a paltry plebeian glossiness or an unseemly whiteness at the edges; in a snowy cravat, which is a serious investment of labour in the hemming, starching and ironing departments; and in a hat which shows no symptom of taking to the hideous doctrine of expedi-

ency, and shaping itself according to circumstances; let him have a parish large enough to create an external necessity for abundant shoe leather, and an internal necessity for abundant beef and mutton, as well as poor enough to require frequent priestly consolation in the shape of shillings and sixpences; and lastly let him be compelled, by his own pride and other people's, to dress his wife and children with gentility from bonnet strings to shoe strings. By what process of division can the sum of eighty pounds per annum be made to yield a quotient which will cover that man's weekly expenses?

Bishops and archdeacons, who earned a considerably higher income, continued to urge their clergy to wear the 'proper and decent apparel' of canon law. As the established Church began to feel threatened by the strength of the Non-conformist brethren, so the movement towards unifying the dress of their clergy became more important. The problem of finding a habit 'preserving always an evident and decent distinction from the laity in their apparel'[2] seemed to be solved if the cassock was worn more generally. Roman Catholic priests were forbidden to wear the cassock out of doors, and the Non-conformists eschewed its use. A religious pamphlet, entitled *The Dress of the Clergy* and undated, but probably from the early 1840s encourages the use of the cassock:

If he adopts the rounded coat with straight collar, which formed the mourning court dress of the last century, he finds that the Quakers and other sectarians have anticipated him even here. The mourner dresses in black like himself, and the tradesman and the farmer wear the same white cravat. Canon 74 would be complied with by the clergy wearing a canonical coat or cassock at ordinary times, superadding to it both on all public solemnities and on every other dress occasion

– the gown of their ministry and degree, the hood, the scarf, and, out of doors, the square cap.... In winter a cassock of cloth or any other warm material, in summer black cashmere, bombazine or silk. In warm weather single breasted and buttoned up and in the cold, as it is generally now made, double breasted, for walking and riding the cassock may be made the length of the ordinary greatcoat and for dress and for solemn occasions it might have that flowing length which seems proper to it.[3]

The author holds up the uniform of the army as an example of dress common to a profession encouraging comradeship and fellowship, and this undoubtedly was the main reason for the desire to create uniformity amongst like-minded clergy. The single-breasted cassock may be the one described by a contemporary report on the 'modern country clergyman': 'He is anxious to show that the church is everywhere.... He is always to be seen in a long single breasted coat, and slouched billy-cock hat, hurrying at a half-run from one end of the village to the other ...'.[4]

The cassock did not become very popular in the first part of the nineteenth century, however, as it was too far removed from fashionable dress, and certainly the single-breasted version came to be associated with the soutane of the Roman Catholic Church and was only accepted by a minority. When Anthony Trollope describes the dress of Mr Harding in *The Warden*, written in 1855, he depicts the costume of the ordinary, old-fashioned clergyman in black frock-coat, black knee-breeches and black gaiters[5] – the 'mourning dress' described in the pamphlet quoted above. He is not particularly influenced by the extremes of the 'low church' Evangelical movement or the 'high church' which originated with the Oxford Movement.

The Frock-coat

The black frock-coat was more popular and was retained by the clergy until the beginning of the twentieth century, only gradually giving way to the shorter jacket of the fashionable man in the 1890s. A passage written in 1894 to help an American distinguish the differing schools of thought amongst the Anglican clergy describes them thus: 'The High Churchman is close-shaven, with a collar, high vest and a long coat....

The Low Churchman, with whiskers and neckerchief, is neatly attired in customary suit of solemn black, desiring to appear, and appearing, more of a minister than the priest; while the Broad

47 Rev. H. R. Haweis, by C. Pellegrini, 1888. Rev. Haweis is wearing a black frock-coat and top hat, the regular wear of the nineteenth-century clergyman who was slower to adopt the short jacket than the layman. The white bow tie and imperial collar indicate that he is of a 'low church' persuasion; the 'high churchman' would favour the clerical or 'dog' collar. Clergy always follow lay fashion in hairstyles and here Rev. Haweis sports a handsome set of whiskers and long hair.

Churchman disports himself in a straw hat and short jacket ... sometimes adorning his countenance with a huge moustache, and looking like a dragon on furlough.'[6]

The Collar and Bands

The vest or waistcoat of the high churchman was cut very high with a band at the neck to support the clerical collar. At the beginning of the nineteenth century all clergymen wore white collar and stock or cravat with a suit, and, usually, white bands with the cassock. When the white bands almost disappeared, the white tie persisted, and it was considered highly improper for the clergy to appear without it.[7] Mr Harding 'somewhat scandalises some of his more hyperclerical brethren by a black neck-handkerchief'[8] and Samuel Butler in *The Way of All Flesh* describes two generations of clergymen being identified by the white necktie. Theobald, the father, in his first living is recognisable because: 'A hard and drawn look begins to settle about the corners of his mouth, so that even if he were not in a black coat and white tie a child might take him for a parson.' When Ernest, his son, and hero of the book, is first ordained, he meets a friend in the street: 'Ernest felt that he quailed when he saw Towneley's eye wander to his white necktie and saw that he was being reckoned up, and rather disapprovingly reckoned up, as a parson.'[9]

Evangelical and low church clergy wore the collar and necktie and the high churchmen adopted the Roman collar sometime after the 1850s. This was the white band around the throat with no pleats or ruffles which was starched, as was the fashionable collar, until it was completely rigid. High churchmen wore their waistcoats cut high to the throat with a gap at the centre front of the standing band in which the clerical collar could be seen. When this gave place to a V-neck waistcoat they filled in the space with a square of black silk which was in line with the Roman practice. At the end of the century low churchmen had also adopted this practice and some Non-conformists followed suit.

The white bands were never completely discarded. Dr Liddon, in his biography of Walter Kerr Hamilton, Bishop of Salisbury (1856–69) tells us that this saintly prelate would not allow his

chaplains to follow the modern fashion of leaving off bands. 'These things are all worth something and it is very difficult, where it is not impossible, to restore anything which has ever been given up.'[10] They were also worn by lawyers, children in parochial charity schools and parish clerks, and formed part of the state dress of the Chapel Royal. The white bands are distinctly English and were retained by the low churchmen and Evangelicals who took them abroad with missionary societies. Bands in France were usually black cloth or crêpe edged in white.[11]

The Senior Clergy

The everyday dress of the senior clergy was more regularly worn. The archdeacon and the bishop in Anthony Trollope's novels are always dressed in clothes suitable to their position. 'A dean or archbishop, in the garb of his order, is sure of our reverence, and a well-got-up bishop fills our very souls with awe. But how can this feeling be perpetuated in the bosoms of those who see the

48 Bloomfield, Manning and Gurney, by G. Richmond, 1840–5. The clerical coat could be cut straight or be cut away like the one worn here by the central figure. The short cassock or 'apron' held at the waist by the broad sash was inherited from the eighteenth century and was worn, especially by bishops and archdeacons, until the 1950s. Gaiters were generally worn with the apron, although they are not indicated in this sketch.

49 *Punch* cartoon, 1889: 'Aesthetics' by George du Maurier. The caption reads:

Mrs van Tromp:— 'Oh, Sir Charles! modern English male attire is *too* hideous! Just look round . . . there are only two decently dressed men in the room!'

Sir Charles:— 'Indeed: and which are they may I ask?'

Mrs van Tromp:— 'Well – I don't know *who* they are, exactly – but just now one of them seems to be offering the other a cup of tea'.

The artistic dress movement considered Victorian fashions very ugly and was trying to re-introduce knee breeches and stockings into men's fashionable dress to replace trousers. Here the waiter in his livery and the cleric in his apron are considered by an American aesthetic to be attractively dressed.

bishops without their aprons, and the archdeacons even in the lower state of dishabille?'[12]

The archdeacon in *The Warden* was always well turned out in his black suit, 'shining black habiliments', which consisted of black coat, decorous breeches and neat black gaiters showing so admirably that well-turned leg. The most important feature of his dress was the shovel-hat, a stiff broad-brimmed hat, turned up at the sides, worn by high ranking ecclesiasticals: 'The archdeacon ... his shovel hat, large new and well-

pronounced, a churchman's hat in every inch, declared the profession as plainly as does the Quaker's broad brim.'[13] The bishop wore the apron, breeches and gaiters, with the knee-length clerical coat. For everyday wear it was black, but for special occasions the outfit was made in purple. Bishops still continued to wear the chimere with the rochet which was noted for the enormity of the sleeves, so large that they had to be sewn directly into the chimere to support the weight. Whether high church or low they were worried by outside influences and sought to protect the Church from extremists. Anthony Trollope's bishop is disturbed by the politics of John Bold: 'The Bishop, in his simple mind felt no doubt that John Bold ... would distribute all tithes among Methodists, Baptists and other savage tribes; utterly annihilate the sacred bench, and make shovel hats and lawn sleeves as illegal as cowls, sandals and sackcloth!'[14] (monastic dress had been proscribed in Britain since the Reformation until just before *The Warden* was written).

In the *Graphic* magazine there is an illustration showing William Howley, Archbishop of Canterbury and the Lord Chamberlain telling the news to the young Princess Victoria of her uncle William IV's death on 20 June 1837. The archbishop is shown with his back to the viewer but he is clearly wearing a grey bobbed wig, gaiters, and a knee-length clerical coat, and is carrying a shovel hat.

The Cassock

The cassock, although it nearly dropped out of use with the ordinary parish parson, continued in use as the requisite court dress of ecclesiastics other than bishops, and together with gown and bands was worn by court chaplains and university preachers. With encouragement from the bishops, Bishop Hamilton (1808–69) was the first to wear his cassock as customary dress.[15] By the end of the century the cassock became universally worn inside church.

In church, cassocks were adopted by the choristers as well as clergymen in the third quarter of the nineteenth century. In St Paul's the boys were first vested in cassock as well as surplice on 27 February 1872. The colours used for cassocks were blue, black, purple and scarlet; scarlet being generally used for ordinary Sundays and feasts, blue, black or purple for weekdays, Advent and Lent. Clergy, deacons, sub-deacons and those in minor orders always wore black; purple was reserved for bishops, who as it has been seen, also wore purple aprons. Rev. Lee, writing in 1877, said that the Bishop of London annually gave a dinner to the Archbishop of Canterbury and his suffragans, at which they all appeared in apron or short cassock of purple silk, with a dress coat of purple cloth.[16] Scarlet cassocks were worn by cardinals of the Roman Catholic Church and by doctors of divinity in several of the foreign universities. The Pope, alone, wore the white cassock. There was a tradition, according to an eminent ritualist, that black was the colour for the ordinary cassock, scarlet in churches which were Royal foundations, purple in Episcopal foundations and blue in churches dedicated to the Virgin Mary. This was not apparently adhered to in practice in all denominations of the Church.[17]

The cassock was usually of the 'Sarum' type, that is double-breasted with no sign of the fastenings on the outside, and held in place at the waist by a narrow leather belt, or a cincture or girdle of the same cloth. The style buttoned down the centre front was not encouraged in the Anglican Church. Rev. Percy Dearmer in his *Parson's Handbook* gives his reasons why there should be no buttons down the skirt. 'The use of buttons renders the cassock inconvenient to walk in, uncomfortable to kneel in, and cumbersome to put on. It would also add to the cost if button-hole making were not so often cruelly underpaid.'[18]

The cassock did not have pockets but instead had slits in the side seams so that the wearer could get to the pockets in the trousers worn underneath. Percy Dearmer recommended that the knickerbockers should be worn under the cassock, to avoid the inelegant sight of trouser cuffs appearing below the hem. However, clergy, choir, and all others who used the cassock rarely

50 Mr Helden, curate of St Mary Abbots, Kensington. Photograph possibly by Lewis Carroll. This Anglican curate is wearing the cassock known as the 'Sarum' style, which is double-breasted and held in place at the waist by a sash. Over this he is wearing a gown with hanging sleeves and bands over a soft wing collar. Although clergy favoured wearing dark suits for everyday wear and reserved their cassocks for preaching and for formal occasions, they were entitled to wear them all the time (Roman Catholic priests were forbidden to wear their cassocks out of doors).

Laurence Sterne.

4 *Laurence Sterne (1713-68) by Sir Joshua Reynolds, 1760. Sterne, essayist, novelist and curate, is seen here in correct Anglican clerical dress of the eighteenth century. His double-breasted cassock, held by a sash at the waist, falls open across his lap and reveals his black knee-breeches and stockings. He wears an open gown and the preacher's scarf which partially conceals the bands at the neck. The sleeves of both cassock and gown are cut loose enough to reveal his white shirt sleeve. On his head he wears the conventional wig of the eighteenth-century clergyman, slightly askew, and the severity of his clerical wear is relieved by the informality of the pose*

5,6 *Ordination of priests (above) and deacons (below) at Limuru, Kenya in 1957. Archbishop Leonard Beecher is shown with ordinands in traditional Anglican clerical dress, with a slight variation in the style of wearing the garments. The priests wear both alb and surplice over the cassock and the preacher's scarf hanging in the normal way. The deacons, in the surplice over their cassocks, wear the scarf in the manner* of the stole of the early Church, a style which had been continued in both the Roman and Byzantine traditions but generally abandoned in the reformed churches. The Archbishop wears a scarlet chimere over a white rochet with the hood (not visible) and tippet or scarf. He carries a pastoral staff and a violet Canterbury or square cap. He also has a pectoral cross*

bothered with such refinements, possibly because there were rarely full-length mirrors in the vestry.

The Gown

Clergy continued to wear the gown with the cassock, the academic gown worn by graduates and the full-sleeved preaching gown by non-graduates. Canon 74 of the Anglican Church shows a certain amount of latitude of style. The black gown was the only vestment, if so it may be called, which was tolerated by any of the Prot-estant Non-conformist sects in the nineteenth century. The leaders of the Methodist movement had worn them, and in individual cases, Presby-terian and Congregationalist ministers wore them while conducting services, with the hood of their degree if they were graduates. (In 1828 the undenominational University College, London, was founded and the 'religious tests' were eventu-ally abolished in 1871 in Oxford and Cambridge.)

The gown was worn in the pulpit when preaching; Charles James Blomfield (1786–1857) who was Bishop of London from 1828 was a 'legalist' and insisted upon the gown's being worn in the pulpit, alleging that the use of the surplice was a departure from the usual practice only found in remote and small parishes. He wrote to the very Rev. Dr Calvert: 'I shall be much obliged to you if you will express to the Manchester Clergy, as opportunity may offer, my particular *wish* that they should wear their *gowns*, and clerical hats, or at least the former, on Sundays. I am quite sure that in a place like Manchester, it is very desirable that they should keep up all the appearance of ministers of the established church.'[19] When the French emigré clergy came over during the revolution (1789 and after) they were surprised to see their English secular coun-terparts dressed more like Benedictine monks.

Hats and Wigs

There were many types of hats worn by the clergy in the nineteenth century, usually black and of a simple style. Apart from the shovel hat already mentioned, the most common style among the lower orders of clergy was the plain hat with a shallow crown and a broad brim, although there are also frequent references to a tall black hat. Towards the end of the century there were attempts to re-introduce the square cap, as proper to the gown and cassock when walking out of doors (and also to squash the introduction of the biretta which was considered foreign to the English Church). Percy Dearmer advocates the square cap in black velvet for bishops and doctors and black cloth for all other clergy, and he says they are obtainable from the Warham Guild, 28 Margaret Street, Oxford Circus, London. He does allow the use of the ordinary broad-brimmed felt hat, as it is 'sometimes a convenient compromise in towns because it is less con-spicuous; and this custom has two centuries of tradition behind it.'[20] Morris and Co. make 'SQUARE CAPS in the original shape: for bishops and doctors, velvet 10.6d. for other clergy, cloth 7.6d.' and a black velvet square cap with Percy Dearmer's name tape inside can be seen at the Strangers Hall Museum, Norwich. (In this collection there are also a shovel-hat made by the ecclesiastical furnishers J. Wippell and Co. Exeter, Manchester and London, described in the label as the 'New comfortable'; and a cloth biretta made in four parts which, although it looks as if it should fold, does not. It has a small 'pompom' tuft in the centre.)

Canon 18 orders that 'No man shall cover his head in the church or chapel in the time of Divine Service, except he have some infirmity, in which case let him wear a night-cap or coif' and these, according to canon 74, could only be made of 'black silk, satin, or velvet'. The hat was strictly for outdoor wear, and as such did occasionally follow fashionable dress. Incidentally, canon 18 may have been responsible for the continued use of wigs into the early nineteenth century, as a means of keeping the head warm. Georgina Sitwell, recalling a typical village service at the beginning of the century, said: 'The service was simple and primitive like the congregation. The old clerk wore a yellow welsh wig in winter to keep his head warm.'[21]

The Surplice

The surplice was worn in rural parishes and at the beginning of the century was often considered quaint and old-fashioned. George Eliot in *Scenes from Clerical Life* admits to 'an occasional tender-ness for old abuses' lingering 'with a certain fondness over the days of nasal clerks and top booted parsons'. She describes the clergyman Mr Gilfil, 'an excellent old gentleman, who smoked very long pipes and preached very short sermons', as wearing the surplice. 'Mr Gilfil would sometimes forget to take off his spurs before putting on his surplice, and only became aware of the omission by feeling something mysteriously tugging at the skirts of that garment as he stepped into the reading desk.'[22]

Gradually the surplice was re-introduced to parishes which had neglected the use of it in the eighteenth century, as part of the effort of revival of good order in the Church. Rev. C. K. Francis Brown in *The History of the English Clergy 1800–1900* quotes from contemporary sources the surprise with which the surplice was received in the first decades of the nineteenth century. In 1838 'I was struck by the preacher preaching in a surplice, an unusual thing I thought in a town church at that time', and in 1843 the Rev. G. M. Cooper introduced it to his parish in West Dean 'to the astonishment of the people as they said they had never seen such a thing before', and again '... when I was in Guernsey 1829–32 I never saw a surplice, the whole of the service of the church being conducted by a black-gowned clergyman.'[23]

The surplice was not always received calmly and in 1840 there were 'Surplice Riots' in the city of Exeter, where the offending vicars were mobbed and pelted with filth and rotten eggs by the irate people. *The Times* defended the conduct of the mob, and bade the bishop put down the 'boyish nonsense' of the young clergyman wearing a surplice. Tom Hood poured scorn on these surplice riots in the well-known lines:

A very pretty public stir
Is making down at Exeter,
About the surplice fashion;
And many bitter words and rude
Are interchanged about the feud,
And much unchristian passion.
For me, I neither know nor care,
Whether a parson ought to wear
A black dress, or a white one,
Plagued with a trouble of my own,
A wife who preaches in her gown,
And lectures in her night one.[24]

The surplice was accepted by most churches in the Anglican Communion by the 1870s, as the rise of the Liturgiologists gave the lower churchmen much more to worry about over the introduction of vestments. In *The Way of All Flesh* when Ernest goes to visit his father after a period of estrangement he notices the difference. He goes to the church on the Sunday

... and noticed that the ever receding tide of Evangelicalism had ebbed many a stage lower, even during the few years of his absence. His father used to walk to the Church through the Rectory garden and across a small intervening field. He had been used to walk in a tall hat, his masters gown, and wearing a pair of Geneva bands. Ernest noticed that the bands were worn no longer, and lo! greater marvel still, Theobald did not preach in his master's gown, but in a surplice.[25]

The surplice was still made open in the front as it had been during the eighteenth century. The Rev. Lee writing his glossary in 1877 said 'Our modern practice of having it made open in front arose, no doubt, in the 17th Century, when it was the custom to wear large wigs, and when the putting on of an old surplice would have disarranged their appearance and endangered their position.'[26]

The surplices in the collection of Strangers Hall in Norwich include two fine examples of nineteenth-century versions which are open down the front. One, from Kirriemuir in Scotland, which has a square neck opening with very fine pleating stitched in place, dates from the first quarter of the nineteenth century. The other, from about 1860, has a label in it: 'Made by J. Wippell and Co. Exeter'. A number, 2402, is inked in. This is also made in plain fine linen. The former has some white embroidery around the neck; there are other examples of embroidered surplices, but this decorative work is always in white, of fine workmanship and probably not visible from a distance. Another type of decorative work was smocking which was a natural way of controlling the fullness of the surplice. The sleeves, usually raglan, were very wide and full, and although the surplice became less full than the eighteenth-century version it always remained a generously cut garment. Percy Dearmer in *The Parson's Handbook* says that the surplice should never button in front and that it should fall to within about six inches of the ground. 'A further cause that has led to the gradual cutting down of the garments is the rage for cheapness, and the desire of the tailor to save as much material as possible. Before vestments became a commercial article they remained full on the continent as well as here.'[27]

The firm of Morris and Co. made surplices as well as embroidered vestments and they appear to have tried to keep to the old styles: 'SURPLICES. With the exception of "choir" surplices these are hand hemmed, and are made to a full flowing graceful pattern. Unless otherwise ordered, Priest's surplices are cut to reach within eight inches of the cassock hem.' For the clergy there are two shapes to choose from: the 'full' shape with sleeves to turn over and the 'Catechism' shape with sleeves to the wrist. The 'full' surplice is slightly more expensive, and these surplices come in a choice of two fabrics, linen and nainsook, of which the linen is more expensive – the full surplice is £1 5s in linen, £1 1s in nainsook and the 'Catechism' shape is £1 4s in linen and £1 in nainsook.

Morris and Co. also provide 'white embroidered surplice collars from 12s. extra.' The servers' surplices are the same shape and price as the 'Catechism' style and also come for 'Lads from 5ft. – 5ft.4' and for boys, getting cheaper as the size gets smaller. The choir surplices which are 'slightly reduced in fullness' also come in three sizes – men's, lads' and boys' – and are the cheapest of all. These too, are offered in both linen and nainsook, and with an extra reduction of 6d per surplice where more than six are ordered. Smocking was from 4s extra.[28]

The Church of England never brought lace into the decoration of the surplice and the cotta was only very rarely introduced in the highest Anglo-Catholic churches. The cotta is the short version of the surplice which has a broad band of lace at the hem and on the lower part of the sleeves, and is generally worn by acolytes and servers. Percy Dearmer dismisses this vestment with one line: 'The Cotta is fortunately not one of the vestments ordered by our Rubric.'

The Alb
The alb had totally disappeared from use in England after the Reformation. Archbishop Grindal in his injunctions to the churchwardens of the diocese of York in 1571 gave a comprehensive list of articles, including albs, which were not only to be disused, but 'utterly defaced, broken and destroyed'. In 1576, when he was made Archbishop of Canterbury, he ordered the same for that province.[29] The alb was re-introduced into general use in the Church of England with the vestments which will be discussed later.

The Rochet and Chimere
Canon law ordained that the rochet should be the proper dress for a bishop whenever he appeared in public. The ordinal of 1662 differed from that previously in use in ordering that a bishop-elect should be presented 'vested with his rochet and that after the examination he should put on the rest of the Episcopal habit.' This cannot mean the cope or the vestment, as they were not especially episcopal. It doubtless refers to the chimere with a scarf or tippet, such as was put on by Archbishop Parker immediately after his consecration on 17 December 1559.[30] The rochet and the chimere went together and have to be dealt with as one. Charles I had decided on the apparel of churchmen in Scotland on 15 October 1633. Bishops were to provide themselves with 'a chymer (that is a sattin or taffetie gown without lining or sleeves) to be worn over their whites at the time of their consecration.'[31] Although the chimere was not mentioned as church dress when the ornaments rubrics were laid down, it had always been considered proper to the bishop when wearing his rochet, so much so that when the sleeves of the lawn garment grew to their enormous size in the late eighteenth and most of the nineteenth century, they were sewn directly on to the chimere.

The rochet of the bishop was a full-length robe made of fine linen or lawn and the sleeves were gathered into a cuff at the wrist with a frill. There was a band of black or red at the wrist which appears to be a detail introduced by the bishops themselves. The black band went with the black chimere which was the standard colour from the establishment of the Church until the latter half of the nineteenth century. 'The red wristband now worn with the red chimere is, unless the prelate be an Oxford D.C.L., a mere folly, perhaps invented by [Samuel] Wilberforce.'[32] There is a late nineteenth-century rochet of pleated linen and lace in the collection at Strangers Hall, Norwich which has both red satin cuffs and shoulder pieces.

The chimere became very narrow in the back when the large rochet sleeves were sewn into it but by the end of the century this practice was falling out of use; certainly by the 1890s writers on ecclesiastical dress were encouraging the idea of returning the sleeves to the rochet. (It must be remembered that the rochet had always been made in a sleeveless form as well as with sleeves, and in this form there was a strong tradition in favour of the rochet for the clerk.)

As they changed the style of the chimere, the prelates introduced coloured robes again. Before the Reformation the 'sleeveless cote' had been made in colours other than red and black, notably green and blue. However, in the nineteenth century the alternatives to black were red and occasionally purple. In the 'official arrangements' for the Lambeth Conference of 1897 it was ordered: 'that when robes are worn, the bishops will wear either the black or red chimere as each may find convenient.' In the event, all the English bishops and most of the others wore scarlet. *The Guardian* newspaper reported on the event on 4 August 1897 'The Archbishop of Canterbury and all the members of the home episcopate, as most of the colonial and American bishops, wore their scarlet robes, but a few appeared in black chimeres, and two or three in violet.' Purple, although the colour of the cassocks of the episcopate, was not approved of and scarlet and black became the common colours (scarlet being reserved for bishops who were also doctors of divinity in theory, if not always in practice).

Wigs

The clerical wig was retained into the nineteenth century by some clergy and clerks but bishops and archbishops were the slowest to relinquish it. The first three decades of the nineteenth century saw the whole bench of bishops in the grey bobbed wig and most voluminous 'magpie' (the nickname for the white rochet and black chimere). Many bishops wanted to discontinue the practice of wearing the wig but George IV (1762–1830) would not permit it. The *Dictionary of National Biography* notes of George Pelham: 'when raised to the episcopal bench he nearly went down on his knees to George III to be permitted to dispense with the wig but the King was inexorable.'[33]

Charles James Blomfield (1786–1857), Bishop of Chester in 1824, and of London in 1828, made vigorous attempts to abolish the episcopal wig, and only gained permission on the accession of William IV in 1830. Gradually all bishops ceased to wear wigs although there are still references to them in the 1850s – Bishop Turton is said to have worn a wig at an ordination in Ely in 1857[34], and George Murray, Bishop of Rochester (1827–60) is generally held to be the last bishop to wear a wig in the House of Lords. (He was the last of a breed who regarded a bishopric as the natural reward for political work and were content with inherited standards.) Archbishops wore wigs for formal occasions (for example, at the wedding of Queen Victoria to Prince Albert in 1840 and at the christenings of the royal children). John Bird Sumner (Archbishop of Canterbury 1848–62) was said to be 'the last wearer of this hideous and uncanonical head cover.'

The Hood and Tippet

With the rochet and chimere of the bishop, and the cassock and surplice of the priest, the hood and tippet or scarf completed the outfit known as 'choir dress'. The hood is not an ecclesiastical vestment but merely part of the academic robes. It has nevertheless been given a quasi-ecclesiastical character in England by canon 58. It was to be worn over the surplice at all choir offices and for preaching. Worn with the hood (which was not really visible from the front – only the black band across the throat holding it in place could be seen) was the tippet or scarf. This was worn over the hood to keep it from riding up, fell down on either side, and hung straight; it was not to be caught by a girdle or held in place by any device. Tyack puts forward the proposition that the black scarf is the contraction of the *cappa nigra*, the decent black cope of Sarum use: 'In the course of time this cope got to be contracted more and more in breadth, until it became a broad band only, generally of black silk, which, under the name of a canon's or chaplain's scarf has lasted to our day.'[35]

The words 'scarf' and 'tippet' refer to the same garment; the alternative name 'stole' is misleading, as this garment has nothing whatever to do with the stole which is part of the suit of vestments. The tippet should be of black silk for those with a master's degree and dignitaries and of black stuff for ordinary clerics, but generally silk was used for all tippets. Morris and Co. advertised 'Tippets or Black Scarves. Ordinary or thin ribbed silk 0.18.6. Very thin silk 0.16.6.' The black tippet was to be the same width throughout although pleats were stitched in at the centre to control the fabric around the back of the neck. Percy Dearmer says 'The stitched gathers at the neck are a modern corruption of the tailors'.[36] The hems could be either pinked or simply hemmed, and the tippet was not to be decorated in any way.

The tippet or scarf is important in choir dress as it is the only vestment that distinguishes the ordained cleric from the laity. (Clerks and choristers who have a degree are entitled to wear the academic hood, and all wear the cassock and surplice.) The wearing of the tippet or scarf by all the clergy was a nineteenth-century development. It had been retained (sometimes lined with fur) in the choir by dignitaries since the days of the Reformation but it was introduced to all his clergy by Bishop Blomfield of London, and the practice quickly spread to other dioceses. J. T. Micklethwaite, writing of the tippet in an article in 1888, says 'thus it comes that the stole is now generally used, though fifty years ago it was as obsolete as the chasuble.'[37]

The Almuce
The almuce of grey fur was re-introduced for the use of senior clergy, the reason given being that as it had not been mentioned in the ornaments rubric of the first Prayer Book it had not been forbidden. This fur shoulder cape with two long tabs at the front was the least popular vestment and was not worn in all churches, although it was always considered acceptable choir dress.

The Choir Habit
Before moving on to the important re-introduction of the wearing of the old vestments in the Anglican Church, it is worth restating the choir habit as set down by Percy Dearmer at the turn of the nineteenth century.

Bishops   rochet, chimere, black silk tippet lined with brown sable *or* rochet (surplice and grey almuce if desired) cope, mitre, gloves and the crozier.

Deans and Canons (with *Prebendaries* if so appointed by the chapter)   surplice, almuce of grey fur, hood of their degree (the almuce replaces the scarf or tippet).

Minor Canons and Chaplains   surplice, hood of their degree, almuce of black fur or of such material as was appointed by authority.

Priests and Deacons (with a doctor's or master's degree)   surplice, hood of their degree, stuff tippet.

Priests and Deacons (non-graduate)   surplice, stuff tippet. (In practice hoods also were worn by the licentiates of theological colleges).

Readers   surplice, with any reader's collar, or ribbon and medal, that may be appointed by the diocese. (In practice readers, clerks and choristers who have a degree, also wore the hood of that degree.)

Parish clerks   surplice or rochet.

Choristers   surplice (the chanters might wear copes also if the officiant was thus vested).

The cassock is usually worn under all of these outfits.

Choir dress, as described above, was accepted by all the Anglican churches, as the clergy felt that these vestments were acceptable according to Church law, and were not 'tainted' by Roman practice. The introduction of vestments had caused much surprise and distress amongst the more 'low church', and by the end of the century the evangelicals had accepted choir dress as a reasonable habit.

Gowns
The Irish Prayer Book of 1877 left out the vexatious question of the wearing of the chasuble and coloured stoles. The minister is required by the 4th canon, 'that only a plain white surplice shall be worn, and the customary scarf of plain black silk, with the hood. The minister is allowed to wear a plain black gown when preaching, but with this exception, "No minister shall wear any

other Ecclesiastical vestment or ornament."'[38] Other Non-conformist sects elected to wear the cassock and gown with bands for important occasions (also with the hood); and the names 'Geneva gowns' and 'Geneva bands' came to be associated with the very garments which the original Puritans and Calvinists opposed.

The moderators of the three Presbyterian bodies in Scotland developed an official costume which became fixed by continuous usage: 'The head of the established church or kirk, wears court dress and an ample gown with full sleeves, the Moderator of the Free Kirk dresses very similarly, while he of the United Presbyterian Kirk uses a Genevan Gown and bands.'[39]

The Cope and Mitre

The cope had always been allowed in the Church of England although it had fallen into general disuse except in the most important ceremonies. The mitre had completely disappeared after the introduction of the clerical wig, although, with the pallium, the mitre could remain as a heraldic device on the coat of arms of a bishop.

Percy Dearmer mentions the mitre quite naturally in conjunction with the cope but it had been a recent innovation and was only accepted by a minority. Edward King, Bishop of Lincoln, usually held responsible for introducing the mitre to the Anglican Church, was an advanced high churchman and was prosecuted in 1890 by the Archbishop of Canterbury (Edward White Benson) and other bishops for ritualistic practices. St Stephen's House, Oxford still has a splendid mitre which was once the property of Bishop King; this is made in the thirteenth-century style, of cream silk, embroidered with pearls and amethysts. The mitre had been tried out previously with ludicrous effect. Rev. C. K. Francis Brown writes of one occasion: 'A Roman Catholic furnisher had sent some mitres down to an episcopal meeting. They reposed upon the hall table. One was placed upon the person of Bishop Ellicott. His grey side whiskers, apron and gaiters could hardly be described as congruous. But when he commenced to walk with defective gait (the result of a regrettable railway accident) the spectacle was generally regarded as unedifying. The mitre was replaced on the hall stand.'[40]

The Reintroduction of Vestments in the 1840s

The Oxford Movement, whose central figures were Keble, Newman and Froude, was not itself concerned with the re-introduction of vestments. The Tractarians (as they were also known) had not been responsible for inventing the fashion for reproducing Gothic architecture for which they have often been blamed – the Gothic movement in ecclesiastical architecture had begun long before 1833.[41] The first generations of Tractarians were singularly indifferent to ceremonial, and Froude never mentions it. John Keble, who was always careful about his personal appearance, did not pay much attention to vestments. When the church he had built was consecrated in October, 1848, 'the bishop forbade the large body of clergy who were to be present to come robed in surplices, but Keble cared little for such details.'[42] He did, himself, wear the surplice, and one of his surplices, together with an M.A. hood and a mortar board, are still kept by Keble College, Oxford. Newman, likewise, did not show much interest in vestments. In his church at Littlemore there was an embroidered altar frontal, worked by his sisters 'of crimson plush velvet', but he never wore the vestments of the Roman Church. He is censured for not wearing a black gown in the pulpit, which hardly indicates an advanced ceremonial, and after his final sermon he 'took off his hood, and threw it over the altar rails, as though to signify that he had finished his work as a teacher in the Church of England.'[43]

Edward Bouverie Pusey (1800–82) joined Newman and Keble very soon after the Movement had been formed and although a great scholar and very earnest in his study of the early Church, he knew nothing about the 'Ornaments of the Minister'. 'Do tell me what a cope is' he is reported to have said one night to Bloxham who was dining with him at Christ Church.[44] He expressed a view that 'It seems beginning at the wrong end for ministers to deck their own persons: our own plain dresses are more in keeping with the state of our Church which is one of humiliation. It does not seem in character to revive gorgeous, or even in any degree handsome dresses in a day of reproach, rebuke and blasphemy: these are not holyday times.' He himself

51 Priest vesting himself for Mass, 1851. The priest, with the maniple on the left arm, is arranging the stole in the form of a cross upon his breast, which will be kept in place by his girdle. His alb is decorated with lace at the hem and at the cuffs, and his amice is quite plain, with no apparel. The cassock seen underneath the alb still has a train, although it is shortened to the instep in the front. The stole and maniple have grown much bigger and are heavily decorated with wide ends and a thick fringe. When the Anglican Church re-introduced vestments at this time, the medieval Church was looked on as the model and not the contemporary fashions of the Roman Catholics.

bishop's expostulations, Pusey said that he thought the decoration could be defended by the ornaments rubric, but that 'we have too much to do to keep sound doctrine – to go into the question of dresses.'[45]

The credit for treating ceremonial seriously belongs to Cambridge, not to Oxford. The revival of ecclesiastical learning, which was so conspicuous a feature of the Tractarian Movement, necessarily made the clergy familiar with the primitive liturgies and with the ancient service books of the Church of England. Contemporary with this revival of liturgical knowledge, there sprung up a widely diffused taste for ecclesiastical design in the fabric and furniture of churches, a taste which was greatly promoted by the works of Augustus Welby Pugin, and by the formation of the Cambridge Camden Society in the year 1839.

The Society was founded by John Mason Neale with others, and it published a magazine called *The Ecclesiologist*, the first number being printed in November 1841. Pusey and the Oxford Movement objected to some of their principles, and the Evangelicals viewed the movement with the deepest suspicion and distaste: 'We poor aesthetical fellows' wrote Benjamin Webb on 31 December 1844 'get kicks from all'.[46] At first, the Society tried to re-introduce merely decent ceremonial and the surplice; Bishop Phillpotts of Exeter in 1840 and Bishop Blomfield of London in 1842 directed their clergy to wear the surplice in the pulpit. The riots which resulted in Exeter have already been mentioned (page 98), and Bishop Phillpotts had to withdraw his order. In 1843 William James Early Bennett introduced a new type of service to St George's, Hanover Square – the clergy and surpliced choir walked to their places in procession. Bishop Blomfield consecrated St Barnabas, Pimlico, on 11 June 1850 and 'the Bishop and clergy walked in procession from the vestry through the street, chanting a psalm with full choir, vested in surplices – a thing I believe not done before.'[47] It was this occasion that provoked the famous statement from Lord Ashley, better known as Lord Shaftesbury, when he was presiding at a Protestant meeting held at the Freemason's Hall later that year on 4 December: 'I would rather worship with Lydia on the banks of the river than with a hundred surpliced

wore only the plain black scarf or stole, over his surplice, though his assistant in the Hebrew professorship (all those who taught at Oxford and Cambridge were in holy orders) the Rev. C. Seager, drew upon himself, and upon Pusey, episcopal censure and suspicion by decorating his stole with a cross at each end. In replying to the priests in the gorgeous temple of St Barnabas.'

Also at this time George Rundle Prynne, a Puseyite, the incumbent of St Peter's, Plymouth from 1845 to 1903, was being vilified by the local newspapers for introducing alms bags, although he only wore the surplice and vestments were being introduced in other parts of Britain. On St Mark's Day 1846, J. M. Neale wrote to his friend Benjamin Webb to persuade him to introduce the cope: 'The greatest use of the cope is, it strikes me, to accustom our people to coloured vestments; once do that and do it on such Anglican grounds as we have [i.e. the ornaments rubric], and the chasuble follows without difficulty.'[48]

The Helston case, decided by Henry Phillpotts, Bishop of Exeter (1831–69) with the advice of his chancellor, was the first occasion on which the ornaments rubric came into dispute in the nineteenth century. The judgement was:

It is the duty of the parishioners to provide the albe, the vestments and the cope. True it would be a very costly duty, and for that reason most probably Churchwardens have neglected it, and Archdeacons have connived at the neglect. But be this as it may, if the Churchwardens of Helston shall perform this duty at the charge of the parish providing an albe, a vestment and a cope as they might in strictness be required to do I shall enjoin the Minister, be he who he may,.to use them.[49]

The period 1857–71 was marked by great development in ceremonial and this included vestments and ornaments of the ritual; the emphasis was being transferred from the inner meaning to the outward expression. The main line of defence was the ornaments rubric which runs as follows: 'And here is to be noted, that such Ornaments of the Church, and of the Ministers thereof, at all times of their Ministration, shall be retained, and be in use, as were in this Church of England, by the Authority of Parliament, in the second year of the reign of King Edward the Sixth.'

On 3 May 1873 a deputation of the Church Association, or as Archibald Campbell-Tait describes them in his diary, 'sixty thousand people thirsting for the blood of the Ritualists', presented a petition to the archbishops of York and Canterbury asking for 'the entire suppression of ceremonies and practices adjudged to be illegal.' The archbishops in their reply discouraged the idea of unlimited prosecutions (an extremely expensive business, as had already been discovered) but agreed that the position was serious. In 1874 Archibald Campbell-Tait, as Archbishop of Canterbury, determined to introduce a bill into the House of Lords, with Queen Victoria's warm approval.[56] The bill, entitled 'An Act for the better Administration of the laws respecting the Regulation of Public Worship' was passed without a division. As a result five clergy were sent to prison for wearing vestments, but the Protestant fury abated and in the next five years there was a growth in toleration.

The extent of the adoption of the Mass vestments can be seen in the report on the Canterbury convocation of 1906.[57] The five bishops involved in this report were: Dr John Wordsworth, Salisbury (the convener); Dr George F. Browne, Bristol; Dr Archibald Robertson, Exeter; Dr Edgar C. S. Gibson, Gloucester; and Dr Frederick H. Chase, Ely. Their aim was obviously to defuse the situation, and gently to inform both clergy and laity how innocuous liturgical vestments were in their origins. They proved there was no direct connection with Levitical (Old Testament) dress, and that vestments were simply the garments of civil life ornamented and beautified, and that the symbolism attached to them, although arbitrary and fanciful, was at the same time quite innocent and uncontroversial. The inevitable reply came from J. T. Tomlinson who published an article entitled 'The Craving for Mass Vestments. An Examination of the report by five bishops to the Convocation of Canterbury on "The Ornaments of the Church and its Ministers"' in April 1908. He agreed with much of the scholarly research done, but still rejected the use of the vestments even after 'the report has "disinfected" these robes of all symbolic meaning.' He maintains that 'the purely antiquarian facts are usefully tabulated in Part I of the Report, and the possession of common sense by the reader will suffice to reject its special pleading in favour of restoring "continuity" with the worst period of downgrade development, rather than the centuries nearest to the Apostles.'

The Church of England took the middle

course, and in the event each parish and its minister chose its own way to worship. The twentieth century started with the three streams of the Anglican Church (high, low and broad) all convinced of the rightness of their own way, with many other denominations including Roman Catholics enjoying their hard-won freedom of education and political and social emancipation, and each was part of an ever-growing missionary tradition, which was second to none throughout the world.

J. M. Neale first wore a chasuble in 1850, a home-made chasuble was worn at Wilmcote, Warwickshire in 1849, and one was used at St Thomas the Martyr, Oxford, on Whitsun 1854. An eccentric clergyman, Rev. R. S. Hawker of Morwenstone, had made for himself a yellow 'chasuble' or poncho, which he wore in church and outside riding his mule. He did not play a significant part in the development of the ritual however, as he denounced the Ecclesiologists in the same breath as the Methodists, and preferred to consider the West Country and himself as part of the pre-Augustinian Celtic Church and thus closer to the Church of the East.

St Saviour's, Leeds, was a very advanced church in ceremonial, and even after clergy had been sacked, the vicar, Mr T. Minster, continued to introduce new ritual. The choir were already in surplices when he put them in cassocks as well in 1848; they put up hangings and had a white altar frontal with a red velvet cross with Agnus Dei (the Lamb of God) embroidered in the centre for Easter. He introduced midnight Mass at Christmas that year, and the clergy wore white stoles. The other parts of full Eucharistic dress were given to them, 'but to avoid disputes as far as might be they were not worn for the present.'[50] The bishop said to Mr Minster: 'You are a plague-spot on my diocese.'

In the two decades following 1850 there were several churches who adopted the full sets of the medieval or gothic vestments. The Rev. Richard Seymour entered in his diary on 6 October 1865: 'Before breakfast walked out and went to St Lawrence's Church [Norwich]: Holy Communion being administered, three priests in chasuble, dalmatic and tunicle. Two others with a long black cassock and very short surplice, and ten acolytes robed as abroad. It was a strange sight but the service was very solemn.'[51]

On 19 October 1866 *The Times* published a leading article attacking St Alban's, Holborn. 'Three of these personages, bedizened with green and gold and yellow and covered with black stripes and crosses, stand with their backs to the congregation ... these gorgeous and flaunting dresses and candles, and odours, and gesticulations, have in them something almost revolting to an English stomach.'[52] In 1868 the Church Association determined to attack St Albans, Holborn, and the case of Martin v. Mackonockie was brought to court. Although vestments were left out of the charge and the Dean of the Arches, Sir Robert Phillimore on 3 February 1870, allowed the vestments, the Privy Council reversed the judgment on 21 February 1871 and declared them illegal. (St Alban's, Holborn, still has a green silk dalmatic, part of a high Mass set, referred to in a letter from Dean Stanley to Archbishop Tait – 'I have seen three men in green' – and a cotta and a biretta that belonged to Father Mackonockie.)[53]

There were many problems as the Mass vestments were introduced. The ornaments rubric was not always clear and there was no special court to deal with doctrinal or ceremonial disputes. Some clergy and churchmen disliked vestments but disliked state intervention even more; some statesmen could not understand what the fuss was all about – the Prime Minister, Melbourne, was heard to remark that things had come to a pretty pass when religion started to interfere with one's private life, which indicates that the statesmen in control were not perhaps the best qualified to deal with ecclesiastical problems.

Much was published, and the argument went to and fro. In 1866 William Milton put the point of view against adopting the chasuble and all that went with it: 'The strict sacrificial vestments are not legal in the Church of England and, I believe, never have been. The cope is now illegal in parish churches. It was excluded by the advertisements of 1565 and nobody has thought of restoring it or sanctioning it since.... The use of surplice and hood is all that is now contemplated and enjoined by statute and rubric.'[54] The Ritualists argued that the correct dress enhanced the ceremony and protested that they were part of a strong British

52 Cope designed by Sir Ninian Cowper and embroidered by the Society of the Sisters of Bethany. English, early twentieth century. When vestments were re-introduced in England with Catholic emancipation and freedom to worship, and the rise of Ecclesiologists and 'high churchmanship' in the Anglican Church, the English talent for embroidery came back into the Church with a large number of banners, altar frontals and vestments being made by laity and religious. Medieval or 'Gothic' styles were used as models and work of a very high standard was produced.

tradition of 'Andrewes, Bancroft, Laud, Wren, Montague and their fellow confessors and we claim, with them, for the English Church, the revival of all the vestments and ornaments to which it can be proved she is justly entitled.'[55]

The Rev. Robert Owen, Fellow of Jesus College, Oxford, was provoked by a letter from the two archbishops and twenty-two bishops protesting against the introduction of the new rituals in 1851. He published a pamphlet entitled *An Apology for the High Church Movement on Liberal Principles* in which he pleaded the use of copes in English cathedrals in the eighteenth century, and said that it was an effort to seek 'the beauty of holiness'. On 17 April 1857 *The Union*, an Anglo-Catholic weekly, urged upon all clergy 'who hold the Catholic faith to commence at once this beautiful and symbolical practice' (of wearing vestments) and the Ritualist Movement had begun in earnest.

Monastic Dress

One of the major alterations in religious life in this period in Great Britain was the large number of religious orders that grew up in the last half of the nineteenth century. In 1800 there were no monasteries or convents in Britain; by 1870 there were 67 communities of men and 220 of women which were Roman Catholic, and 60 houses of Anglican nuns. Male orders were slower to start in the Church of England, but were eventually also numerous. The traditional habits were observed, and where new orders were set up they did not deviate from the general rules of white, black, brown or grey, simple wool habits with cowls for the men, veils for the women, and sandals. Each order had its own style of dress and they were too many to describe individually here.[58] Novices nearly always wore white veils and professed nuns generally wore black over a wimple or binder of white.

Ecclesiastical Embroidery

The introduction of vestments gave extra momentum and work to the Arts and Crafts Movement, and the strong tradition of embroidery, which had never died out, found new impetus in the making of vestments. As well as their main work of prayer and works of charity the convents provided both embroidery schools for the production of the new vestments and also the opportunity to wear them. J. M. Neale who founded the Sisterhood of St Margaret, East Grinstead, in 1854, celebrated in a chasuble, and there is a green chasuble with outlined orphreys that belonged to him preserved there today. Their embroidery school opened in 1866. The elaborate cream and gold chasuble and stole of Canon W. J. Butler is still preserved at the community of St Mary the Virgin, Wantage, which he founded in 1850, and there are many other communities which still own the vestments made, often by their predecessors' hands, at this time.

It has been said that the first English-made vestments used by the Roman Catholic clergy after Catholic Emancipation in 1829 were made by the costume workshops of the Royal Opera House, Covent Garden, because there was no tradition of vestment making in England.[59] Certainly Planché took enormous pains to get accurate vestments when they needed to be created for the stage, travelling to the Continent to do his research if necessary. He had been sent to Rheims to research the pageant to celebrate Charles X's coronation, which was performed on 10 July 1825 at the Royal Opera House. A. W. N. Pugin took great trouble to study the history of ecclesiastical vesture and also designed vestments and ornaments. The high standard of both scholarship and workmanship were to combine together to create beautiful embroideries (it is interesting to note that generally it was a man that designed and women who spent the many hours of painstaking work that was needed). Sir Ninian Cowper did many of the brilliant designs which were worked by the school of needlework set up by the Society of the Sisters of Bethany in Lloyd Square, London. William Morris, who had, incidentally, gone up to Oxford intending to become an Anglo-Catholic clergyman, was interested in all forms of church furnishings and his firm William Morris & Co. was to become one of the firms which supplied vestments to the Church. Very early on in the existence of the company, the Exhibition of 1862 brought it to the notice of G. F. Bodley, the architect who was then entering his great church building career.[60] William Morris did not design vestments (neither did he design clothes or the fabrics for them) but he did design altar frontals and took an interest in the art of embroidery, particularly Opus Anglicanum, taking part in the work himself. His daughter, May Morris, took over the embroidery workshops when she was 23, in 1885, and the importance of this section increased.

In 1854 the Ecclesiastical Embroidery Society was formed by Agnes Blencowe (who had made working patterns of flowers drawn full-size from medieval vestments and furnishings which had been published by the Ecclesiological Society in 1848) and the sister of George Street, the Gothic revival architect. The aim of this society was to 'supply altar cloths of strictly ecclesiastical design either by reproducing ancient examples or by working under the supervision of a competent architect'. In 1863 the Society joined forces with the Wantage Church Needlework Association, which consisted of the exterior sisters and friends of St Mary's House, Wantage, Berkshire.[61]

The School of Medieval Embroidery run by the Sisterhood of St Katharine in Queen Square, Bloomsbury, specialized in ecclesiastical needlework. In 1880 the *Magazine of Art* recorded: 'There are at present 15 workers in this school, who undertake the execution of orders for embroidered stoles, orphreys, chalice veils, maniples, chasubles, banners, altars frontals, etc. for those churches in the Church of England in which such accessories of ritual are used.'[62]

Many vestments from this period are dated or have a documented history, and even from relatively little-known workshops a very high standard of embroidery was produced. A beautiful chasuble with matching stole and maniple, now kept by St Mary, Walsingham, Norfolk, has an embroidered inscription inside the chasuble which says 'To the glory of God and in loving memory of Susan, Mother Superior of the Community of St Peter who entered into rest on the feast of the conversion of St Paul 1887 R.I.P.'.

The Morris company catalogue of vestments shows that the company allowed as much individuality for each customer as was possible, providing a variety of silk backgrounds in a choice of the four liturgical colours, with either highly decorated or simple embroidery provided beautifully finished, or started in floss if the parish wished to embroider the design themselves.

SPECIMENS OF HAND EMBROIDERED STOLES

Stoles embroidered or started in floss on silk damask to suit the various seasons, also with a simple cross or emblem if preferred.

Prices according to work

There are broad and narrow stoles, with embroidered bookmarks to match; maniples; apparels for both amice and alb; dalmatics; Gothic chasubles and copes also included in this catalogue.

With the growing demand for vestments and ornaments various ecclesiastical outfitters sprang up to fulfil the need. Wippells had been founded

53 The Ecclesiastical Council at Rome, 1869. This procession of bishops entering the council chamber, carrying their mitres, shows how large the vestigial hood had grown. Trimmed with fringe, it reached excessive proportions in the nineteenth century and looked more absurd as the cope became much shorter. The rochets are trimmed with broad bands of lace at the hem (and also on the cuff although they are not seen here) and the cassocks have lost the long trains they had in the seventeenth and eighteenth centuries.

as early as 1789, the Wippells having been an established family of wool merchants since the seventeenth century. Thomas Pratt and Sons were founded in 1851 and Mowbrays, originally a bookshop, was founded in 1858. Vanpoulles, founded by a Frenchman Maurice Vanpoulle opened in Vauxhall Bridge Road in 1908.

The introduction of mass-produced vestments meant that the art of embroidery was not always upheld, the liturgical colours became formalized far beyond the intentions of the Ecclesiastical scholars who had first advocated their use, and the shapes were not always as graceful as those vestments that were made especially for an individual. However, it brought vestments within the price range of parishes who had neither the skill nor the desire to make their own, and the tailoring of suits and cassocks was of an extremely high standard. These professional ecclesiastical outfitters brought a unity of style of vestments throughout the country, and became the arbiters of fashion and ecclesiastical dress regulations.

Anglican clergymen had the choice of wearing all the vestments that were in use in the reign of Edward VI, and this meant the 'highest' churches could be very similar to the Roman Catholics in their worship. The Roman Catholic hierarchy was re-established in 1850 and in that year the pallium was sent from Rome to the Archbishop of Westminster. However, despite increased ease of communication, professional ecclesiastical vestment makers, and regular synods and convocations, the dress of the clergy continued to be diverse and individual and the use of vestments, although enormously increased, was still not universal. Bishop William Stubbs, though a high churchman, did not much care for the outward and visible side of advanced churchmanship, and when some enthusiastic ladies wished to make him a cope he was heard to declare that he would much rather have half a dozen new shirts.[63]

CHAPTER NINE

The Protestant Churches
in the Twentieth Century
1914–1970

IN THE LAST CHAPTER emphasis has been put on dress as an identifying badge of the type of churchmanship of the wearer in the Church of England; the Non-conformists or free churches must now be looked at in more detail. A satirical article in *The Tatler* indicates how clothes and religion had become intermingled and with the large number of different schools of thought, dress was the best guide. A character called Pasquin of Rome writes to Isaac Bickerstaff:

There is one thing in which I would desire you would be very particular. What I mean is an exact list of all the religions in Great Britain, as likewise the habits, which are said to be the great points of conscience in England, whether they are made of serge or broadcloth, of silk or linen. I should be glad to see a model of the most conscientious dress amongst you, and desire you will send me a hat of each religion; and likewise, if it be not too much trouble, a cravat.[1]

Quakers
The broad-brimmed black hat of the Quaker has already been referred to, and was the most distinctive part of their dress in the seventeenth and eighteenth centuries. It was plain and untrimmed and the brim was uncocked because Quakers, along with the Baptists and the Mennonites, excluded buttons, ribbons and superfluous fastenings for the sake of decoration. 'With Quakers it is a point of their faith not to wear a button or a loop tight up; their hats spread over their heads like a penthouse, and darken the outward man, to signify that they have the inward light.'[2] Independents, Presbyterians and others had adopted simplicity of attire as one of their cardinal principles, and emphasized plainness to an extreme. When Charles II asked William

Penn what were the real differences between their religious beliefs the Quaker is reported to have replied 'The difference is between thy hat and mine; mine has no ornaments.'[3] There was another difference. Quakers did not reserve special dress for the ministers or hierarchy, but all wore these simple garments, taking the basic cut from contemporary fashion but excluding all the trimmings. William Penn wrote in 1693 in *Some fruits of Solitude*: 'Chuse thy cloathes by thine own eye, not anothers. The more simple and plain they are the better. Neither unshapely, nor fantastical; and for Use and Decency, and not for Pride.'

The black hat was worn indoors as well as outside (fashionable hats had been worn indoors in the seventeenth century when Quakers first adopted this fashion), but Quakers refused to doff their hats to anyone. Consequently, they often got into trouble in court and in 'polite society'. They continued this practice undeterred, and only removed their hats to pray. 'Charles II once granted an audience to the courtly Quaker, William Penn, who, as was his custom, entered the royal presence with his hat on. The humorous Sovereign quietly laid aside his own, which occasioned Penn's enquiry "Friend Charles, why dost thou remove thy hat?" "It is the custom" he replied "in this place, for one person only to remain covered."'[4]

George Fox, the founder of the Society of Friends, or Quakers (1624–90) was originally in the habit of attending the Church of England. If he approved of the doctrine being expounded he removed his hat; if, however, the preacher uttered unwelcome sentiments he solemnly put it on as a protest. The plain dress of the Quakers had more in common with the Baptists than the Puritans.

Quakers wore their hair long and accepted wigs readily, although a document in 1717 inveighed against 'men's extravagant wigs and wearing the hair in a beauish manner.' It grants that 'modest, decent or necessary wigs might be allowed.'

The clothes of the Quaker are described in more detail elsewhere[5] but there are important points to be drawn out. There are similarities between the regulations of the Society of Friends and the early monastic orders, emphasizing decency and cleanliness, avoiding fashion and using plain fabrics (from about 1693 figured, striped or flowered stuffs, cloths or silks were generally condemned). The colours chosen were black, browns and greys and undyed stuffs were preferred whenever possible. John Woolman, a tailor, wrote a journal in which he clearly expresses the dilemma facing him. In 1760 when he was forty years old, he was anxious about wearing clothes and hats that had been dyed. By 1762 he had a beaver hat in the natural colour and reports 'Some Friends were afraid that my wearing such a hat savoured of an affected singularity'.[6]

The Quaker wore the simplified version of the coat, vest and knee-breeches for a longer time than fashion commanded (and in America for even longer than in England) but slowly the style of clothes changed as fashion changed, often only when the particular garment became completely obsolete and therefore difficult to obtain. When the heavy beaver hat could no longer be acquired the Quakers did not go to the trouble and expense of having them specially made and by the end of the nineteenth century, when everyday dress had the simple styles approved by the Quakers, they simply ceased to wear special identifying dress.

Female Quakers adapted contemporary fashions in the same way as the men, simplifying and removing all fripperies, although they did originally wear more coloured fabrics. The scarlet mantle was common among Quaker women from the seventeenth century (in 1678 George Fox bought red cloth for a mantle for Margaret Fell who was to become his wife). In the eighteenth century the green apron became popular among Quaker women. The Women's Quarterly Meeting of Lincolnshire, held on 21 April 1721 stated 'We think green aprons are very decent and becoming to us as a people.' In 1735 a young Friend, Mary Drummond of Edinburgh, was given an audience with Queen Caroline: 'The Queen seemed much pleased with her plain dress, and green apron, and often said she thought it exceedingly neat and becoming.'[7]

In the eighteenth century the Friends wore coloured aprons while the fashionable lady wore white aprons. In the nineteenth century this was reversed, and the Quaker women wore their aprons white or sometimes black when coloured silk aprons were sported by the fashionable. They had always worn white neckerchiefs when bodices were cut too low for modesty and propriety.

Generally Quakers, Baptists and Presbyterians always avoided the tendency to create their costume into a uniform, unchanging and arbitrary, which was against the principles of simplicity and meekness of their foundation. However, they were strict and until the early nineteenth century it was possible for an individual to be totally disowned by the Friends for wearing fashionable dress if it was considered to go against the Society's principles.[8]

Methodists

John Wesley regretted that he had not made a regulation about dress. He wrote in his journal 'I might have been firm (and I now see it would have been far better) as either the people called Quakers or the Moravians; I might have said, this is the manner of our dress, which we know is both scriptural and rational. If you join with us, you are to dress as we do, but you need not join us unless you please; but, alas! the time is now passed.'[9]

In the twentieth century the Methodist minister has the right to wear (although he is not obliged to) the dress of the Evangelical clergyman of the Church of England, which was current at the time of the death of John Wesley in 1791. The clerical collar and bands, the cassock, the gown and the hood of his or her degree are all worn, if so desired, and sometimes the surplice, but certainly not the Mass vestments.

The Salvation Army

Another group of Christians who adopted singular dress for men and women, laity and clergy, was the Salvation Army. They had always dressed

54 A Salvation Army band. From the early days the members of the Salvation Army were enthusiastic about wearing a uniform and before it was possible to create a regular uniform they would dress in an approximation, to tell the world they were soldiers of the Lord.

uniformly, and the evangelists of the Christian Mission had worn 'suits of clerical cut, with frock coats, tall hats, black ties and carrying umbrellas, the last named for leading singing during processions rather than for use in wet weather. The wearing of white ties and the use of the title "reverend" were forbidden'.[10] When the Christian Mission became the Salvation Army it was recognized that a uniform of a military type should be adopted, and in November 1878 Mrs Booth wrote that it had been finally decided to adopt uniforms and 'put the finishing touch to the military tactics which had infused into the Mission such a spirit of hopefulness and agression.'[11] Uniforms for all sorts of occupations had become accepted in society – postmen, policemen, bellboys and schoolboys had all been given a distinc-

tive style of dress. Although unique in ecclesiastical dress, the Salvation Army is itself unique, and the adopting of this strict style of dress suited their mission. 'When on duty at the Army, the Salvationist Lord Mayor was dressed no better and no worse than the street sweeper who played beside him in the same band.'[12] Originally the uniform was improvised with tin labels and home-made badges and no attempt was made to regularize the uniform until the 1880s. At first the jerseys (for women) guernseys (for men) and bands with the words 'Salvation Army, Blood and Fire' were blue, but by 1882 these were all changed to red (the bands were to be worn around the hat or around the arm). The colours of the uniform and the flag were red, blue and yellow and the 'Army ribbon' a tricolour of these primary shades, was introduced in August 1882.

Mrs Booth and her daughter Emma, the training principal, designed the 'Hallelujah bonnet'. A simple black straw bonnet trimmed with a plain, pleated band of black silk around the crown, it had to be suitable for uniform wear and also cheap, strong and large enough to protect the heads of the wearers from cold as well as from brickbats and other missiles. The bonnets were already old-fashioned and did not meet with instant approval, but were accepted because they were distinct from mere wordly fashion.

The actual design of the uniform is not fixed by general regulation, but by instructions (minutes) issued from time to time by the Chief of Staff by order of the General. In England the Salvation Army has the right to use any designation, uniform or badge that was in use when the Chartered Associations (Protection of Names and Uniforms) Act was passed in 1926. Elsewhere the uniform varies according to the circumstances. For example the sari, the dhoti and the turban have been adopted by Salvationists in India; in other tropical countries uniforms are made from materials light in colour and texture and sun-helmets replace the cap, and in arctic conditions furs are worn.[13]

Women's Dress

The mid-nineteenth century witnessed a revival in the part played in Church life by women. The Quakers and the Salvation Army had valued them as individuals within the movement with special dress required. The Anglican Church had introduced religious orders in which the nuns accepted traditional habits special to their order. In 1861 in north London, a deaconesses' institution consisting of Elizabeth Ferard, Ellen Meredith and Anna Wilcox was set up at 50 Burton Crescent, near Kings Cross. Elizabeth Ferard was the first episcopally ordained deaconess in the English Church since the Reformation, and by 1872 the order had been fully restored and was generally much approved of. In 1871 some general principles were set out and signed by the archbishops of Canterbury and York, and eighteen bishops. The only rule set down about their costume is the simple instruction 'No b. A Deaconess should wear a dress which is at once simple and distinctive' and this was repeated in 1891, in the same words, in the resolutions passed by the Upper House of the Convocation of Canterbury on Sisterhoods and Deaconesses.[14] The dress was probably similar to that of profes-

sed sisters, and was not in any way a uniform in the nineteenth century, as each institution designed its own distinctive costume. They seem to have favoured blue as it was adopted as the traditional colour when the Chapter and Council of the Order finally decided in 1944 that 'the normal choir dress should be a long cassock with veil or soft square cap (the Canterbury Cap), and that, at present a surplice should only be worn at the desire of the incumbent.'[15]

The cassock was generally of the Sarum style – double-breasted but with only the two buttons at the very top, on either side of the neck, visible. The collar band followed the style of men's clerical wear with a space at the centre front for a white band to be visible. At the waist a girdle of black or navy silk or cotton cord was worn, each end being finished off with a tassel. After the War deaconesses could wear the cassock short for convenience (they wore it about their daily routine, and not just for church), and the sleeves could be shortened to just below the elbow, but this was a matter of personal preference and no rules were set down.

In 1944 it was decided that deaconesses should adopt a common cross, and a silver cross incorporating the Chi-Rho as the central monogram between the Alpha and the Omega was selected. These early Church symbols were suitable as the order of deacons, including women, was one of the very earliest orders in the Church, and the cross corresponded to a design found on a gate used by deaconesses at St Sophia, Constantinople. The first person who had worn this cross was Dorothy Batho, a divinity specialist at Roedean, who was ordained in the diocese of Chichester and wore it in 1931.[16] The cross comes in the form of a badge which is pinned on the cassock or lapel; the deaconess also wears a pectoral cross which can be of this design or an individual choice.

Ecclesiastical Colours

The use of coloured cassocks for choirs had been introduced in the nineteenth century, and bishops had always had the right to wear purple cassocks even though they had not used this privilege for the full-length garment. At the beginning of the century the 'royal scarlet' was introduced as the colour reserved for cassocks worn by those in cathedrals, churches and chapels of royal foundations (known as 'Royal Peculiars') The royal livery was scarlet and traditionally red was reserved for Chaplains in Ordinary to the royal family. However, from the Reformation until 1903 black was preferred, and it was in the reign of Edward VII that scarlet was re-introduced. The King's Chaplains drew the Lord Chamberlain's attention to the fact that they wore red cassocks at the King's coronation in 1902, although the 1903 edition of *Dress at Court*[17] makes no reference to cassocks being any colour other than black. In 1908 Edward VII especially instructed the Bishop of London in a letter that scarlet was to be reserved for royal chaplains and the edition of *Dress at Court* for that year specifically states that they should wear red cassocks. The clergy at St George's, Windsor, wear 'Murray' and are thus slightly different from the other Royal Peculiars. With this cassock a scarlet 'Canterbury cap' and white gloves should be worn.

55 Morse. English, about 1905. This morse in a gold frame backed on silver and set with emeralds surrounding a translucent enamel of the Crucifixion with the four emblems of the gospel writers combines traditional themes with contemporary (art deco) design.

Gloves

Gloves had been part of the dress of clergy during the nineteenth century; not only senior ecclesiastics such as bishops, but the ordinary parish priest would wear kid gloves in church, especially when preaching. This habit, which was not governed by any regulation, had died out by the end of the century.[18] Black gloves were worn in winter by evangelicals, bishops and residentiary canons. White gloves were more common and were sometimes reserved for summer wear, but it must be emphasized that this was a personal choice of the clergyman and no hard and fast rules ever applied. As late as the coronation of George V in 1910, Dr Carr Glynn wore purple gloves, which were not the real episcopal gauntlets but an expression of his own taste.[19]

Regulations on Clerical Dress

From the 1860s there had been attempts to regulate the dress of the clergy in the Anglican Communion. A Royal Commission of Ritual was appointed on 3 June 1867 as a result of the confusion arising from the judgments in ritual cases. The Public Worship Regulation Act was passed in 1874, and with the subsequent imprisonment of five clergy between 1878 and 1887 (see

page 104) the Act became discredited and ritual prosecutions declined in number. The attitude of the bishops towards the law is put clearly in this quotation from a certain Bickersteth, in the matter of the parish of Tedburn St Mary:

With regard to wafer bread, lighted candles on the Holy Table in the daytime, and the vestments complained of, I have stated to Mr Tothill that they are, in my judgment, contrary to the laws and usages of the Church of England, and are therefore not only inexpedient but wrong. I earnestly hope that the rector will yet see it his duty to submit to my admonition as his Father in God. But in the present state of the law, I fear that prosecutions in the Courts on such matters of ritual only aggravate the evils they are intended to suppress.[20]

Things were so bad that in 1904 a further Royal Commission on Ritual Matters was appointed 'to enquire into the alleged prevalence of breaches or neglect of Law relating to the conduct of Divine Service in the Church of England and to the ornaments and fittings of churches; and to consider the existing powers and procedure applicable to such irregularities, and to make such recommendations as may be deemed requisite for dealing with the aforesaid matters.' The commission was composed mainly of laymen and held 118 meetings, interviewing 164 witnesses. The report which they issued declared that 'the law of public worship in the Church of England is too narrow for the religious life of the present generation. It needlessly condemns much which a great section of Church people, including many of her most devoted members, value.' In 1906 Edward VII gave to Randall Thomas Davidson, the Archbishop of Canterbury, and to the convocation, authorization to prepare a new rubric 'regulating the ornaments (that is to say the vesture).'[21]

The two world wars and internal disagreements delayed the settling of the ornaments rubric. World War I caused a major crisis for the clergymen, who had not fought a war for many centuries. Although some enlisted and served as combatants, many acted as chaplains. Randall Thomas, the Archbishop of Canterbury, wrote: 'By every line of thought which I have pursued I am led to the conclusion ... that the position of an actual combatant in our Army is incompatible with the position of one who has sought and received Holy Orders.'[22] Clergy who had worn civilian dress did not give a second thought to wearing military uniform suitable to their rank, with only the white clerical collar and black stock indicating their position. Wherever possible the formalities were observed, surplices and scarves were worn at services and the ritual was maintained, but obviously this was not always possible, and clergy did the best that they could under the different circumstances. Vestments were certainly no longer a priority in the minds of the churchmen. Siegfried Sassoon, in the final section of the memoirs entitled *Sherston's Progress* reports that back in France he attended a church parade addressed by a bishop in uniform '(a fact which speaks for itself ...)'.[23]

On 21 January 1937 convocation dress, that is formal dress for civil occasions especially convocation, was agreed on in York.

That the House adopts the regulations regarding Dress laid down in this Report.

1. That the dress to be worn during the sessions of

56 Rev. G. E. Mayo, R.A.F. When the clergy entered the armed forces during the two World Wars they adopted the uniform of their service and rank but retained the clerical collar and black stock as identifying emblems. Wherever possible they would wear cassock and surplice for services but when they had to dispense with these under duress, they did.

Convocation shall consist of Cassock with girdle or belt (in the case of bishops, deans and archdeacons the so-called short cassock or 'apron' shall suffice), gown of the academic degree of the wearer, or in the case of non-graduates the preacher's gown, hood corresponding to the academic degree, black scarf, bands and either a square 'college' cap or a Canterbury cap. It should be noted that the scarf according to Canon 74 should be of silk for a graduate and stuff for a non-graduate.

Doctors in Divinity or other faculty may wear either full dress or the habit of their degree.

The Doctors of the University of Oxford have three costumes:

1. Full dress, consisting of a scarlet gown with full sleeves. All doctors in whatever faculty if in Holy Orders should wear the scarf and tippet of Canon 74 and bands: Doctors in Divinity wear their cassocks also. Hoods are not worn with full dress.

2. The habit viz: cassock, bands, M.A. gown with

the sleeves poked through the arm holes of the habit or chimere, hood and scarf.

3. Undress viz: cassock, bands, M.A. Gown and scarf. (Doctors at Cambridge wear the hood over the scarlet gown in full dress.)

2. That the dress so prescribed be worn by those members who accompany the President and their Lordships of the Upper House and the Prolocutor on those occasions when an address should be presented to the Crown, unless other instructions be received from the Lord Chamberlain.

The Committee recommend that the Synodical Secretary, if not a member of the House should wear the dress prescribed in paragraph 1. above.[24]

Work on the ornaments rubric continued and in 1947 a report was prepared – 'The Canon Law of the Church of England Being the Report of the Archbishops' commission on Canon Law together with proposals for a Revised body of Canons.'

57 Archbishop Leonard Beecher and clergy at the consecration of St Walstan's, Rongai, Kenya. As this service is one of consecration the clergy wear choir dress, cassocks and surplices with the hoods of their degree. These hoods are academic and can be worn by laity as well as clergy; different colours and fabrics indicate the degree and university but have no ecclesiastical significance. The archbishop on the right is in rochet and chimere with his black tippet or scarf and hood (which is partly hidden).

1. Every Minister when saying or singing Morning and Evening Prayer (*in Church*) – [pencilled in] shall wear a cassock, and a surplice (to be provided and kept clean at the charge of the Parochial Church Council) together with a scarf and hood of his degree. (Lyndwood, p. 237: 1603. Canons 25, 58.)

2. At the Holy Communion, the celebrant, as also the gospeller and the epistoler, if any, shall wear with the cassock either a surplice with scarf or stole, or a surplice or alb with stole and cope, or an alb with the customary vestments. (Advertisements (1566) 11.1603. Canons 24, 25.)

3. For the occasional offices the Minister shall wear a cassock and a surplice with a scarf or a stole. (Lyndwood, p. 249, 1603. Canons 25, 58.)

4. At Baptisms, Marriages and other appropriate times a cope may be worn at the discretion of the Minister.

In 1969 the whole exercise was completed and the final form of the ecclesiastical dress worn at Divine Service in the Church of England is as follows:

B8 Of the vesture of ministers during the time of divine service.

1. At Morning and Evening Prayer the minister shall wear a cassock, a surplice, and a scarf; and for the occasional offices a cassock and a surplice with scarf or stole.

2. At the Holy Communion the celebrant, as also the gospeller and the epistoler, if any, shall wear with the cassock either a surplice with scarf or stole, or a surplice or alb with stole and cope, or an alb with the customary vestments.

3. On any appropriate occasion a cope may be worn at the discretion of the minister.

4. When a scarf is worn, the minister may also wear the hood of his degree.

5. The Church of England does not attach any particular doctrinal significance to the diversities of vesture permitted by this Canon, and the vesture worn by the minister in accordance with the provisions of this Canon is not to be understood as implying any doctrines other than those now contained in the formularies of the Church of England.

6. Notwithstanding the foregoing provisions of this Canon no minister shall change the form of vesture in use in the church or chapel in which he officiates unless he has ascertained by consultation with the parochial church council that such changes will be acceptable: provided always that in the case of disagreement the minister shall refer the matter to the bishop of the diocese, whose direction shall be obeyed.

Outdoor Dress

The outdoor dress of the clergyman continued in the nineteenth-century fashion of sober and conservative contemporary dress. The soft white tie of the lower churchman, the Evangelical, disappeared almost completely during World War 1 when all clergy adopted the stiff clerical collar set into a black front or bib, a square of silk or cotton which tucked under the waistcoat, or a specially made shirt which was plain in front and buttoned up the back. This clerical collar, dubbed the 'dog-collar', proclaimed the ordained minister and as a general rule the higher (or deeper) the collar the lower the churchmanship of the wearer and the lower (or narrower) collar proclaimed the high churchman or the Roman Catholic priest. This white band probably became stiff-starched at the same time as the fashionable collar was stiffened and worn as a separate item, attached to the shirt with collar studs. When the collar in ordinary dress became soft and attached to the shirt, the clerical collar remained as part of the clergy 'uniform'. Collars did not, however, continue to be made only of fine linen and boil-starched; paper disposable collars were made and nylon and polythene were readily accepted as alternatives as

soon as they were available. Collars could come in any size but normally the suppliers offered them in 1 inch, $1\frac{1}{4}$ inch, $1\frac{1}{2}$ inch, $1\frac{3}{4}$ inch and 2 inch depths and provided stocks or shirts that could accommodate these collars.

After World War 2, certainly from the 1950s, some clergy left off wearing the collar, except for specific Church occasions, as they felt that it created a barrier between them and the laity. When they adopted the collar and tie it was completely indistinguishable from ordinary lay dress; there was not a revival of the white tie of the nineteenth-century Evangelical. The stocks were squares or shield shaped and lay flat on the chest, held in place by the waistcoat or cassock worn over the top. There was never any front fastening and as a rule they were completely plain, although occasionally they could be pleated.

The vest-stock was an efficient way of combining two garments and ensuring a neat, clean look when worn with a suit. Made on the same principle as a waistcoat but without the centre fastenings, it had two small pockets just above the hem on either side and was cut straight across at the bottom with an adjustable strap at the back. Vest-stocks were generally made of black and could be of wool, cashmere, alpaca, poplin or corded silk. Anglican clergy generally wore the collar so that it was visible all the way round but the 'Roman' style of a black band of the cloth revealing the white collar centre front was also offered as an alternative.

Shirts made to go with the collar were a later introduction but were very useful and popular. They had to open in the front, but this was usually hidden by a fly-opening. From the 1960s these shirts were made in blue or grey as well as black, and grey became a popular colour with some clergy for stocks and occasionally cassocks as well.

The frock-coat was still being made for the clergy well into the 1940s but it was never as popular in the twentieth century as the lounge suit, which was generally black or grey but could be of any colour or fabric – there were no regulations governing this. The reputable church furnishing suppliers produced catalogues illustrating clerical frock-suit, dress wear, lounge suits, tropical dress and overcoats and raincoats and could supply everything from hand-embroidered vestments to black socks and braces.[27] These catalogues have proved to be, to a certain extent, the arbiters of taste and fashion for clergy at least in the first half of the twentieth century, supplying as they did Roman Catholics, Anglicans, Methodists and laity with cassocks and surplices to order. Some styles invariably became adopted by different sects and to an extent, although traditions were always maintained, there was some flexibility in choice. The 'Roman' or 'Latin' cassock, for example, was single-breasted with buttons down the front and usually made with a short cape; the 'Sarum' or 'Anglican' cassock was the double-breasted version held at the waist by a narrow belt. Both of these styles have existed, and still do, side by side in the Church of England.

In the Anglican tradition white cassocks were allowed for clergy in the tropics, and in the 1970s the white or off-white cassock-alb replaced the traditional black cassock and surplice in some churches. The alb, the surplice and the cotta continue in use, made in fine linen, or lawn, but also in polyester/cotton mixtures for easy care. The busy clergyman (or perhaps his wife) has welcomed man-made fibres for their crease-resistant nature and also because they are so much cheaper than the traditional fabrics. In the first half of the twentieth century the evangelical (who so despised the surplice a hundred years before) tended to favour the long surplice with the big full sleeves and the high Anglican preferred a short surplice or a cotta. (This, as with almost any generalization about clothes, can be furnished with exceptions that prove the rule.)

Episcopal Dress in the Twentieth Century

Bishops, deans, archdeacons and provosts continued to wear the 'apron' and gaiters throughout the first half of the twentieth century, even introducing this strange garb into the colonies. The evening dress suit for the provost of the Episcopalian cathedral in Edinburgh, now at the Strangers Hall Museum, Norwich, consists of a black wool frock-coat lined in black silk and with the label in it of 'Adeney & Son of 16 Sackville Street, Piccadilly, London, W.' The apron, breeches, cummerbund and stockings are all black, and so are the buckled shoes which have the date 1908 written in ink on the tan lining. The buckles on the breeches and the shoes had once belonged to Dr Swayne, formerly Bishop of Lincoln. The outfits which had belonged to Lord Fisher of Lambeth (Geoffrey Fisher, who became Archbishop of Canterbury in 1945) are similar in style and manufacture. All these clothes were tailor-made; the breeches and gaiters have the Wippells label and it is written in ink that they were made especially for Fisher as archbishop. With this collection is a stringed top hat in a leather box marked 'Bishop of Chester' (where he had been previously).

Dr Fisher, as Bishop of Chester, was wearing his apron and gaiters at home in his study when the author's father (the Rev. Gordon Mayo) went to see him before being accepted for ordination in 1938. Dr Crick, who succeeded him as Bishop of Chester, caused quite a stir by being the 'first bishop to be seen in trousers'! (*c.* 1942). Leonard Beecher, the first Archbishop of East Africa, wore the apron and gaiters and so did his archdeacons, and they did not pass out of general use either in Britain or abroad until the late 1950s and 1960s.

The dress of the Anglican bishop in the twentieth century basically follows the traditional form. The apron and gaiters gave way to a lounge suit worn with the clerical collar and purple stock and the pectoral cross – which is commonly worn with everyday dress, as well as with both choir habit and vestments. It is not a symbol of jurisdiction and so can be worn even when visiting another see: 'Professor Norman Sykes tells me that when the Archbishop of York arrived in New York last year the press photographers gave him a great welcome. When Dr Temple posed for his picture one of the photographers, noticing his pectoral cross, said, "lean forward please, all the ladies will want to see the charm on your chest."'[26]

In addition to the purple cassock for general use, a bishop should have a black one to wear in Advent, from Septuagesima to the end of Lent, and also at services for the dead and on non-liturgical occasions. The choir habit consists of the rochet, black chimere and black silk scarf. If the bishop wears the red chimere it is proper to wear it with the purple cassock, although the cassock is mainly hidden by the rochet (whose wristbands take the colour of the chimere). The bishop should never wear an academic hood with either the red or the black chimere. An alternative style of choir dress is a short rochet and a shoulder cape, apparently following an American fashion[27], which is useful when the bishop is going to put on a stole to preach, to assist in the administration of Holy Communion, or to perform a simple act of dedication.

When the bishop is celebrating Holy Communion solemnly and at ordinations he wears full pontificals, but if he celebrates the Holy Communion simply he can just wear the chasuble, stole and maniple. When he is officiating at the Communion at a procession, at the occasional offices and at Matins and Evensong he wears the cope over his rochet (leaving off the chimere). With the cope the bishop usually wears the mitre. This should *not* be made to match the cope or set of vestments. A bishop should have two, preferably three, mitres (although this tradition is falling into disuse):

a. The Simple Mitre; made of white silk or linen, without embroidery or orphreys. This should be worn at services of the dead, on Good Friday and Easter Even. When a bishop, who is neither celebrating nor officiating, wears the mitre in the presence of the diocesan, he should use the simple mitre.

b. The Golden Mitre; made of white silk embroidered with gold, or more commonly of cloth of gold, without orphreys. This should be worn at most, if not all, other services. Because it is worn so often, the bishop would do well to have a second of these for special occasions.

c. The Precious Mitre; also made of white silk, embroidered with gold or cloth of gold, but adorned with orphreys and with precious stones. This is worn *only* when the bishop officiates solemnly at Matins or Evensong, or when he celebrates or presides solemnly at the communion; and is never used in penitential seasons, when the vestments are purple. Its use might well be restricted to Christmas, Easter, Whitsun, Ascension Day and occasions of major importance, such as an ordination.

Because of its weight, it may be found convenient to wear the precious mitre only in procession to and from the chancel, and at certain points in the service noted in the text. The golden mitre will then be worn during the rest of the service. The fact that the precious mitre is often too heavy for the bishop to wear it throughout the service is the sole reason why it is exchanged for the golden mitre on these occasions. If the bishop does not possess a precious mitre it is pointless to pretend that some other mitre is 'precious' simply in order to use two mitres during a ceremony.[28]

The bishop also has a ring which can be on either the first or third finger of the right hand and is put on over the glove, when one is worn. The bishop may have two pectoral crosses, one for everyday use and the other reserved to wear with his vestments, which can be laid out with them before the service. Gloves are also part of the pontificalia generally worn in conjunction with the mitre. When the bishop celebrates the gloves are removed at the offertory. The bishop carries the crozier or pastoral staff which is not only a distinguishing mark of the episcopate but also a sign of jurisdiction.

Liturgical vestments, once adopted in the Anglican Church, underwent no major change of function or in the manner of wearing, and such changes of decoration were due entirely to fashion. The maniple was often discarded, but the stole, chasuble and dalmatic could be decorated by embroidery, appliqué or enriched by the textile used, and both amateur and professional embroiderers made vestments. Liturgical colours were adhered to with more universal thoroughness than ever before in their history, with the stole often matching the chasuble and dalmatic, and sometimes the mitre matching the cope; this had no precedence in early Church vestments but sprang from the nineteenth-century desire to formalize the sets of vestments.

CHAPTER TEN

Roman Catholic Vestments in the Twentieth Century 1900–1980s

THE ROMAN CATHOLIC CHURCH had developed much stricter rules on dress and materials even though these were not always adhered to. *Ecclesiastical Dress* by de Montault, translated by Walter Conan[40], shows how complicated and detailed the regulations were and has footnotes which indicate on how many occasions they are either unknown or ignored; for example, in Chapter One, General Principles – Materials, 'Velvet is reserved as the prerogative of the Pope. Its use, even in accessories, is a flagrant usurpation.' The footnote says 'What would de M. [de Montault] say to the very common use in Ireland of the velvet birretta and stock by parish priests and others? (Ed.)'.

Moire (watered silk) belongs only to Cardinals. *No one* else is entitled to its use (in Ireland it had also been used in purple for bishops); Silk is the symbol of the Pontifical Court, and no one has any right to its use but those who form part of it, such as Bishops and Prelates assisting at the throne. Otherwise it is only used in accessories; Wool – the rule is strict on this point. The garments of a bishop can only be in wool (cloth or merino). Silk is the exception in certain cases, and even then does not extend to the Cappa (this rule is, as regards Ireland at least, not observed at all).[41]

Cardinals wear red, a scarlet colour, which is different from the cerise, crimson or aramanth colour of the bishops. Purple is also worn by bishops and by the Pope. The items of costume should be similar in texture and colour – a purple mozetta should not be worn over a black cassock, and the one should not be of silk if the other is of wool. The cassock, or soutane, is made in black for priests and lower clerics; white for the Pope (and Cistercians, Dominicans and Praemonstrat-ensians, etc.); brown for Carmelites, Franciscans, Capuchins, etc.; violet for bishops and red for cardinals. In countries with Protestant majorities the cassock is reserved for inside the church, and the ordinary suit with the collar and black stock is outdoor dress; in predominantly Catholic countries the priest will wear his black cassock in the streets and about his daily business. (In wartime, officer and soldier priests and military chaplains were obliged to celebrate Mass without putting on a cassock when circumstances were difficult.) Laymen who are employed in churches – sacristans, cantors, servers, organist or choir-master – are obliged to wear the cassock during the performance of their duties. The cassock is not specific to any religious order and as such is not blessed at ordination, but a formula for blessing this clerical dress, if it is wished, has been introduced in the New Roman Rite.[42]

The Soutane

At the beginning of the twentieth century the Roman soutane was cut full and was not tight fitting but it has gradually become a more tailored garment with no train. The front is cut in one piece, without a waist seam. The buttons are of silk, and convex in shape. The sleeves are straight with a turned-back cuff. The collar is cut away in front to allow the clerical collar and stock to be seen. The buttons are very small and as a result they are set quite close together, leading to a potentially time-consuming ordeal for the priest in a hurry to get dressed. As a result the buttons are not always functional but can be sewn on to the outer side of the front opening which conceals a zip fastener,[43] or large more infrequent buttons, or hooks and eyes. The soutane with a small cape and oversleeves was called the zimara, but is now more commonly called the soutane or Roman cassock.

There were five kinds of soutanes worn by bishops and prelates at the turn of the century:

1 The episcopal soutane, which was of purple silk, with a train and trimmed with cerise silk. The trimming consisted of buttons, buttonholes, bindings for the edges, top stitching on hems; the linings and facings and cuffs were all of cerise silk, which was also used to line the train.

2 The soutane of the mantellone prelates, – of purple, the same as **1** but with no train, and the trimmings were all of purple.

3 The mourning soutane was black, with a train, and trimmed with purple, the cuffs being of purple silk. It was used by bishops except at Rome, where a violet costume is worn on all occasions because of the Pope's presence which calls for a special etiquette and solemnity. By 1960 mourning was no longer observed (in clerical dress) and bishops only wear black for Good Friday and when the Holy See is vacant.

4 The house soutane was black without a train, trimmed with cerise, and this style became outdoor dress for the bishop by the 1960s, worn with a violet sash and violet fringes.

5 The house soutane for mourning was black, without a train, trimmed with purple, but with black facings. It was used by bishops and mantelletta prelates.

The zimara comes in two types corresponding to **4** and **5**, trimmed accordingly in cerise or purple. By 1960 the bishops used only two cassocks: **4** the house soutane and **1**, a purple or violet cassock trimmed with cerise silk which is worn when a bishop is officiating or present at a liturgical ceremony. In 1952 the train of the cassock was abolished for all ecclesiastics, even for cardinals, by decree of the Sacred Congregation of Rites.

In the early part of the century three cinctures were worn for different occasions. Cinctures are broad bands of fabric made double and fastened by strings. The two ends hang down to about the knee on the left side. The first type is of violet silk ending in violet fringes, for house use; it is worn with the black cassock. The second is similar but the ends finish in violet tassels; this is choir dress

and worn with the violet cassock. These two violet cinctures survive but the third, of black silk with tassels, was for mourning and ceased to be worn when wearing mourning was abandoned. (The custom of going into mourning ceased in the twentieth century, mainly because of World War I.) The cincture came to be made to fasten with hooks and bars when the strings or ties were found to be inconvenient (in any case the fastenings are hidden).

Episcopal Dress

For outdoor dress the bishop wears a skull cap, biretta or hat. The biretta is the oldest type of headwear and was made of thin cardboard covered in silk or merino. The older usage was a black biretta lined in cerise or green for bishops and purple for mantellone prelates. It was made to fold in some countries (France and Ireland for example). Purple was introduced as the correct colour for the biretta and the skull cap in the twentieth century and the skull cap eventually replaced the older style by the 1960s. For ordinary dress the three-cornered hat was replaced by the pontifical hat which is round, with a small, low crown and a wide, flat brim. The outside is of black cloth and it is lined with silk varying in colour. It is edged with a wide ribbon, green or purple, and two silk cords hang underneath each side; they are held in the middle by a slide, which tightens under the chin, and is finished by a single tassel which falls on the breast. Green is the colour used by bishops and green with gold in the cord by patriarchs and nuncios; prelates who are not bishops use purple. This hat is worn by bishops in processions in Rome at the time of the Pope's installation, in their own diocese at the solemn entry into their episcopal town, and when going from the palace to the cathedral to officiate. Although it is not liturgical and is therefore dubbed 'ordinary' in terms of dress the hat was considered a very special item of dress, and like the cardinal's hat it was attached to the foot of the bishop's deathbed or catafalque, and finally hung above his tomb in the vault of the cathedral.

The plain white linen collar and purple stock are worn, and purple stockings with black shoes which may have gold or silver gilt buckles. For outdoor dress the pectoral cross is suspended on a chain and at celebrations a cord of green and gold, with a tassel of the same colour, is substituted for the chain, the tassel hanging at the back.

For choir dress the bishop wears a rochet, but of a very different sort from that of the Anglican. The Roman Catholic rochet is shorter (about knee-length) and the body of it is made of finely pleated lawn or cambric. At the hem there is a deep band of lace and there are deep cuffs of lace. There are also lace insertions at the neck and shoulders. The lace on the sleeves is lined with a

58 Archbishop Fisher and Cardinal Heenan, Lambeth Conference 1968. The Archbishop of Canterbury, Geoffrey Fisher, is in a type of black clerical hat with a broad brim that is held up to the crown by ties. He wears the stiff clerical collar known as the 'dog collar' and a black clerical coat with a band. Under this he is wearing the short cassock, or apron and gaiters, which are not visible in this photograph. His Roman Catholic counterpart, the Archbishop of Westminster, Cardinal Heenan, is in a red biretta and a soutane and sash. They are trimmed with red as he is a cardinal and the pectoral cross denotes that he is a bishop. They are both in the formal outdoor dress of their branch of the Church.

fine silk the colour of the soutane to which the wearer is entitled. In mourning or during a vacancy of the Holy See, the rochet is not pleated and has no lace. Over the rochet in choir, and also over the soutane alone, a short cape called the mozetta is worn. It is furnished at the back with a small hood and fastens down the front with a row of tiny buttons. It allows the rochet, especially its lace, to be seen. Made of violet to match the cassock, it is trimmed with cerise and has a cerise silk lining.

When a bishop is outside his diocese or is without jurisdiction, he wears the mantelletta, a cloak reaching to the knees, with a standing collar, hooked at the neck and open in front, without buttons; at the sides two vertical openings are provided for the arms. This covers the rochet and thus makes him significantly different from the resident bishop. Made of violet cloth and lined at the collar, shoulders and down the front in cerise silk, the mantelletta matches the cassock.

The cappa, the large formal mantle, was originally of violet wool lined in cerise silk, summer and

winter. However it was often made entirely of silk, despite the fact that silk was by right reserved for a bishop who was a member of the papal court. It has a large hood or 'chaperon' of ermine in the winter and cerise silk in the summer (in both cases lined in violet). It also had a long train which was either held up by a cleric called a train-bearer or was carried in a twist, 'tortillon', suspended by a ribbon from the left arm. The Sacred Congregation of Rites ordered the shortening of the train in 1952. The cappa is always violet-coloured even when the bishop wears a black cassock; the mantelletta and mozetta are black and trimmed with violet silk, during penitential seasons (Advent, Lent, Ember days) and at all funeral offices. The biretta and skull cap are violet for all seasons.

The dress of the regulars (those from religious orders) who have been promoted to the rank of bishop is much simpler. They wear the violet skull-cap or biretta but keep the colour of their religious habit for the choir and outdoor attire, without any violet ornaments. They do not wear the rochet although they may wear a surplice when the Pope is officiating. The colours worn by the various orders are:

Monks of Vallombrosa Augustinians Benedictines Basilians	Black
Camaldolese 'Mercedaires' Premonstratensians Trinitarians Monks of Mount Oliver	White
Trappists Cathusians Cistercians	White, but the mantelletta, mozetta and cappa are black (the cappa has a white hood)

Dominicans: as above but with white trimming of the mantelletta and mozetta. The cappa is all white (1960)

Sylvestians: blue

Franciscans: blue/grey (blue cendree) (1929); cinders (a type of ash-brown) (1960)[44]

Capuchins: brown

Carmelites: brown with white mantelletta and mozetta. The cappa is brown with ermine in winter and in summer white silk replaces the ermine.

The episcopal insignia are the throne, the ring, the cross, the pectoral cross, the ombrellino, the hat, and the coat of arms. The ring is made of gold (symbolizing charity) with a large jewel in the centre which may be of any colour, except sapphire which is reserved for cardinals. It is surrounded by diamonds unless the bishop is a regular. It is received during the bishop's consecration and is a sign of authority and power (this dates from when the ring was a seal). The pontifical ring worn when bishops officiate in a solemn manner should be slightly larger in diameter so that it may be worn over the glove.

The pectoral cross is not strictly insignia as at the time of their consecration bishops receive it from the hands of the master of ceremonies and not from the consecrating prelate. It is, rather, an emblem of traditional devotion and can be worn anywhere as it is not a token of jurisdiction.

When the bishop celebrates at High Mass (called Pontifical Mass) he wears sandals, stockings (buskins), rochet, amice, alb, girdle, pectoral cross, stole, tunicle, dalmatic, chasuble, gloves, mitre and ring (pontifical), the colour being prescribed by the Church for that particular feast. He carries the crozier and the maniple is put on his left arm after he has said the opening prayers at the foot of the altar. For Vespers or Benediction of the Holy Sacrament, the sandals, gloves and tunicle are not used. The mitre comes in the same three forms as described above in the section on the dress of the Anglican bishops (page 120), that is, simple, golden and precious.

The Archbishop

The archbishop (patriarch or primate) wears the same as the bishop in all respects but there are two honorary distinctions attached to the archiepiscopal rank: the use of the pallium and the privilege of having the cross borne in front.

The pallium has become much smaller and like an emblem, rather than a garment. It is a narrow band of woollen cloth worn on the shoulders with a pendant strip falling on the breast like a collar. It is still decorated with black crosses and is treated with more reverence than any other item of dress.

Two white lambs are blessed by the abbot of the canons regular of the Lateran in the basilica of St Agnes without the Walls, on the feast of the saint, 21 January, after he has sung Pontifical Mass. The lambs are then presented to the Pope who blesses them again from the palace window. They are then given into the care of the Benedictines of Saint Cecilia in the Trastevere who must feed and shear them. Their fleece is used to make the palliums which are blessed by the Pope or a bishop on 28 June in the Vatican basilica on the vigil of the feast of SS Peter and Paul and are laid on their tombs for a night. They are then given to a prelate appointed to keep them until such time as they are given to the next new metropolitan archbishop.

Cardinals

The dress of cardinals is distinctive as scarlet is reserved for them, and over the centuries a complicated formal etiquette was created. At the beginning of the century they had nine separate outfits:

1 Ordinary costume
2 Street costume
3 Travelling costume
4 Visiting costume (*costume d'etiquette*)
5 Ceremonial costume
6 Choir costume
7 Pontifical costume
8 Special costume
9 Costume of regulars

The red cassock had been conferred by Pope Boniface VIII in 1294 and subsequently scarlet became the cardinals' special colour, not to be confused with the cerise of bishops. They were entitled to wear purple on occasions but had virtually ceased to do so by the twentieth century. (Etiquette was so strict that it was necessary to issue a pamphlet every year to show day by day whether they should wear red or purple.) If the cardinal is a bishop he can wear the pectoral cross suspended by a gold chain or a red and gold cord with pontificals. He wears vestments proper to his position as bishop, priest or deacon, and his mitre is, properly, white damask with red trim. Most of the rules which apply to bishop's costume are the same for the cardinal; the biretta and skull cap are scarlet even for regulars; the scarlet trimming is

the same as the cerise trim for bishops; the soutane is the same cut, as are the mantelletta and mozetta (although cardinals wear the mantelletta and the mozetta together in the presence of the Pope). The use of watered silk is special to the College of Cardinals and no cardinal carries a crozier (as he does not have jurisdiction over a diocese). Cardinals have a red hat edged with gold braids for officiating at very solemn ceremonies but the 'cardinal's hat' received from the hands of the Pope at the Consistory has become a mere emblem or ornament to the position and is never worn. The hat is made of red cloth with a very wide brim and ornamented with thirty red tufts, fifteen on each side. The crown is extremely shallow and the heavy cords ending in tassels were formerly used to tie this headgear under the chin. It is exhibited at the cardinal's home when he is alive and at his death it is placed at the lying-in-state. Finally it is hung on the vault of the cathedral, if the deceased is a resident bishop or archbishop.

The Pope

In the first half of the twentieth century the Pope's soutaine or cassock was made of white wool or white silk with a watered silk cincture provided with a fringe of gold. A plain white skull cap completed the simple outfit of the Supreme Pontiff. For more solemn audiences he wore a rochet (of fine pleated linen and lace) and a short red velvet cape fringed with ermine in winter and scarlet satin in summer. A soft red velvet cap with the same trimming could be worn at this time. The Pope wears red shoes of velvet or leather embroidered with a cross in gold. The hat of the Pope was of red felt, covered in red silk, with the brim turned up at the sides, edged with gold braid and encircled with a cord hung with golden tassels. When the Pope left his apartments he wore a red stole.

The pontifical ring is of gold set with a precious stone that was often engraved. A ring special to the Pope is the 'fisherman's ring' so called because it is engraved with the picture of the apostle St Peter in a boat casting his nets. This ring is personal to the Pope, and has his name on it; since the time of Leo X, 1521, it has been broken at his death.

The Pope's pallium was the same as that of the archbishops and he used the three mitres. At one time he also had the tiara, the three crowns symbolizing imperial, royal and sacerdotal power, but the wearing of the tiara fell into disuse as the role of the Pope as temporal prince became less significant. The vestments of the Pope were not essentially different from those of a bishop, with some notable exceptions.

The *falda* was a long white skirt of silk with an extremely ample train which fell around the feet at all sides and had to be held up at the front and back by ecclesiastical dignitaries when the Pope was walking. The first mention of this garment is made in relation to St Pius V's accession in 1566, but it is difficult to date precisely when and how it originated.[45] Its origins were probably purely practical, this simple vestment being easy to wash and keep clean, and the extra length being a sign of dignity.

Another garment peculiar to the Pope which dates back to the twelfth century was the *fanon*. This word can also be used for the maniple, the corporal and a piece of silk held by the bishop. The links between these are very tenuous but *may* have their origins in the handkerchief or napkin, a cloth used for keeping things clean, giving protection from dirt. The fanon of the Pope was a cape tied round the neck which was like two superimposed mozettas, ornamented with white and gold stripes, joined together by a purple cord. A shining cross was embroidered on the breast which the cardinal deacon kissed when placing this vestment on the Pope. The fanon was put on after the pectoral cross over the alb; the upper cape was lifted up and covered the Pope's head until he was fully vested. The fanon finally came down over the chasuble like a cape.[45]

Vestments of the Mass

The vestments of the Mass in the first half of the twentieth century were unaltered except in details of cut and decoration and need only a brief outline here. With these vestments the priest, deacon and sub-deacon wore the alb with its amice and girdle. The Latin Church had had a highly decorated belt embellished with embroidery and sometimes pearls and precious stones, but this gave way to the simple cord. The tunicle was worn by the sub-deacon, or an ordained cleric taking over his functions (except on the Sundays of Advent and Lent and other penitential days). There was still a tendency to make this vestment identical with the dalmatic despite the attempts of liturgiologists to make it closer to its original form which was shorter and with longer, narrower sleeves. The decoration should be of the simplest. The tunicle was also still worn by those of episcopal rank under the dalmatic and chasuble.

In the seventeenth and eighteenth centuries the dalmatic had undergone dramatic changes except in Italy. The garment had been split completely up both sides and in some cases the sleeves only remained in vestigial form, fastened with ribbons. (The tunicle did not completely follow the dalmatic in this extreme form.) In the nineteenth and twentieth centuries the original style was restored in many places, after a certain amount of pressure from eminent ritualists. Clavi reaching from each shoulder to the hem front and back were the only decoration proper to the dalmatic, and the traditional trim of fringe has disappeared completely in some cases. The deacon wore the dalmatic on feast days and on other occasions he wore the stole in the manner special to his rank. The dalmatic was the second vestment of the episcopate.

The use of the chasuble for celebrating Mass is obligatory. In the eighteenth century it had reached its most curtailed shape, being reduced to a mere tabard in some cases. In the mid-nineteenth century Dom Gueranger, the restorer of the liturgy in France, revived the use of large chasubles in his abbey at Solesmes. Regular and secular clergy and bishops followed his example, and gradually the softer, larger chasuble returned into general use. It is interesting to see how the term describing this style changed as the history of vestments became better understood. In 1863 the Congregation of Rites was consulted about chasubles and the expression 'Gothic' chasuble was used, a badly chosen term, as there was no special type produced in the thirteenth, fourteenth and fifteenth centuries – only new styles of decoration. In 1925 a decree mentions the 'ancient' shape and in 1957 'vestments of the primitive shape' is the description used. The new chasubles, large, supple and light, are probably closer to the *casula* of the early Church, although heavier fabrics, brocades and damasks, were still popular.

The stole and maniple, the insignia of office, remained essentially the same as before. The subdeacon at his ordination received the maniple and retained it on proceeding to other major orders. In the same way, when he became a deacon the bishop invested him with a stole which was retained until episcopacy, even though it was worn in a different manner in each rank. The maniple still retained the memory of its original function, that of the napkin carried by those who serve at table; the bishop received his maniple at the moment when he went up to the altar (except at Masses of the dead); the priest did not wear a maniple at the marriage ceremony until he went to celebrate Mass; the deacons at the throne of a solemn ponitifical Mass wore no maniple, because they had no function to perform at the altar during the holy sacrifice, their duties being done by more senior ecclesiastics.[47]

In 1959 Pope John XXIII announced the plan to reform the Code of Canon Law and on 3 February 1983 Pope John Paul II received the solemn presentation of the New Code and for the first time permission was granted to translate it into the vernacular. Canon 929 states that 'In celebrating and administering the Eucharist, priests and deacons are to wear the sacred vestments prescribed by the rubrics.'

The Roman Catholic Church has returned to the basic principles concerning dress that were practised in the early Church. The rules are kept simple and to an extent flexible, with guidelines set down for instruction. 'In the body of Christ not all members have the same function, and this diversity of ministries is shown externally in worship by the diversity of vestments. At the same time, the vestments should contribute to the appearance of the rite itself.' The conference of bishops may determine details, such as adaptations for special occasions or regional usages and propose these to the Apostolic See. The nature of the fabrics used, whether natural or man-made, is left to the discretion of the conference of bishops but there is guidance in the simple instruction: 'The beauty of the vestment should derive from its material and form rather than from its ornamentation. Ornamentation should include only symbols, images or pictures suitable for liturgical use, and anything unbecoming should be avoided.' Traditional colours are to be maintained and they are listed as white, red, green, violet, black and rose, while vestments for special occasions have no special colour ordained, merely that they should be the most noble.

The Alb

The instructions are consistently simple and in all ways follow the instructions of the early Church, maintaining tradition but allowing flexibility at the same time. The alb is common to all ministers and the cincture or girdle is always worn with it although the amice (which no longer always serves a practical purpose) is often left off. The alb is always worn under the chasuble or dalmatic, or when the stole is worn instead of either of these two vestments. The surplice, worn over the cassock, can be worn by lesser ministers at the Mass or at less important services.

The Chasuble and Dalmatic

The chasuble is proper to the priest who celebrates Mass and is worn over the alb and the stole. At major services when there are more clergy celebrating the Eucharist than vestments the concelebrants may omit the chasuble and wear the stole over the alb, but the celebrant must always wear a chasuble. The deacon wears the dalmatic over the alb and stole.

The Stole

The stoles continue to be worn by different ranks of minister in the different ways. The priest wears his around his neck and hanging down the front, pendant if worn over a surplice, crossed on the breast and tucked into the cincture when worn with the alb. The deacon wears it over his left shoulder, fastened at the right side. The two stoles are different garments and given at ordination: the deacon, dressed in an alb, is given the dalmatic and stole as a sign of office; the priest is dressed in an alb and deacon's stole and receives the chasuble, a new stole (sacerdotal) and a linen gremiale; he then discards the deacon's stole.

The Cope

The cope is worn by all ministers in processions

and other services where prescribed, and during the many international visits of Pope John Paul II it has become the custom for all bishops within a see to have identical copes for the large processions which are televised and broadcast worldwide.

★   ★   ★

The dress of ecclesiastics of all denominations has lost none of its importance in the passage of time, although the emphasis has changed. The Church in the second half of the twentieth century, of whichever denomination, has retained the tra-ditions while adapting the fabrics and fashions to contemporary taste. The cassock–alb of the Anglican man or woman is perhaps the most dramatic innovation, but even this is a natural development of a garment. The Church no longer puts such a large part of its wealth into its buildings, ornaments and vestments as it did in Britain in the twelfth, thirteenth and fourteenth centuries (and in Roman Catholic Europe until the nineteenth century); but the dress of the ministers of whatever denomination is as important as it has ever been in the Church's complex history.

Glossary

Accaby (also Acca)   A rich figured silk stuff, decorated with gold, used in the fourteenth century.

Acolyte   An inferior officer in the Church who attends the priests and deacons, and performs subordinate duties such as lighting and bearing candles etc. He would now be known as a 'server'. The name is derived from the Greek 'ακολουθος and Old English *colet*.

Aire (also Air; Eastern Orthodox: Aer)   A cloth to cover the paten and chalice. It was usually of silk but could be a linen napkin embroidered with coloured silks. It was used in Bishop Andrew's chapel and in Canterbury Cathedral before the Rebellion (1647).

Alb (also Alba, Albe, Album, Tunica Alba, Chiton Poderes, Camisa, Alba Dalmatica; Eastern Orthodox: Sticharion)   The alb started off as everyday wear and as the *Alba dalmatica* – a white linen tunic with sleeves – was a popular garment in Rome *c.* AD 100. The Green name *chiton poderes* indicates that it was ankle-length, and it was held in place at the waist by a girdle, in which form it has survived to the present day. In the fourth century we see it worn as an undergarment by the bishop and deacons in the St Vitale mosaics, and by the fifth century it has become a specifically Christian garment. In 824 Amalarius of Metz speaks of the alb as a 'camisa'. All ranks of clergy wore the plain alb until the eleventh century when changes occurred in the West. The cassock (adopted from Barbarian dress in the sixth century) had been lined in fur to suit the colder climates of the countries of Northern Europe and

the surplice developed – a shorter overtunic with wider sleeves to accommodate the bulky cassock. When the alb was worn it became decorated with embroidered panels – apparels (*paramenta*) (q.v.) on the cuffs and at the hem. The alb was always worn under the tunicle, dalmatic, chasuble or cope and always with the amice and the girdle. The alb with the amice, apparels and girdle, was also the regular dress of the acolytes at Mass, Lauds and Evensong. By the time of the establishment of the Church of England the alb was called a 'vestment' and included the amice and girdle as part of the suit. In 1549 the Book of Common Prayer required a 'white albe plain' (that is, without apparels) with a vestment or a cope. However, the alb was abolished in the ornaments rubric of the Book of Common Prayer of 1552, leaving the cassock and rochet for the bishop and cassock and surplice for the other clergy as the required wear in church. By 1559 the Prayer Book allowed for the wearing of an alb and a chasuble or cope at the Eucharist and this was confirmed in 1604 when canon XXIV ruled that the principal minister at the Communion in cathedrals and collegiate churches should wear a coloured cope over a plain alb. However the new Protestantism in England neglected the alb, with Non-conformists losing it altogether and the Anglicans generally preferring to wear the cassock and surplice; the alb was retained by the Roman Catholics and the 'high church' Anglicans. The alb has survived in England, both as the long white loose tunic worn over the cassock and in a more tailored form known as the 'cassock-alb' which is, as the name indicates, a compromise between the two garments, generally in white or natural cloth.

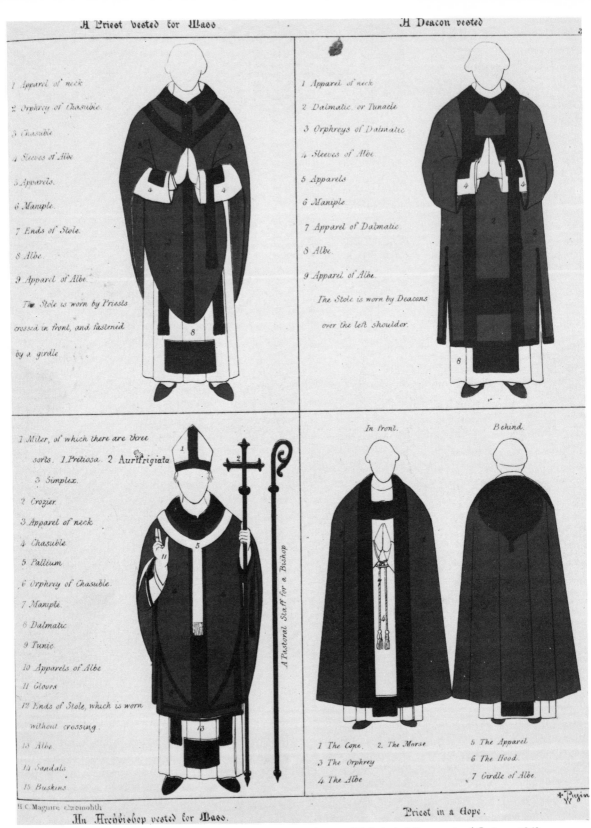

A Priest vested for Mass

1 Apparel of neck
2 Orphrey of Chasuble
3 Chasuble
4 Sleeves of Albe
5 Apparels
6 Maniple
7 Ends of Stole
8 Albe
9 Apparel of Albe

The Stole is worn by Priests crossed in front, and fastened by a girdle

A Deacon vested

1 Apparel of neck
2 Dalmatic, or Tunacle
3 Orphreys of Dalmatic
4 Sleeves of Albe
5 Apparels
6 Maniple
7 Apparel of Dalmatic
8 Albe
9 Apparel of Albe

The Stole is worn by Deacons over the left shoulder

1 Miter, of which there are three sorts. 1 Pretiosa 2 Aurifrigiata 3 Simplex.
2 Crozier
3 Apparel of neck
4 Chasuble
5 Pallium
6 Orphrey of Chasuble
7 Maniple
8 Dalmatic
9 Tunic
10 Apparels of Albe
11 Gloves
12 Ends of Stole, which is worn without crossing
13 Albe
14 Sandals
15 Buskins

A Pastoral Staff for a Bishop

H C Maguire Chromolith

An Archbishop vested for Mass.

In front.   Behind.

1 The Cope.   2. The Morse   5 The Apparel
3 The Orphrey   6 The Hood
4 The Albe   7 Girdle of Albe

+Pugin

Priest in a Cope.

59 Ecclesiastical vestments as illustrated in A. W. N. Pugin, *A Glossary of Ecclesiastical Ornament and Costume*, 1868.

60 The alb: the exhumation of St Hubert, by a follower of Van Der Weyden, after 1437. The two tonsured priests lifting St Hubert from his tomb are wearing the alb with the amice at the neck and the girdle at the waist. Apparels can be presumed to be on the hem as they can be seen on the wrist of the younger priest. The two priests wear their stole correctly crossed at the breast, and the bishop in cope and mitre on the left has his hanging pendant. The man holding the bishop's cope back from his arm is wearing a surplice, the development from the alb.

Almuce (also Amess, Almutium, Caputium)
This garment originated as a protection for the head and shoulders against the cold in the medieval church, and in the course of time became a mark of rank and distinction. Originally a lined hood or a fur scarf worn over the surplice, it emerged as a fur-lined hood with two ends hanging down in front and was regarded as part of

the choir habit. Hierarchical significance was established in the type and colour of the fur – grey squirrel being the highest rank and reserved for bishops and canons in the cathedral. The choir vestment of all dignitaries until the fourteenth century, it was superseded by the mozetta for the bishop, archbishop, cardinal and Pope but retained by canons. In the fifteenth century the almuce was hung over the left arm as a sign of office, and continues to be worn in this way in France and on the Continent by the canons. In 1549, in St Paul's Cathedral, it was recorded that minor canons were wearing tippets like other priests instead of their almuces, thus marking the transitional stage. The almuce was discontinued in the established Church under Elizabeth I and was replaced by tippet and hood.

Amice (also Amess, Amita, Amyss, Anabolagium, Humerale, Superhumeral) The amice is a rectangle of white linen worn as a neckcloth, probably originally for the protection of the more important vestments from the effects of perspiration. The name is derived from the Latin *amictus* (amicio = I wrap round). Originally the amice was put on after the alb but eventually it was the first vestment to be donned. Covering the head and shoulders, it was crossed over the breast and held in place by two long tapes around the body. It was then rolled back over the vestments and the

61 Almuce: Trinity altarpiece (wings closed). Sir Edward Bonkil – first provost of the Collegiate Church of The Holy Trinity, Edinburgh, by Hugo Van der Goes (active 1467, died 1482). Sir Edward wears a fine linen surplice over a fur-lined cassock, and carries on his left arm the fur almuce. In this form the original fur hood has changed into a mark of rank, an emblem of distinction rather than a practical garment, and is often part of the dress of canons. Sir Edward has a small tonsure, and the angel seated at the organ is wearing an alb, an amice and girdle.

62 Amice: the tomb of Bishop Thomas Bekyngton, Wells Cathedral. The square of white linen worn round the neck of the clergy is put on first but appears over the top of all the vestments covering the neckline of the alb and as in this case, the chasuble as well. The broad band of embroidery on the outside edge (known as the apparel) gives the stiff collar-like appearance and the soft folds of linen can be seen at the front and inside. Bishop Thomas Bekyngton is also wearing a mitre with lappets, or infulae.

head left uncovered for celebration (on the Percy Tomb at Beverley it covers the head). The amice develops slowly as a Mass vestment from the seventh century; mosaics at Ravenna and elsewhere show that it was not worn before the sixth century, and in the Eastern Church it has never been an official vestment. Ordo Romanus Primus (*c.* 800) refers to the amice as being part of the Pope's vesture and indicates that sub-deacons wore amices only when the pontiff was vested in a dalmatic (Ordo IV). The amice developed into a hood in the tenth century in order to protect vestments from the fashionable long hair and as all vestments became more elaborate, the amice was furnished with an apparel which formed a decorative panel when it was in place. In 1549 the Act of Uniformity refers to 'vesture appropriate'; the amice (with the girdle) is understood whenever the alb is mentioned and loses the apparel where the expression 'an albe plain' is used. Despite the fact that it is not mentioned specifically in the ornaments rubric we know that in Queen Mary Tudor's reign there are records of orders to purchase altar-cloths, albs and amices, so it was not lost at this period. Wherever the alb has been worn subsequently the amice is generally also

63 Alb, amice and girdle: detail of angel from the Gorges tomb, Wraxall, Somerset. Angels are frequently represented in the alb with its necessary adjuncts, the amice and the girdle. This set of garments is always worn under Mass vestments, by all ranks of clergy, and can also be worn by those who have not been ordained. They are specifically religious garments but not sacerdotal so were often used for the dress of angels in paintings, sculptures and needlework.

included although with the modern 'cassock-alb' it is not often worn and is no longer regarded as a necessary part of the suit.

Analabys (Eastern Orthodox) A kind of scapular worn by monks in the Greek Church.

Anchorite (also Ancret, Hermit, Recluse; f. Anchoress, Ancress) A person who has withdrawn or secluded himself from the world, usually for religious reasons.

Annulus An episcopal and pontifical ring generally worn on the third finger of the right hand, but also worn on the forefinger, especially in the fifteenth to seventeenth centuries.

Apparel (also Paramenta, Parure) A decorative embroidered panel applied to the alb and the amice.

Archbishop In dress the archbishop is only distinguished from the bishop by the pallium (in the Roman Church) and the cross-staff carried in the left hand instead of the pastoral staff or crozier.

Archdeacon As the *oculus episcopi* it was the task of the archdeacon to make a yearly visitation of the parishes within his jurisdiction during which, among other duties, he was to enquire whether the divine office was carried out in worthy fashion. The short 'apron' cassock and gaiters became the regular dress of the archdeacon from the eighteenth century until the 1950s; this type of dress had developed because it was convenient for travelling.

Armariorium A wardrobe in the treasury of cathedrals and monastic churches, for storing the Eucharistic and other vestments.

Armenian Church Tradition has it that four apostles brought the Christian faith to Britain – SS Bartholomew, Thaddeus, Simon and Jude, but St Gregory the Illuminator (third century), a prince of the Armenian royal house, is generally held to be the founder of the Church. He had been converted in Caesarea and until the middle of the fifth century the Armenian Exarch (the Kath-

64 Apparel: cushion embroidery, cut from an orphrey. This small embroidery of an archbishop, dating from the great period of Opus Anglicanum, shows the apparel of the amice standing out around the neck, and the apparel at the hem of the alb (the lowermost garment) and at the wrists. These panels of decorated needlework were applied onto the alb and were often of great value, incorporating pearls and jewels. With a fifth apparel at the chest, they were supposed to represent the five wounds of Christ.

olikos) was always ordained by the Exarch of Caeserea. Since 491 the Church of Armenia has been in schism with Caeserea and with the Church of the Empire (the Eastern Orthodox Church). The principal vestments are:

Saghavart: a cap or crown, elaborately designed and colourful.

Shapik: this corresponds to the alb, but is fuller and usually of silk.

Porurar: a type of stole. The head is put through a hole in the upper part of the vestment and the rest hangs down in front. It is usually made of expensive brocade and often bejewelled.

Goti: a richly embroidered girdle which secures the stole to the alb. A large white napkin is attached to the left side.

Bazpan: two slips of brocade on wrists which were once the towels that correspond to the forerunner of the maniple.

Varkas: a garment which resembles a small amice with a stiffened collar, from which a breastplate embossed with jewels may be suspended; it is said to derive from the Jewish ephod.

Mitre: the metropolitan wears a gold mitre and a triple pallium.

Crozier: the pastoral staff.

Schoorchar: a cope, but corresponds to the chasuble in liturgical use. Two strips of embroidered fabric, often showing pictures of saints, were attached to the shoulders of the schoorchar of the bishops.

Konker: Epigonation (q.v.); lozenge-shaped piece of stiffened material suspended from the left-hand side of the girdle.

Kogh: a veil decorated with a gold fringe that covers head and shoulders.

Deacons wear the shapik of linen or silk and the stole is worn over the left shoulder.

Armilla Part of the insignia given to the British Sovereign at coronation, shaped like a stole. In 1485 at the coronation of Henry VII 'the King ... shall take armyll of the Cardinall ... and it is to were that armyll is made in the manner of a stole wovyn with gold and set with stones (Rutland Papers 18)' (*O.E.D.*). It also means a bracelet: 'The armil or bracelet was looked upon by the Anglo-Saxons as one of the badges of Royalty (Rock, *Church of Our Fathers*)', 1849 (*O.E.D.*).

Aspinet (also appinet) A kind of silk cloth.

Austin Friars (also Eremites, Black Canons) An order founded *c.* 1250. They wore a black gown with broad sleeves, held with a leather belt and a black cloth hood; the under-dress was a white cassock.

Baculus Pastoralis *See Crozier.*

Bands Two strips of white material falling from the collar. They are a development from the falling collar, hanging in two strips down the

65 Bands: George Berkeley, Bishop of Cloyne (1685–1753), by J. Swibert, *c.* 1732. The Bishop of Cloyne is in informal clerical dress; he has removed his wig and has a soft black nightcap over his shaved head. He is wearing the double-breasted 'Sarum' cassock with the turn-back cuffs of the Anglican Church and at his neck the linen bands, the mark of the professional man, worn by clerics but also by lawyers and academics.

front, and were adopted as conventional dress by the clerical, legal and academic professions in the early eighteenth century. Parish clerks and dissenting ministers also appeared in gown and bands. (They are not a development from the amice as some writers have thought.) They were also known as Geneva bands.

Baptismal Garments (also white garments) After the immersion and the washing, the candidate was dressed in a white garment, as a sign of innocence and purity. It is known that by the fifth century the neophytes wore their baptismal robes for the whole of Easter week, changing back into their ordinary clothes on Low Sunday. (E.J. Yarnold S.J., *The Study of the Liturgy*).

Baptists Founded *c.* 1633. The most distinctive principle of the Baptists is that they only permit baptism for adults. An offshoot of the Brownists, they formed into a distinct community in the reign of Charles I and have since formed various groups: Anabaptists (from the Continent), General Baptists (also called Armenian Baptists) and Strict and Particular Baptists.

Baudekin (also Baudekyn) The name given to precious stuffs often used for vestments and altar hangings. It is extremely rich fabric composed of silk interwoven with threads of gold, resembling brocade. It is said to have derived its name from Baldeck or Babylon. Henry III (1207–72) appears to have been the first English monarch to wear cloth of baudekyn, but it was probably known for some time before on the Continent.

Beards There have been no official rulings on the wearing of beards and moustaches, clergy generally following the conservative fashions of the day. In the West it has usually been the fashion for the professional classes to be clean-shaven and in pictures we find beards only worn by the early Benedictines, the Hermits and the Capuchins. The clergy in Elizabethan England are often shown with trimmed beards and Victorian clerics often sported whiskers or side-burns.

Benedictines Most monastic orders were based on the rule of St Benedict, the code for the religious life which made him the patriarch of Western monasticism. Almost all that is known of his life is found in the dialogues of St Gregory the Great, Pope from 590 to 604. He was born *c.* 480 in Norcia, south-east of Perugia soon after the collapse of the Roman Empire, and decided to devote himself to the spiritual life. Although he founded many monasteries his name is always linked with Monte Cassino, in Campania. He died in 543 or 547, and his sister Scholastica, a well-known nun who died *c.* 543 was buried with him. The rule emphasized manual labour as well as prayer and contemplation, and set down special regulations for dress and how and when to wear the various garments. The keynote was simplicity and practicality rather than hardship or particular

austerity, and traditionally Benedictines wore black.

The *cowl* of which St Benedict speaks was a garment, possibly a casula or early undecorated chasuble, fitted with a hood (*vestis cucullata*). For monks it would probably be made of a rough fabric and possibly of skins of animals (cf. the melota – μηλωτή – sheepskin of Eastern monks). Between the ninth and twelfth centuries the casula was slit along the sides and the two parts fastened at intervals by bands or straps called 'St Benedict's stitches'. Cowls with sleeves, at first quite narrow, were in use as well from the tenth century.

The *scapular* replaced the cowl, originally for travelling or manual labour. It was a length of cloth with a hole for the head, worn as a protective garment. There does not appear to be any mention of a garment of this name before St Benedict.

The *tunic* was worn under the cowl or scapular by day and as sleepwear at night, still girt with belts and cords (*cincti cingulis aut funibus*). Some abbots were allowed by special privilege to use the mitre and crozier, and other parts of episcopal costume.

Most monks went barefoot or wore sandals of wood or leather. St Benedict mentions *pedules* and *caligas*; the former are probably stockings or light indoor footwear and the latter working boots.

The clothes were not the property of the individual monks but issued to them as and when they needed them for travelling abroad or for extra warmth in winter.

Berettino A red hat worn by cardinals, granted by Pope Paul II in the third quarter of the fifteenth century.

Bindae The cloth (or wimple) passing over a nun's head to cover the hair and then folded under the chin; it is made of white linen.

66, 67 A Benedictine monk and nun. The monk wears a full black habit of wool with wide sleeves and a cowl pulled over the back of his head, barely covering the tonsure. The nun wears a similar habit with a black veil over a white bindae and gorgette, the linen covering the head and throat. She carries a rosary, and they both hold a book, probably a missal.

68 Bindae: Mater Dolorosa, by Dietric Bouts (active 1457, died 1475). The bindae, or white veil, is made of linen and folded elaborately to cover the hair and the throat. It should cover the forehead and here is worn properly, not like that of the prioress in Chaucer's *Canterbury Tales* and others mentioned in the fourteenth and fifteenth centuries. The raw edge at the bottom edge has been blanket-stitched. The black veil is worn by the professed nun in many religious communities (the novice wearing white).

69 Biretta: Archbishop Fernando de Valdes, by Diego Velasquez, after 1639. This portrait shows the biretta as it stiffens and grows more formal on the Continent. The biretta of the Roman Catholic Church has three raised parts (four being reserved for the headwear of doctors) and in this respect, and in the fact that it became a solid shape, it is completely different from the square cap of the Anglican Church.

Biretta A stiff three-cornered hat or cap developed from lay-dress and adopted by clergy for general use; it has limited liturgical use. In the latter half of the fifteenth century the skullcap developed four corners and this 'square cap' was worn by many ecclesiastics by the middle of the sixteenth century. In 1604 bishops, dignitaries, graduates and all other clerics were required to wear the cap. By 1640 on the Continent the biretta had assumed the solid shape that we still recognize in the Roman Church, but in England it assumed a more flexible form. Both in England and elsewhere it was worn over the skullcap; and the mortar-board of the end of the seventeenth century apparently combined the square cap and the skullcap in one piece. The biretta is tradition-ally red for cardinals, green or purple for bishops and black for canons. The Rev. Percy Dearmer tried to re-introduce the square cap in the late nineteenth century, and where it was used it was called the 'Canterbury cap'.

Birrus (also Byrrus) A short cloak adopted in the Middle Ages as an ecclesiastical vestment, resembling the mozetta.

Black Canons See *Austin Friars*.

Black Friars See *Dominicans*.

Boy Bishop (also Episcopus Puerorum) A singular custom that possibly arose in the thirteenth century. On the feast of St Nicholas (6 December) the choristers chose one of their number to be bishop until the Night of Holy Innocents Day. He was properly vested together with some of the other boys who assumed the roles of canons. Archbishop Cranmer forbade this custom, Mary I restored it, and Elizabeth I abolished it. Boy bishops are mentioned in inventories, for example from the small parish of St Peter Cheap in 1431 'ij childes copes for S. Nicholas wᵗ j myter, j tonicle, l chesebie iij feeble aubes for childer and a crosse for the bysshopes'.

Bracile   A belt or girdle worn during the day by monks to hold the knife and the handkerchief, etc.

Broad Stole   Worn like a stole but in fact a chasuble rolled up by the deacon in penitential season. Amalarius of Metz reports that at the Mass in Rome the deacon removed his paenula before the gospel and thenceforth rolled it in such a way that he could wear it with his stole over the left shoulder and under his right arm.

Burse   A square case used as a receptacle for corporal and pall.

Buskins   Knee-length stockings worn by bishops, archbishops, cardinals, the Pope and some abbots in the liturgical colour of the day.

Caligae   Short boots over which bishops' sandals were fastened.

Callotte   A skull-cap worn by the Pope and other dignified ecclesiastics. That worn by the Pope is either white or red.

Cambucca   See *Crozier*.

Camisa   A shirt or undertunic made of linen.

Camister   Thieves' cant – a clergyman or minister, taking *camis* in the sense of 'surplice'.

Cammaka (also Camaca, Camlet)   A fine cloth originally made of camel's hair by the orientals, and afterwards of silk only. Many church vestments were made of this material during the reign

of Edward III (1327–77) (E. Ashdown, *British Costume during the Nineteenth Century*, 1910).

Canon   By the eighth century the canonical life (*canonica vita*) began to prevail. Clergymen (including clerks in minor orders) lived with others in a clergy house, or – in later times – in one of the houses within the precinct or close of a cathedral or collegiate church, and ordered their lives according to the canons or rules of the Church. Since the Reformation canons, with the dean at the head, have constituted the body of resident ecclesiastical dignitaries who manage the cathedral and who formally elect the bishop. By the Cathedral Act of 1840 the number of residential canons was reduced, in many cases to four, and the non-residents were deprived, with some exceptions, of their emoluments, though they are still called prebendaries. See also *Canons Regular of St Augustine* and *Praemonstratensian Canons*.

Canons Regular of St Augustine   An order founded about 1060 whose members wore a white full-sleeved tunic, under which was a black cassock. The cloak and hood were also black; they also adopted the square cap. A leather girdle passed around the waist.

Canopy   A covering or awning held over the sacraments, relics and dignitaries.

Canterbury Cap   See *Square cap*.

Cantor (also Precentor)   A dignitary in cathedrals who leads and directs the choir, etc. A term for the lay singer in the Eastern Orthodox cathedrals.

Cappa   See *Cope*.

Capuchin   A friar of the Order of St Francis, of the new rule of 1528, so called from the sharp-pointed capuche, adopted first 1525 and confirmed to them by Pope Clement VII in 1528.

Capuchon (also Capuche)   A hood of a cloak or a tunic, generally worn by monks and friars.

Caputium   (also   Capputium,   Capuche,

Capuchon) The hood at the back of a cope, cloak, mantle, scapular or mozetta; also the hood or cowl worn by monks.

Cardinal **1** A dignitary of the Roman Church next in rank to the Pope, and from whose ranks the Pope is chosen. The sacred college of cardinals alone have the right to elect the Pope since the third Lateran council in 1173. A cardinal can be bishop, priest or deacon. If the cardinal is a bishop he may wear a pastoral cross (q.v.) but does not carry a crozier (q.v.) which is a sign of jurisdiction. The colour red was conferred to cardinals for their cassock, stockings, gloves and hat by Pope Boniface in 1294, although they probably had already worn red customarily.

2 A title given to two of the minor canons of St Paul's Cathedral and still retained, deriving either from their serving at the chapter or cardinal (i.e. chief) Mass celebrated daily in pre-Reformation times, or from *cardinales chori*, the four cornermen or principal men in choir; this title was given in the fourteenth century and is unique to St Paul's.

Cardinal's Hat The cardinal's hat is proper to St Bonaventura and St Jerome. St Bonaventura is distinguished by the Franciscan girdle and absence of long beard.

Carthusians An order founded in 1084, whose members wore a white cassock and hood, and over this a white scapular with two very prominent bands joining the front and back portions. The cloak, if worn, was of black material. The Carthusians were very austere and, alone of all the monkish orders, shaved the whole head as an outward sign of their austerity.

Carmelites An order of mendicant friars founded in 1209. Their first habit was white

70 Cardinal: St Jerome, ascribed to Battista Moroni (active 1546–7, died 1578). St Jerome, who is often depicted as a hermit with a lion, is here seen in full cardinal's robes but with a long flowing beard which signifies his life as a hermit. He wears a scarlet *cappa clausa* with side slits for the arms to come through. Under this is a pleated rochet of fine white linen which is not trimmed with lace, and under that a red cassock. His white gloves have a soft cuff which terminates in a tassel, which is here used decoratively but was originally the end of a cord securing the gloves on the hand. The shoulder cape is furnished with a hood (the *caputium*) which is here worn over the head, under the large red hat. This hat eventually became too large and too flat to be worn and was just used as an emblem.

71 Carthusians. These unfortunate Carthusians are wearing the habit and over that the scapular worn by most monastic orders for working and outdoor use; it is here kept close at the sides by bands of fabric, sometimes known as 'Benedict's stiches'.

throughout but during the latter part of the thirteenth century their cloaks were particoloured, white and red. These, however, changed back again to all white, with a brown choir cloak for the Great Office.

Cassock (Roman Catholic: Soutane) The cassock is an ankle-length sleeved tunic which can be held at the waist by a narrow belt, or buttoned from neck to foot, and may be of any colour. Its form and use demonstrate the difficulty of classifying the garments worn by clergy. It is universally worn by clergy underneath the Eucharist vestments and all other liturgical garments but it is not in itself a vestment; although worn as an undergarment in services, it is also an overgarment for wear indoors and outdoors; further the cassock is not an exclusively clerical garment and may be worn by servers, choristers and vergers. Unlike the vestments, the cassock does not come from the dress of the Graeco-Roman world, but is adopted from Barbarian dress. In the sixth century the lay fashion had been for shorter tunics and the clergy, in deference presumably to their

more dignified position in the world, retained the older form of a full-length tunic. The Council of Braga in 572 ordered the use of the cassock, and in the colder climes of the northern European countries they could be lined in fur or sheepskin (*pellicea*). In the early thirteenth century many English bishops attended the 4th Lateran Council of Rome which forbade red and green cassocks for priests and lower clergy, allowing bishops to wear any colour. Several councils since have established black for the clergy, red for cardinals and purple for bishops, and white for the Pope. The general cut of the cassock has not altered very much although the full cassock with a train was fashionable for prelates in the fifteenth and sixteenth centuries. The cassock became the regular indoor and outdoor identifying dress of the clergyman and in 1604 canon VXXIV forbade beneficed clergy to go out in public 'in their doublet and hose without coats and cassocks'. Together with gown, hood and spare cap this comprised the outdoor dress of the clergy until the beginning of the nineteenth century. In the eighteenth century the Anglican clergy wore a surplice and stole over a black cassock for church. A major change in the cut of the cassock as outdoor dress occurred in the eighteenth century when it was shortened to form an 'apron' for horse-riding bishops, deans and archdeacons and together with corresponding gaiters, forms an outfit still affected by some dignitaries, although this style never replaces the traditional ankle-length cassock. The Roman Catholic cassock or soutane is usually singlebreasted with a row of many buttons down the centre front, distinguishing it from the Anglican or 'Sarum' style which is double-breasted and held in place by a sash or a belt. The decline in the practice of wearing a cassock as distinctive outdoor dress by clergy of the Church of England coincided with the emergence of the clerical collar in the nineteenth century. In World War I clergy serving in the armed forces established the compromise of wearing the collar with the uniform of the service and reserving cassocks with surplices for services.

Casula See *Chasuble*.

Cenobite (also Coenobite) A monk who does

his service in a monastery under a rule and an abbot, living in a community as opposed to an anchorite who lives in solitude.

Chaplain (also Capellanus)   Originally 'cappelani' were those who had charge of the sacred cloak of St Martin; in medieval England the word meant a chantry priest:

1. Generally, a priest or a clergyman or a minister of a chapel.

2 Specifically a clergyman who conducts religious service in the private chapel of a Lord, Sovereign or high official, of a castle, garrison, embassy, college, school, workhouse, prison, cemetery or other institution.

3 A nun who recites the inferior services in the chapel of a nunnery. Chaucer, in the Prologue to the *Canterbury Tales*, refers to 'Another Nonne also with hire hadde sche, that was hire chapelleyn'.

Chasuble (also Casula, Paenula, Infula)   The chasuble became the principal vestment used by the priest for the celebration of the Mass, and originally developed from the practical travelling cloak, the paenula, which was generally worn in the Graeco-Roman world by both sexes and all classes. This was made from a semi-circle or more usually two quadrants of woollen material with the two edges sewn together to form a conical or

tent-shaped cloak, a hole being left for the head. The tent-shaped cloak or casula (literally 'little tent') has seams running vertically down the centre front and back and these were strengthened by narrow strips of braid, known as orphreys. By the sixth century the cappa was in regular use, and by the seventh century the name chasuble or casula came into use in the Church. The first chasubles would have been wool, either undyed or dyed purple and unadorned, and by the eighth century we see the emergence of the chasuble as the distinctive outer garment of the presiding celebrant at the Eucharist˙ (Ordo Romanus Primus). The dalmatic and tunicle also became vestments at this time and in the ninth century it became generally accepted that the priest wore the chasuble over the alb, the deacon wore the dalmatic and the sub-deacon wore the tunicle. The next development in the shape of the chasuble occurred over the next centuries as the vestments began to be made of richer fabrics (the Church became wealthier and silks became cheaper and more readily obtainable in the period of the 'flowering of English art' – Opus Anglicanum). Medieval chasubles were originally of more or less conical form, and subsequently nearly all were curtailed at the sides, e.g. the Clare chasuble (fig. 15). One practical reason for this is the elevation of the host in the Eucharist, where the priest raises the bread above his head at the altar. The rubrics of the Roman missal direct the deacon or acolyte to raise the chasuble at the moment of elevation, meaning presumably, the cloth covering the arms. This would be satisfactory with a garment made from wool, but as the vestment became more elaborate and heavy – by the thirteenth century the chasuble was established as a 'rich and high-priestly ornament, no longer merely a garment of clothing', elevating the host meant the chasuble became cut away at the sides, leaving the arms free. Eventually it was found to be more convenient to make this reduced chasuble by joining two shield-shaped

72 Chasuble: Flemish ms., 1290. Both the bishop (with the crozier, or pastoral staff) and the archbishop (with the cross staff) are wearing the chasuble over the alb, amice and dalmatic. These chasubles have simple orphreys and are otherwise undecorated, although they are lined in a different colour.

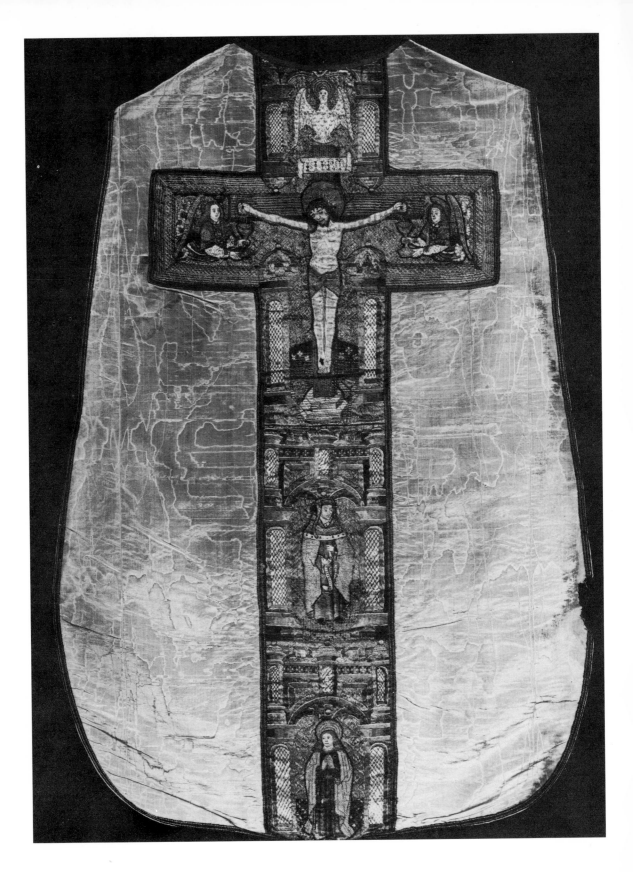

pieces of material along the shoulders. The seams of such chasubles are not usually decorated, but non-functional vertical orphreys are often applied to form a kind of cross front and back. The 'shield' shape or 'violin' shape was prevalent at the time of the establishment of the Church of England. The Roman Catholic Church retained the vestments and in the seventeenth century the chasuble continued as a vehicle for display, a Baroque ornament. In the Church of England the chasuble was re-introduced in the mid-nineteenth century by the emergent 'high Anglicanism' in the form of the Ritualist Movement; this caused much distress within the Church but succeeded in firmly re-establishing vestments for some clergy. J. M. Neale was wearing vestments in the 1850s, and by the end of the century mass-production of vestments by commercial firms had confirmed their popularity. The neo-medievalism of the Cambridge Ecclesiologists and the Ritualists led to the advocacy of the so-called Gothic chasuble with matching stole and maniple, a romantic but not historically accurate interpretation of the early vestments. Vestments in the twentieth century, both mass-produced and hand-made, are reverting to the simple shape of the earlier period, and are being made of simpler fabrics. The reasons are directly the reverse of the reasons for the growth in elaboration: the Church is poorer, or less willing to spend money on garments, and the stuffs are more expensive.

Chimere   A silk or satin sleeveless gown, black or scarlet, worn by Anglican bishops and doctors of divinity. The name may be derived from the Spanish 'Zammarra' which can be found in the twelfth century as a short cloak worn by bishops when riding horseback. In a longer version it became part of the customary attire of bishops on

74 Chimere: W. C. Magee, by C. Pellegrini, 1869. The chimere is the sleeveless gown worn over the rochet by bishops and archbishops in the Anglican Communion. Over the top of this is worn the preaching stole which Bishop Magee is clutching with his left hand.

both liturgical and civil occasions. In the eighteenth and nineteenth centuries the chimere acquired the full lawn sleeves of the rochet, which had grown so big and full that they were sewn into the sleeveless chimere. The sleeves are gathered into the wrist in a band from which a frill emerges. This is the vestigial remains of the Elizabethan frill that was worn by all clergy in common with contemporary fashion; the red wristband worn with the red chimere appears to be a mere foible, perhaps invented by Samuel Wilberforce (1805–73).

Chirothecae   The embroidered gloves worn as part of the Episcopal costume.

73 This chasuble has an embroidered orphrey in the shape of the Cross, the symbol of redemption. Angels collect the sacred blood and the figures of the beloved disciple John and the Virgin Mary are below the crucified Christ, a theme that recurs more than any other on the orphreys of the chasuble, the official Mass vestment. This chasuble of watered silk has been curtailed at the sides, which leaves the arms of the priest officiating free for the elevation of the host.

Chiton Poderes　See *Alb*.

Chrisome　A white cloth or robe put on newly baptised persons by the priest as an emblem of innocence. Children that died within a month of being baptised were buried in their chrisome robe and called chrisome babies.

Cidaris (also Cydaris, Ydaris)　A cap used by bishops before the emergence of the mitre. The word is of Semitic origin and referred to the cap of state of the Persian rulers.

Cingulum　See *Girdle*.

Cistercians　An order founded in 1098. They built their first monastery in England in the early part of the twelfth century and although reformed Benedictines they wore a white cassock with cape and a small hood; when at public prayer a white gown was thrown over these, and when abroad a black one.

75 Cistercian nun: Virgin and Child with a nun (detail), by Joachim Patenier. This nun, who is probably the donor of the panel, is wearing white, the official colour of the Cistercian order, with a black veil, worn by the professed nuns of every order.

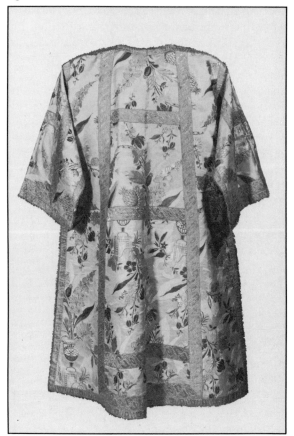

76 Clavi. The clavi are the woven bands used to decorate the dalmatic from the earliest days of the Christian Church (and before) and continued to be the decoration special to this vestment.

Clavi　The decorative woven or embroidered bands found on early tunics, dalmatics and paenulas.

Clerical Coat　The outdoor dress of clergy; a form of conservative fashionable coat in a dark colour, usually black.

Clerical Collar　A white stiffened band of linen or cotton, or more recently nylon or even polythene, worn instead of fashionable neckwear. In the late nineteenth and twentieth centuries this can sometimes be the only identifying item of clothing worn by the clergy. It has come to be known colloquially as the 'dog-collar'.

Cluniacs　An order founded in 910 at Cluny in France. They were first introduced into England at Lewes in Sussex, where a priory was founded in 1077. Being a reformed order of Benedictines, the Cluniacs retained the black dress.

Colet (also Collet) A shortened form of acolyte (q.v.). It is not clear whether the loss of the 'a' was due to aphesis or to mistaking it for the indefinite article – a–collyt.

Collare A richly ornamented collar or tippet, which was sometimes placed over the upper part of the chasuble. It was also known as 'the Flower' (D. Rock, *Church of Our Fathers*, 3 vols, 1849–52).

Colours, Liturgical Although all vestments were originally plain and white, coloured fabrics

77 This ivory comb, carved with scenes from the Bible, was kept in the church specifically for use by the priest after he had fully vested, as almost all liturgical vestments are put on over the head.

and embroideries were soon introduced. By the twelfth century the following colours had been established:

Black: Masses for the dead; Good Friday (silver not gold trim).

White/gold: Christmas and Easter; Epiphany.

Red: apostles; martyr saints (except female virgins); Pentecost.

Violet: Lent; Advent; Rogation days.

Green: Trinity; less traditional, but serves as the all purpose colour.

Blue: no liturgical significance but very popular colour especially in the fourteenth- and fifteenth-century inventories and found in Old Sarum Rite; associated with churches named for Mary.

White: Feast of Virgin Mary; virgin saints.

It would appear, however, that it was not until the end of the nineteenth century in England that these colours were taken too seriously; individual

churches preferred to use their best vestments for the important festivals irrespective of colour.

Comb Combs are frequently mentioned in inventories of church furniture, and can be exceedingly beautiful in design. Although of no liturgical significance they were intended for the use of officiating clergy before entering the choir and would be necessary as so many vestments are put on over the head.

Congregationalists See *Independents*.

Cope (also Cappa, Capa) A ceremonial version of an outdoor cloak worn during the latter days of the Roman Empire. It is basically a semi-circular piece of cloth held together at the front by a clasp or a 'morse'. The cope is worn at non-Eucharist ceremonies (i.e. baptism, marriage and procession) in the place of the chasuble. It may also replace the dalmatic or tunicle since its use is not restricted to bishops and priests. It was in regular use by the end of the sixth century when it was known as the cappa (a topmost garment), had a functional hood and was made of a thick black woollen material (*cappa nigra*). This continued to be worn in the choir and outdoors as a protection against the cold in the Middle Ages and through to the present day as the clerical cloak fastened at the throat by a chain and hook and worn over the cassock. As the cope became an increasingly ceremonial garment, the hood ceased to be functional and was eventually reduced to a triangular or shield-shaped decoration at the back. A certain variation in style has occurred (usually dictated by the type of fabric used) but apart from the reduction in the hood to a vestigial flap there has been no substantial change in its form; the employment of silks and other expensive materials runs parallel with the development of the chasuble. The cope has become liturgical but not sacerdotal and is made in the colour appropriate to the season or to the position of the wearer. In the West the cope is a general ecclesiastical robe of splendour and has never been a distinctive clerical vestment; it is not blessed, nor solemnly given during ordination and no symbolic meaning has been given to it. In the Book of Common Prayer, 1549, the parish priest is ordered to wear a vestment (i.e. chasuble, stole and maniple) *or* a cope. Although this was withdrawn in 1552, in 1604 the ornaments rubric ruled that the principal minister at the Communion in cathedrals and collegiate churches should wear a coloured cope over a plain alb. This custom is still observed in some cathedrals and ex-collegiate churches in spite of the fact that a cope is an extremely inconvenient garment in which to perform the Eucharist actions and gesture.

The Coptic Church Alexandria was one of the earliest cities to receive the new Christian faith, and tradition said that St Mark the Evangelist had been its first missionary and first bishop. Pantaenus (died *c.* 212) founded at Alexandria a school that became the first Christian university, which boasted such scholars as Clement of Alexandria (died 217) and Origen (died 254). In the fifth century the Coptic Church, as it came to be known, broke with the Church in Europe and since then has been separate from both the West (Rome) and the East (Constantinople). The vestments are similar to those of the Byzantine (Eastern Orthodox) rite but the Coptic priest has an amice. It is much larger than the Western amice, made of white linen embroidered with two large crosses. One end hangs down the back, the other is wound round the head to form a hood. Other vestments are:

Burnus: a cope which serves the same function as a chasuble.
Omophorion: a pallium, which may be worn by bishops. It is of wool but is much longer than the Western pallium.
Saccos: a form of dalmatic worn by bishops. It is very elaborate and usually heavily decorated.
Tailasan : a broad strip of embroidered material ending in a hood, worn by dissident priests. While dissident priests wear a turban out of doors, the Catholic clergy wear a cylindrical black hat over which the bishops wear a veil.

In the Coptic liturgy the celebrant must be barefoot during the celebration of the Eucharist.

Corporal A square piece of white linen upon which the chalice and the host rest during the Eucharist.

Cotta A shortened form of surplice, either with or without sleeves. It can be edged with elaborate lace.

Cowl (also Caputium, Coule, Cucullio, Cucullus, Cuculle, Goule) Originally merely a cap or a hood covering the head and the nape of the neck, the ordinary headgear of peasants and children. It was adopted by the monastic orders and subsequently meant the whole garment with the hood attached.

Cross Staff A tall stick ending in the form of a cross, borne by archbishops and the Pope in procession.

Crozier (also Baculus) The pastoral staff held by the bishop in his left hand. In the thirteenth century archbishops and the Pope began to carry a cross-staff instead. The crozier is often an elaborately worked symbol of the shepherd's crook, an indication of the pastoral responsibilities of the bishop, and by the sixteenth century crozier was the common name of the episcopal crook. Many nineteenth-century ecclesiastical antiquaries have erroneously transferred the name to the cross borne before the archbishop.

Crutched Friars (also Crossed Friars) Founded *c.* 1250, they were so called because they wore a red cross on the back and breast of their blue habit.

Cucullus See *Cowl.*

Cultellus A knife worn by monks for use in the refectory and elsewhere.

Dalmatic (also Alba Dalmatica) Both the dalmatic and the tunicle are essentially variant forms of the *alba dalmatica* and therefore share a common origin with the alb (q.v.). ('Dalmatica'

78 Coptic stoles. The stole on the left is the epitrachelion used by the Coptic Church in Egypt, showing the form of the Eastern stole which is sewn together up the centre front with a shaped opening for the neck. On the right is a Slavonic stole from the seventeenth century, broader than the Western stole but a similar shape. Both are decorated with figures of saints, a style of decoration popular in the Western church until the fifteenth century.

79 Processional cross: champiere enamel on copper gilt set with pastes. French (Limoges), thirteenth century. The processional cross is held by or carried before an archbishop or if he is present, the Pope.

80 Crozier: head of pastoral staff, made of ivory. English, School of Canterbury, *c.* 1180. The pastoral staff or crook is carried by a bishop as a symbol of his responsibilities to his 'flock' and as a representative of Christ, the Good Shepherd.

81 Crozier: a bishop blessing – centre of a triptych in ivory. French, thirteenth century. The bishop, vested for Mass in chasuble with mitre, alb and amice, holds his pastoral staff in his left hand and blesses with the right hand. His fringed maniple is seen clearly but his stole is invisible as the dalmatic is full-length and covers it.

82 Dalmatic: St Stephen – alabaster statuette. English, fifteenth century. Stephen, the first Christian martyr, who was stoned to death (Acts of the Apostles 6 and 7), was named first of the seven deacons chosen by the apostles to look after the needs of the Greek speaking widows among the Christians at Jerusalem. As a deacon he is represented wearing the dalmatic, alb and amice. Clavi and fringing are painted on the dalmatic and apparels are painted on the alb and amice. He carries a book and the stones of his martyrdom.

would seem to indicate an origin in the region of Dalmatia, but this would be long before the garment took on any ecclesiastical significance.) In second-century Rome the dalmatic was a wide-sleeved overgarment, popular in a shortened version, and appears to be the garment worn by some praying figures in the catacomb frescoes. Having been accepted by the patriarchs in Rome it was first conferred as a mark of honour on bishops, then on archdeacons and later on deacons. By the fourth century the dalmatic worn over the alb was the garb of bishops and deacons (St Vitale mosaics). Pope Silvester (314–35) is said to have conferred the dalmatic onto Roman deacons and although all ranks of clergy wore it, it became the regular costume of the lowest ordained minister by the ninth century. In the fifth century the Pope and the Roman deacons wore the dalmatic of white linen adorned with vertical purple stripes (clavi) back and front from the shoulders to the hem and round the bottom of the sleeves, and the use of the dalmatic was later granted by the Pope as a privilege to the bishops and deacons of other churches. The dalmatic was longer than the tunicle, with wider and shorter sleeves. It was shortened and split down the sides to facilitate walking, and eventually split right up to under the arms. By the nineteenth century sleeves became no more than vestigial flaps but now the former pattern has been restored. From the tenth century the dalmatic was made of richer fabrics and was elaborately decorated, most notably with fringes, tassels, orphreys (or more properly clavi) and apparels. With the chasuble and tunicle the dalmatic is regarded as a festal vestment and not to be worn in penitential seasons, and it may be noted that during the coronation ceremony the English Sovereign is vested in a dalmatic.

Damask A fabric frequently used for vestments. Originally from Damascus it is a rich silk or other textile figured by using the sateen effect of the warp or the weft interchanging in a special design.

Deacon A sacred order in the Church, next in dignity to that of a priest, and whose duties are to be an assistant to the sacerdotal and episcopal orders.

Dean The first dignitary of a cathedral, the head of the chapter. Except in cathedrals served by monks, the office of dean has existed since 1086.

Diaper, Diapered A two-coloured sheen produced by the interweaving of threads. A linen cloth is woven in a pattern, formed by the different directions of the threads throwing off

83 Dalmatic: Butler-Bowden cope (detail). St Laurence, carrying the gridiron, the emblem of his martyrdom, is here shown tonsured and wearing the dalmatic of the deacon. The apparelled amice and alb are clearly represented but there is no maniple; both ends of the stole are shown below the hem of the dalmatic as if it was worn in the manner of the priest and not over the left shoulder and caught at the right side which would be correct. This is probably the embroiderer's error – Laurence was certainly a deacon.

light from its surface in such a way as to give a diapered pattern, with the spaces between the lines filled up by parallel lines, a central leaf or dot, etc.

Discalced   Strictly speaking barefoot (O.E.D.: discalceate – unshod, barefoot). Most discalced orders usually wear sandals of leather or wood.

Dominicans   (also Black Friars) An order founded in 1215. They wore a white tunic fastened with a white girdle, over which was worn a white scapular. The overgarment was a black mantle and hood and the shoes were also black. Lay brothers wore a black scapular. They were also known as 'fratres de picâ' – magpie brethren – because they wore black and white.

Echarpe   A scarf worn by some canons regular, not to be confused with the stole.

Encheirion   (Eastern Orthodox) Originally a handkerchief, it took on the same liturgical meaning as the maniple of the Western Church in the ninth century and becomes a regular item of episcopal dress in the eleventh century. It hangs from the girdle.

Encolpium   A golden cross worn by bishops and some other dignitaries of Rome. It hung upon the breast.

Ephod   The 'breastplate' of the Levitical priest. A Jewish priestly vestment without sleeves or side seams, it is fastened by buckles at the shoulders and by a girdle at the waist.

Epigonation   (Eastern Orthodox) This developed from the encheirion (q.v.) and is more clearly a badge of rank. It is a stiff, square-shaped ornament suspended from the girdle by one corner. It was generally worn by bishops but its use was extended to priests.

Epimanikia   (Eastern Orthodox) Cuffs, possibly derived from those worn in civil dress. They appear in the eleventh century and at first were probably reserved for bishops. Later they became a liturgical vestment worn by both bishops and priests.

Episcopal Vestments   Of or pertaining to a bishop.

1 The buskins and sandals	8 The dalmatic
2 The amice	9 The gloves
3 The alb	10 The chasuble
4 The girdle	11 The mitre
5 The pectoral cross	12 The ring
6 The stole worn pendant not crossed like that of the priest.	13 The pastoral staff or crozier
	14 The rochet
	15 The cappa magna
	16 The cope
7 The tunic	17 The gremiale

(A.W.N. Pugin, *Glossary of Ecclesiastical Ornament and Costume*, 1868)

Epitrahelion   (Eastern Orthodox; also Epitrachelion; Peritrachelion) The equivalent of the stole, primarily a vestment worn by priests.

Eremites   See *Austin Friars*.

Ermine   A fur with associations of purity, royalty, etc. It is the winter fur of the stoat which is wholly white except for the tip of the tail which is black.

Escalope   The shell emblem of St James the Great, worn as an insignia by pilgrims.

Ethiopian Vestments   These are Coptic in origin:
Alb: usually white or coloured silk, as is the *amice*.
Stole: of the Byzantine pattern.
Girdle: confines the alb.
Cuffs: used extensively and confine the sleeves of the alb.
Kabba or *Cappa*: resembles a cloak with a hood, that falls to just below the knees. The cappa of the priest is often ornamented on its upper part with small gold silver bells.
Lanka: a shoulder cape with five short pendants.
   The outdoor dress of a cleric consists of a cassock over which is worn a wide-sleeved coat. A round flattened cap is also worn.

Falda White papal vestments for solemn occasions, worn over the cassock.

Fanon Orale
1 A sacred vestment for bishops only, an oblong piece of stuff possibly evolved from the amice.
2 A thin veil or mantle fastened around the Pope's neck when he celebrated pontifical High Mass as a special addition to the vestments.
3 A napkin, mappula or maniple.
4 A corporal.
Fanon when appearing in English inventories generally means a maniple.

Femoralia Breeches or drawers. *The Oxford English Dictionary* describes femorals as 'clothing for the thighs – breeches'. See Leviticus 6:10: 'The priest shall be revested with the tunike and the linnen femoralles'. (Douay Bible 1609).

Firmaculum A cope-morse or clasp.

Franciscans (also Grey Friars) Founded in 1208, this order was first introduced into England in 1223 at Canterbury. They originally wore a long loose grey tunic girded with a cord, and a hood or cowl and cloak of the same colour. In the fifteenth century the colour was changed to brown. The feet were bare or protected by sandals. The Franciscan nuns or Poor Clares wore the same but with a black veil instead of a hood.

Fringe An ornamental border or edging, originally the ends of the threads that formed the stuff, fastened together to prevent further unravelling. A fringe is often found on the dalmatic from the ninth century.

Fustian A cloth with a linen warp and cotton weft; some sorts included worsted. Woollen fustians were made at Norwich as early as 1336.

84 Franciscan: St Francis in meditation, by Francisco de Zurbaran *c.* 1639. St Francis in meditation is shown in the patched habit of the friar. The hood is stitched on to the habit and the whole outfit is made of rough brown wool, the colour of the Franciscan order by this time (it was originally grey). His girdle made of rope shows three knots, indicating the three vows of poverty, chastity and obedience.

Fustian was favoured by the Norman clergy and the Cistercians were forbidden to make vestments of anything but linen or fustian.

Gaiters Leggings protecting the shin from ankle to knee and buttoned up the outside. They form part of secular dress adopted by clerics in the eighteenth century when they shortened the cassock to the 'apron' style.

General Baptists (also Unitarian Baptists) A sect which sprang up in the early years of the Reformation.

Geneva Gown A black preaching gown with academic associations worn by clergy of the reformed Church, originally adopted by Calvin in sixteenth century. It was an open black gown in silk or wool with wide sleeves.

Gilbertines An order founded in 1139 by Gilbert of Sempringham. The canons were dressed in black cassock and hood and white cloak; the nuns in black tunic, cloak and hood. First the cloak, and later the hood were lined in lambskin. The canons wore beards, unusual in holy orders.

Girdle (also Cingulum, Cincture) The cingulum or girdle became accepted as part of the Christian vestments with the *tunica alba*. It is normal to wear a girdle of some sort with the classical alb for the sake of convenience, thus when the *tunica alba* became a vestment it was accompanied by the customary cingulum and was recognized as such in the eighth century. From the tenth century the girdle took the form of a broad belt or cincture of white or coloured material, and could be embellished with woven or embroidered designs and sometimes with precious stones or metal threads. In the Latin and the Anglican Church this has been replaced by a long white rope or cord with tasselled ends. It is put on immediately after the alb and the ends of the stole

85, 86 Gilbertines: A canon and nun of the order of St Gilbert. The black veil of the nun and the cappa and hood of the canon are lined in fur. The Gilbertine canon wears a beard, a distinctive feature of this order.

are tucked under or through it and are thereby held in place.

Gloves   Pontificalia (i.e. worn by bishops), they were originally white to signify purity but eventually assumed the liturgical colour of the day.

Gothic Vestments   Eucharistic vestments based on a medieval type re-introduced in Britain in the second half of the nineteenth century.

Gremiale
1 A square or oblong piece of silk worn by the Roman bishop on his lap whenever he sat down during the intervals of High Mass and at ordinations to prevent the chasuble from being soiled by the holy oils.
2 A white cloth fastened over the head and around the throat and breast of a nun. It was worn under the velum (q.v.) or dark cloth on the head.

Grey Friars   See *Franciscans*.

Habit   A sleeved tunic worn by those in holy orders – originally undyed and of coarse stuff.

Hassock   A cushion for kneeling on in church.

Hood
1 A head covering attached to a cloak or cowl etc.
2 A piece of cloth lined with special colours hanging from the shoulders down the back, worn by graduates. (See *Tippet*.)

Houseling Cloth   A cloth spread before the communicants, to collect up any crumbs of the sacred host if they fall to the ground. It has now generally fallen into disuse.

Humerale   See *Amice*.

Humeral veil
1 A cloth or shawl covering the shoulders and hands, worn by sub-deacons when handling sacred vessels.
2 An oblong scarf worn round the shoulders at certain times during the Mass and used in the elevation of the host to prevent contamination by the fingers of the officiating priest.

Independents   (also Congregationalists) Founded *c*. 1616. The name Congregationalist is a nineteenth-century term, but the sect was founded in the seventeenth century. Its fundamental principle is that every individual group of Christians worshipping together is an independent body with the right of electing and deposing its pastors, settling points of faith and exercising discipline over its own congregation. Robert Browne in the seventeenth century first formulated this system and the sect was known as the 'Brownists' until about 1642.

Infula
1 The bands, lappets or pendants hanging at the back of the cidaris or mitre (both q.v.).
2 Medieval Latin for chasuble, used in fourteenth-century inventories.
3 Occasionally, a mitre or a head covering.

Kalyptra   (Eastern Orthodox) A headdress worn on ceremonial occasions. It was black if the wearer had been a monk before his elevation and white if he had been a layman. As in the Roman Church priests celebrate the Eucharist with their heads bare. After the seventeenth century Byzantine bishops began to wear the mitre.

Lappets   (also Infula, Stola) Two tabs of cloth, sometimes decorated, which fall from the back of the mitre.

Lector   The second of the minor orders whose principal office is to chant the lessons in the Mass on certain days, to read the lessons of the first nocturn at matins, to read the text for the preacher, and to bless the bread and the new fruits.

Linostole   A surplice (from the Greek λινον – linen and στολὴ a robe).

Liturgical   Pertaining to or connected with public worship.

Mandelion   (Eastern Orthodox) A towel used by a bishop.

Mandyas (Eastern Orthodox) A cloak or mantle worn by monks and bishops in the Greek Church in their civil costume. It could be elaborate with squares of coloured fabric (*potamoi* or *pomata*) stitched on as signs of episcopal dignity, or a plain dark mantle, an alternative to liturgical vestments.

Manicatus Furnished with long sleeves.

Maniple (also Sudarium, Fanon, Manipulus, Mappula, Mantile, Manvale Sestace, Pallium Linostinum; Eastern Orthodox: Epimanika, Epigonation) This vestment derives from the mappa, a practical rectangle of linen which developed into an emblem of rank in pre-Christian Roman culture. The mappa was held in the right hand of the consul who waved it as a sign for the games to start. Correspondingly, the maniple of the Pope in the seventh century was used as a signal for the beginning of the Stational Mass. The mappa was a folded handkerchief normally carried in the hand (there being no pockets in classical dress). The Roman deacons carried their napkin (*pallium linostinum*) in the left hand or over the left forearm; and by the ninth century it had developed into the maniple (*manipulus*) and was worn on the left forearm. Perhaps through confusion with the handkerchief (mappa, mapula, sudarium) the two were merged into one vestment, and adopted by sacred orders all over the West. Archbishop Stigand in the Bayeux Tapestry carries the maniple in his hand. The maniple underwent the same transformations as the stole (q.v.) in terms of decoration and colour from the tenth century, and the stole and maniple were generally made as a set.

Mantellone (Roman Catholic) An ankle-length sleeveless garment or mantle in purple worn by chamberlains and papal prelates of inferior grade. Two four-inch strips of material hung from the back of the shoulders to the hem.

87 Maniple: St Cuthbert in episcopal robes adored by a monk. St Cuthbert in full episcopal robes is raising his right hand in blessing and it is this arm that is bearing the maniple. This is correct according to early Christian usage, although usually the maniple is worn on the left arm.

The wearers were sometimes called *monsignore di mantelloni*.

Mantellum

1 A long red mantle worn by a cardinal over his rochet.
2 A short mantle with armholes, reaching to the knees and with a centre front opening.

Maphorium (Eastern Orthodox) A long, narrow scapular, square at the hem.

Melota (Eastern Orthodox) A nightdress or travelling garment made of animal skins worn by Eastern monks. The name derives from the Greek word for a sheepskin, μηλώτη.

Mendicant Orders A name applied to those religious orders which lived entirely on alms – Franciscans, Dominicans, Carmelites and Augustinian Hermits.

Methodists A general name for a number of sects which are derived from, more or less directly, the confraternity formed in the year 1739 by John Wesley, fellow of Lincoln College, Oxford. In 1794 resolutions were passed, including one that 'All ecclesiastical titles such as Reverend, etc., shall be laid aside, as also gowns, bands, etc.' This was so as to cause no division with the established Church of England. Generally following the evangelical branch of the Anglican Church in matters of special dress, the Methodists did not introduce any regulations concerning vestments.

Mitre The origin of the mitre is obscure but by the eleventh century it emerged as the distinctive liturgical hat of bishops. It started as a simple conical cap of white linen with two lappets hanging down the back; in the twelfth century there was a centre dent running front to back in the cap, and a century later the dented cap was being worn the other way round and the present form of a tall divided hat began to develop. In the thirteenth century three types are recognized in Roman ceremonial corresponding with different degrees of ceremony – *mitra pretiosa*: jewelled; *mitra aurifrigiata*: decorated without jewels; and *mitra simplex*: the simple mitre. The wearing of a mitre is not restricted to bishops in the West, and some abbots and cardinals have been granted the privilege. In the Anglican Church after the Reformation, although still part of episcopal insignia, it was seldom worn except at coronations until the reign of George III. Its use has now been revived.

Mitred Abbot   An abbot entitled or privileged to wear a mitre invested by the Pope. The first example is in 1088 when St Hugh, Abbot of Cluny received the episcopal mitre from Urban II. Although some mitred abbots remained in their monastic habit some became indistinguishable from ordinary bishops, as they wore complete pontificals.

88 Mitred abbot: Abbot Willimus. Abbot Willimus is dressed as a monk in habit with the cappa and his only ornaments are the attributes of a bishop – the mitre, the crozier and a morse.

Morse (also Firmaculum, Nouche)   The clasp or fastening on the cope, often made of precious metals, enamelled and set with jewels.

Mortar Board   A popular name for the academic or college cap, which consists of a stiffened skull cap surmounted by a square board, the whole being covered with black cloth; it developed during the sixteenth century.

Mozetta   A short hooded cape worn over a cope by the Pope, cardinals, abbots, bishops and other dignitaries of the Roman Catholic Church. Serving the same function as the almuce (q.v.), it is lined with fur in winter and silk in summer, and is derived from the choir cape or cappa. The mozetta covers the trunk of the body and is fastened down the centre front by a line of buttons.

Nouche   See *Morse*.

Novice   A name given to those preparing to take monastic vows. Preceded by the postulants since the eighteenth century.

Offertory Veil   See *Sudarium*.

Omophorion (Eastern Orthodox)   Similar to the pallium (q.v.) of the Anglican Church.

Orale   See *Fanon*.

Orarion (Eastern Orthodox)   A stole worn by deacons. See *Orarium*.

Orarium (also Orarion, Vexillum)
1 A scarf of plain silk affixed to the crozier.
2 Strictly a napkin or handkerchief, it was the

89 Morse: SS Gregory, Maurice and Augustine, by the Circle of the Master of Liesborn. Pope Gregory on the left in the triple tiara and carrying a cross staff has an elaborate morse with a small Biblical scene within an architectural arch. His cope has an orphrey decorated with gems and a fringe at the hem; his dalmatic is made of a silk brocade with a large pattern worn over a plain alb (although the amice has an apparel). Augustine is dressed in his monastic habit with a cope and a mitre. His morse is a quatrefoil shape set with gems, and his orphrey is a woven braid.

early name for a stole. In the Eastern Orthodox Rite it is specifically the stole of the deacon.

Orb   A globe surmounted by a cross, which forms part of the Coronation regalia.

Orders
1 To take orders – to become ordained in the Christian ministry.
2 Holy orders – bishop, priest and deacon, also sub-deacon in the Roman Catholic Church. In the Catholic Church the minor orders are those of acolyte, exorcist, reader and doorkeeper.
3 Monastic orders – a fraternity of monks, friars and nuns.

Ordinary
1 A rule, ordinance or ordinal. A formula or rule prescribing a certain order or course of action.
2 An officer in a religious fraternity having charge of the convent.
3a) A diocesan officer appointed to give criminals their final prayers and to prepare them for death.
  b) The chaplain of Newgate Prison, whose duty was to prepare prisoners for death.
4 A rule prescribing, or book containing, the order of divine service, especially that of the Mass.
5 Of a judge: having regular jurisdiction especially empowered, ex-officio, to take cognizance of spiritual or ecclesiastical cases.

Ordination (Roman Catholic)   Deacons receive the stole, dalmatic and gospel book. Priests receive the stole and chasuble and the people's offering of bread and wine, in paten and chalice. Bishops receive the gospel book, ring and pastoral staff. The principal consecrator puts the mitre on the candidate but without formula.

Orphrey   A piece of woven or embroidered fabric decorating Eucharistic vestments. Often including gold thread, they are assumed to have taken their name from *auriphrygia* or Phrygian gold.

90 Mozetta: Pope Julius II, by Raphael. Pope Julius wears a red fur-lined mozetta with hood over his white silk cassock and sleeveless rochet.

Orthodox Vestments   Orthodox vestments have undergone a parallel evolution with those of the Western Church, differing because of rite and taste, but basically being the same garments. They developed from the same ordinary Roman dress of the first three centuries and are used on similar occasions. The biggest difference is that there is no sequence of liturgical colours (those of the West developed after the schism) and the vestments are generally white or red and have become stiff with heavy gold embroidery. The split between East and West became permanent between the ninth and eleventh centuries but there had been many breaks before, and the development of vestments probably became independent from the sixth century.

Paenula   A travelling cloak from which the chasuble (q.v.) is derived. The term is often used to describe the chasuble in the early period.

Pall
1 A covering for a coffin.
2 A second corporal for covering the chalice.
3 A linen cloth for covering the altar.
4 An ornamental cloth to hang in the choir on festivals.
5 Often used to mean the pallium (but not in this book).

Pallium (Eastern Orthodox: Omophorion)
1 A long woven band or scarf of white wool marked with six dark crosses, and worn around the neck and shoulders with the ends hanging down in various ways, by patriarchs, archbishops and some other bishops. In the Roman Catholic Church it has developed into the form of a circular strip with two bands hanging down front and back, but in the Ravenna mosaics the bishops all wear a straight band looped over the shoulders with the ends hanging down front and back from the left shoulder. It is still worn in the Eastern Orthodox Church and called the omophorion. The pallium, with the orarium or stole, originated in the early Christian Church in Rome. In 395 the Codex of Theodosius ordered a scarf or pall of several colours to be worn over the paenula by senators. Shortly afterwards this civil ornament became a distinctive badge of episcopal status. In

91 Orphrey: Canon Bernardinus and three saints. Left wing of an altarpiece, by David. St Martin, on the left, has a plain cope with elaborately embroidered orphrey and hood, fastened with a large morse. The orphrey is decorated with figures of saints in niches. The mitre is seen in profile and the lappets or infulae can be seen as purely ornamental appendages, also heavily decorated. St Bernard in the centre is in his habit with cowl. The donor, Canon Bernardinus, kneeling in the foreground, is wearing a fine pleated surplice with very wide sleeves over a fur-lined cassock. St Donation has a matching cope and chasuble of silk brocade and a piece of this fabric has been used for the apparel of the alb. The orphrey is much less elaborate in comparison and the morse is decorated with the figures of the Virgin and Child and two angels.

the West the custom grew up of reserving the pallium to archbishops, who received it directly from the Pope as a sign of his jurisdiction. Although on the Continent some bishops received the pallium, in Great Britain only archbishops of the Roman Church have ever been invested with it.

2 An imperial robe donned by the English monarch at coronation.

Pallium Linostinum   See *Maniple.*

Pannus   See *Sudarium.*

Paramenta   See *Apparel.*

Parure   See *Apparel.*

92 Pallium: group of ecclesiastics, Psalter of Henry of Blois, *c.* 1140–60. The two figures vested for Mass are both wearing the pallium, the attribute of the archbishop, over the chasuble and the dalmatic. The only decoration of the pallium, which is always made of white wool, consists of crosses, and these vary in number. The archbishop on the right has a small fringe at the bottom and his chasuble is decorated with a collar or 'flower'.

Pastoral Staff   See *Crozier.*

Paten   A vessel or plate upon which the consecrated bread is placed.

Pectoral
1 A morse of either metal or embroidery.
2 The front orphrey of a chasuble.

3 The apparels on the breast of some albs and tunicles.

Pectoral Cross (Eastern Orthodox: Stauros) A cross worn by the Pope, archbishop and bishop, upon the breast suspended by a chain or a cord.

Peristera (Eastern Orthodox) A white woollen filet thrown over the head or cap and resting on the shoulders.

Phelonion (Eastern Orthodox) A chasuble worn shorter and squarer than that in the West. The term phelonion for the specialized form of paenula affected by the Byzantine clergy was in general use at least as early as the beginning of the ninth century, when the patriarch Nicephorus sent Pope Leo III, with an accompanying letter, a white sticharion, a brown phelonion, an epitrachelion and an encheiron. (Regestes No. 382; PG 100, 200). Generally the phelonion of members of the ministry, other than priests and bishops, is less ample.

Phrygium (also Tiara) A pointed or domed cap worn by some bishops before the mitre became established. The triple tiara of the Pope was the phrygium with three crowns.

Pilch A thick garment made of skins (worn by anchorites, etc.).

Planeta See *Chasuble*.

Pluviale A large cloak to protect against the rain– the precursor of the cope.

Polystavrion (Eastern Orthodox) A specialized form of the phelonion – decorated with large, usually plain, crosses all over the garment.

Pontificalia The insignia of the Pope or pontiff, also used by bishops and priests. 'When I got to Ockham I was enquiring after an inn to set up my horse and dress myself that I might wait upon my lord in potificalibus' – Samuel Kerich, *Memoirs of a Royal Chaplain* 1729–1763, p. 25.

Postulant A name given to a person undergoing the first period of preparation for taking monastic vows.

Praemonstratensian Canons An order founded *c.*1130 and sometimes termed the white canons. They wore cassock and tunic and round cap, with a long cloak and hood, all of which were white. The abbots did not use any episcopal insignia.

Prebendary A clergyman attached to a cathedral of the old foundation or to a collegiate church, who formerly enjoyed a prebend (Latin *praebenda* – a stipend). The modern title is honorary canon.

Precentor (also Cantor) The leader of the choir, taking a personal care of the music of the church. The only precentors now recognized by the Anglican Church are those of cathedral and collegiate churches.

Processional An office book containing litanies, hymns, etc., for use in religious ceremonies.

Pudding-sleeved Gown A gown with a large bulging sleeve drawn in at the wrist, which was adopted by Protestant clergy.

Presbyterians Founded 1662. There was a definite Presbyterian Church set up in Wandsworth as early as 1572 but it was promptly suppressed. Initially close to the Anglican Church as they believed in a national church, they did not approve of the higher offices such as bishops and archbishops. Despite their support for the new established Church they found no concessions were made to their feelings about the episcopacy at the Restoration of the Monarchy. The Unitarians can be considered heirs to the early English Presbyterians. The Presbyterian Church of Scotland which was organized within the nineteenth century has its antecedents within Scotland.

93 Praemonstratensians: a canon regular of the order of Praemonstre. This canon is carrying the fur almuce on his left arm in the traditional manner of canons. He wears a form of surplice and a high formal type of biretta.

Purificator A small square of linen used to wipe the Eucharistic vessels.

Pyx A receptacle for either relics or the reserved sacraments.

Quakers (1650–56; also Society of Friends, Pennsylvania 1682) The organization of the Society of Friends grew up naturally with meetings held to exercise restraint upon promiscuous preaching, but without the formal constraints of the established Church in services and ceremonies. The three-fold hierarchy of bishop, priest and deacon has a counterpart among Friends – ministers, elders, and overseers. The Society of Friends developed a recognizable distinctive form of dress from the beginning, eschewing the elaborate, decorated, be-ribboned fashions of the day and preferring simple clothes with no ribbons or buttons, made of sensible, usually dark, fabrics. The men wore their hats uncocked, that is to say the wide brim was not tied or pinned up to the crown in the manner of a tricorne or a bicorne and this distinctive fashion was often mentioned by contemporary writers. Special provision was made for Quakers by the Toleration Act 1688.

Rationale Anciently worn by bishops, it has been so long obsolete that it is hard positively to identify it. It was worn upon the breast by bishops at Mass in imitation of the ephod (q.v.) of Levitical priests.

Regnum See *Tiara.*

Religious This term is sometimes used as a substantive word, in the Roman Catholic Church, for persons engaged by solemn vows to the monastic life.

Reliquary A receptacle for relics.

94 Rochet: William Boyd Carpenter, Bishop of Ripon. This photograph taken in the 1870s shows William Boyd Carpenter in the rochet of the Anglican bishop, with the chimere and scarf. The sleeves, although still full, are not of the extreme size of the eighteenth and early nineteenth centuries. The rochet covers the cassock and is made of white linen.

Rhabdos (Eastern Orthodox; also Bakteria, Dikanikion) A non-liturgical staff – an episcopal attribute and generally a sign of authority.

Ring Worn on the third finger of the right hand, the ring is a token of spiritual marriage with the Church by all those in holy orders. Rings grew to be of very large proportions and when worn with gloves were put on over the top. They were worn from the seventh century or even earlier.

Rochet The rochet, the surplice and the cotta are three developments from the alb that formed choir dress to be worn over the cassock. The rochet is now worn by bishops and clerical dignitaries and took the form of an overgarment with either narrow sleeves or no sleeves at all. Its purpose originally was to serve as a dustcoat. In the thirteenth century it was in general use by clergy, sacristans and servers but it became the prerogative of bishops, cardinals and canons regular. The rochet of the Anglican bishop (worn under the chimere) acquired full lawn sleeves, gathered at the wrist, which became so voluminous in the eighteenth century that they were sewn on to the chimere. Bishops apparently abandoned the rochet and chimere as their ordinary dress after the Great Rebellion (1647) and adopted ordinary clerical dress for everyday wear, retaining the rochet and chimere for more formal occasions.

Rochetta The Roman Catholic version of the rochet, a tunic of fine linen or lace, falling a little below the knees, having sometimes tight sleeves and sometimes none. It was worn by cardinals, archbishops, bishops and some canons regular.

Rosary A set of 150 beads divided into 15 groups or decades of 10 beads each. Usually the decades are separated by one larger bead. Attached to this string there are five other beads, two large and three small and a crucifix; this is a complete rosary. The rosary in common use has only five decades.

Rural Dean An ancient title in the Church of England. The chief duty is to visit a certain

95 Rosary, enamelled gold. English, late fifteenth century. This rosary consists of 50 oval Ave beads, six lozenge-shaped Paternoster beads and a large rounded knob. These are decorated with small figures of saints.

96 Saccos: The First Council of Nicaea, 325, by Michel Damaskinos. Dignitaries of the Church are seated here wearing the saccos with various styles of decoration. They are wearing the omophorion or pallium, folded and draped over their shoulders with the ends falling front and back; the ends of the orarium and stole appear below the hem of the saccos, over the alb or sticharion.

number of parishes and report to the bishop.

Saccos (Eastern Orthodox; also Sakkos)   A garment resembling the dalmatic but worn only by the highest dignitaries. Originally a penitential garment, it had become a peculiarly solemn vestment in the thirteenth century and lost its original associations, and became reserved to the patriarch. By the fifteenth century it was worn by all archbishops. There are a great many variations of decoration in the saccos, as there are on the polystavrion (q.v.): discrete crosses, an overall pattern of black and white crosses, crosses in circles, crosses formed in gammas (the Greek letter Γ). It is square in shape, cut away at the sides and with relatively short sleeves.

Samite   A very rich silk material, either a velvet or a silk interwoven with gold, or worked in embroidery. It was used during the Middle Ages.

Sandal   See *Sendall*.

Sandals

1 Leather or cloth straps holding a protective sole in place, worn by monks and friars, even when they were officially 'discalced'.
2 Liturgical shoes worn by bishops, archbishops, cardinals and the Pope, made of cloth or leather in the colours of the day.

Sacerdotal Of priestly duties, vestments etc., from the Latin *sacerdos*, a priest.

Sarcenet (also Sarsenet) A fine soft silk fabric. The word is derived from the medieval Latin *pannus saracenicus*, literally 'saracen cloth'. It was translated as 'taffetas' by Palsgrave in 1530.

Say A cloth of fine texture resembling serge, until the sixteenth century sometimes partly of silk, subsequently entirely of wool. As a wool cloth it was used for linings, by the religious (q.v.) for shirts, and by the Quakers for aprons, for which purpose it was usually dyed green.

Scapula (also Scapular) A tabard worn over the habit, which comes in many shapes. Originally one length of fabric with a hole for the head, it is generally worn outside the girdle.

Scarlet Cloth The most expensive form of woollen cloth.

Sceptre The staff in British coronation regalia.

Sendall (also Sandal) A light thin stuff of silk or linen. When it means linen or lawn it was often used for a shroud or as a dressing for wounds. The Biblical origins mean linen (σινδον fine linen). 'And the body taken, Jospeh wrapped it in a clene sendel, or lynnen cloth' (Matthew 27:59, Wycliffe Bible).

Sindon A fine thin fabric of linen, a kind of cambric or muslin, sometimes interchangeable with sendal (q.v.). 'Joseph taking the body, wrapt

97 Scapula: 'Hanging out the Clothes'. The scapula is worn as a protective covering when the monk or nun is at work or abroad. The hood here is attached to the scapula; it is generally attached to the uppermost garment worn. Here the scapular is kept in place by the narrow leather belt.

it in cleane sindon' (Matthew 27:59, Rheims Bible).

Soutane (also Sottane) Generally Roman Catholic. A long black cassock (q.v.) with a single row of small buttons down the front.

Square Cap (also Canterbury Cap) A square cap that developed in the fifteenth century and was adopted by churchmen in the new Anglican Church. It was discarded when the clerical wig became regularly worn, and was re-introduced at the end of the nineteenth century.

Stauros (Eastern Orthodox) A pectoral cross.

Sticharion (Eastern Orthodox) A long tunic worn by all ranks of the clergy and others involved in the ceremonies. It corresponds to the alb and is sometimes purple rather than white.

Stole (also Stola, Orarium) A narrow strip of material worn over the shoulders in various ways as an indication of the rank of the wearer. The Christian origins are derived directly from a scarf worn by Roman officials as a sign of rank – the stole and pallium have a common origin as a status symbol. In the Theodosian Codex 395 senators and consuls were ordered to wear a coloured scarf or pall over the alb and paenula as a badge of office. Dignitaries in the Church probably adopted it at the same time – and had already forbidden the wearing of an orarium to the minor order of sub-deacons in 372 at the Council of Laodicea. Religious symbolism soon appeared: in the first half of the sixth century Isidore of Pelusium said that the orarium in white wool was a symbol of the lost sheep around the good shepherd's shoulders (see p. 19). A priest wears the stole around the back of his neck and when worn over the alb it is crossed on the breast and held in place with the girdle; over a surplice the ends are allowed to hang down vertically. A bishop always wears his stole in the latter manner and has the pallium over, not under, the chasuble. The deacon wears a stole over the left shoulder and joined at the right side. In origin it is probably a napkin or towel and occurs in pagan representations of religious and domestic service, but perhaps had already passed out of practical use when it was adapted as the distinctive attribute of deacons. In the ninth century the stola received by deacons at ordination was the same vesture as the orarium (the priest's and deacon's equivalent of the pallium of

the bishop). As with other vestments of the Church, the stole was originally a plain fabric but in the tenth century it had become a very elaborate piece, a fine example being St Cuthbert's stole and maniple (c. 909–16). As it became customary to embellish the stole so the ends became wide to accommodate the decoration; in the Baroque period the stole became very short. When stoles came to be made of coloured material they were originally, like orphreys and apparels, in contrast to the colours of the vest-

98 Soutane: two priests in the south of France. The soutane is distinguishable by the single row of buttons down the centre front. The neckband is cut so as to reveal the clerical collar and although the soutane is perfectly acceptable as outdoor wear it can be covered by a coat or black wool cope or cloak when the weather is cold.

99 Stole: Marriage of Philip Duke of Burgundy to Marguerite, daughter of Louis, Count of Flanders. The tonsured priest is wearing the plain alb (with no apparels) and amice and girdle. The stole is worn in the correct manner for a priest, crossed over the breast and held in place by the girdle, which is worn low on the waist in an old-fashioned conservative manner when compared with the higher waistline of the bridegroom. The priest is not wearing the chasuble and maniple which are specifically Eucharistic vestments and would only be worn if he was officiating at the altar.

ment, but in the post-Reformation period when the sequence of liturgical colours was stabilized, stoles were worn in the same colour as the chasuble or dalmatic. In the evangelical sector of the Anglican Church the stole is the only item of the early suit of liturgical vestments which is generally found acceptable. In the nineteenth century during the Gothic revival stoles were again lengthened and commonly decorated with three crosses (not a very Gothic form of decoration) one in the centre back (which a high churchman would kiss before putting it on) and one at each end. The stole was often made with the maniple but when that passed out of general use the stole continued as an unbroken link with the clothing worn in the time of the first Christians by secular man.

Subcingulum
1 A girdle.
2 An ornamental addition to the bishop's girdle which hung down upon the left side.

Sub-deacon
The first of the Roman Catholic minor orders whose offices in church are to wash the altar cloths and corporals; to give the chalice and paten to the deacon at the proper times; generally to minister to the deacon in the Mass; and to chant the epistle. Sub-deacons wear the tunicle.

100 Surplice: St Christopher's Church choir, 1954. Short surplices over cassocks have been a very popular style of dress for church choirs in the twentieth century.

Succingtorium
A sash worn by bishops and high officials in addition to the girdle.

Sudarium
(also Sudary, Pannus, Offertory Veil)
1 A scarf of silk or linen which was cast about the shoulders and in the ends of which the hands of those who carried certain objects ceremonially were muffled.
2 See *Vexillum*.

Superhumeral
In the Old Testament this word is the usual translation for the ephod. It is sometimes used for the archbishop's pallium and sometimes for the amice.

Surplice
The surplice is a modification of the alb and worn over the cassock. It grew fuller with wider sleeves, originally to accommodate the fur-lined cassock or gown worn by the clergy in colder northern countries. As such it was shorter than the cassock and not girt at the waist and retained this form even after the cassock became a

much slimmer garment. In the eleventh century the surplice replaced the alb for non-Eucharistic worship and continues to be worn to the present day. With the cotta and the rochet it has remained pure white and is a liturgical garment although not blessed. Worn by all degrees of clergy, it was ordained for the priest and lower clergy in the Church of England in 1552 when the alb, vestment and cope were abolished. The surplice is also worn by those not ordained, i.e. the vergers, choristers and servers.

Syrian Church   The Syrian liturgy is possibly the oldest formal liturgy and was supposed to have been composed by St James the Less, the first bishop of Jerusalem. The Syrian Jacobites derive their name from another James (Baradeus) who died in 578. Vestments include:

Kuthino: a long flowing tunic which may be of any colour and can be composed of linen, cotton or silk. It corresponds to the alb.

Zunnoro: a cincture or girdle of embroidered stuff and secured by two clasps. It is not worn by the lower orders.

Uroro: stole; a broad strip of material with an aperture of the head, elaborately adorned and covered with crosses. The priest wears it after the Byzantine fashion, the deacon wears his on the left shoulder falling to the hem before and behind, rather like the Russians. The archdeacon wears it in the Latin fashion secured on the right-hand side; the sub-deacon, on the left shoulder with hanging part behind, brought around under the right arm and thrown back over the left shoulder. Readers wear the stole around the waist, with the two ends crossed and then brought up over the breast and tucked behind in the part that forms the belt.

Zendo: the cuffs on the alb.

Phaino: a cope-like garment corresponding to the chasuble.

Masnaphto: the hood worn by Syrian bishops. When the mitre is worn the hood is folded across the shoulders.

Mitre: worn by Catholic Syrian bishops.

Eskhimo or *schema:* a small hood, which varies considerably in decoration. It is worn by both Catholic and Jacobite bishops.

Aba: a black cassock worn by Jacobite secular priests together with a wide-sleeved open gown.

Kawock: a black turban worn with the aba.

Tarbush: a black head covering ornamented with seven white crosses. It is worn by Jacobite priests during the liturgy, removed at the Gospel and from the Preface until the Ablutions.

Sushepo: Syrian bishops bless the faithful with a small hand cross to which is attached a veil. This is carried in the right hand and kept in a small pocket.

Tassels   Tassels are used for the ties of dalmatics and tunicles, sometimes for the ends of stoles, maniples or gloves, and generally at the ends of a girdle, or cord. See p. 39 for the rare use of this word to describe solid ornaments used possibly to attach the morse to the cope.

Tiara (also Regnum)   The triple papal crown – processional headgear for the Pope. The domed hat with single crown was worn by Pope Innocent III (1198–1216) and was an emblem of the temporal power of the Pope. Boniface VIII

101 Tiara: captured Templars before Pope Clement and Philip IV. The triple tiara of the Pope is worn for civil and temporal occasions and not for religious ceremonies. Here Pope Clement with a cardinal and the king with an advisor are sitting in judgement on the Knights Templars brought before them. The Pope is wearing a fur-lined cappa with a large matching hood and has no vestments or ornaments of his sacred office.

(1294–1303) added the second crown and Urban V (1362–1370) completed its decoration with the final coronal.

Tippet and Hood The tippet is the long black scarf worn by clergy over the surplice. The exact origin of this is obscure although it is probably derived from the medieval hood, the extensions of the cape hanging down the front being the tippet and the poke hanging at the back becoming the hood. In any case the hood and scarf would appear to be separated parts of the same garment just as the collar and tie are derived from the single neckerchief. The tippet and hood replaced the almuce by the sixteenth century and became recognizable wear of the new Church of England. In the fifteenth century the hood was commonly worn over the surplice, and was adopted by the universities as a token of graduation. It was given distinctive colours and linings and was accepted in its academic form in the emergent Anglican Church as part of the choir habit of the clergy. In 1549 the Book of Common Prayer recommends the hood as 'seemly' for preachers. In 1604 canons XXV and LVII order it for all graduate ministers, and non-graduates are ordered to wear a tippet instead. Canon LXXIV orders all clergy to wear a tippet over a gown as outdoor wear, and the tippet and hood became established wear. In the nineteenth century when the high church movement moved back to the wearing of vestments the original tractarians were conservative and both Keble and Newman celebrated in surplice and hood at the north end of the altar.

Tonsure A shaved head – a preparatory rite, or disposition for receiving orders.

Trinitarian Friars (also Maturines) An order who dressed in white, with an eight-pointed cross of blue and red.

102 Vexillum: the St Hubert crozier. Flemish, mid-sixteenth century. The small bishop in the centre of this pastoral staff is shown in chasuble, dalmatic alb and amice, with mitre and crozier; hanging from this is the vexillum, the cloth which protected the precious metal from the perspiration of the hand, and helped the grip of the bishop.

Tunica Alba See *Alb*.

Tunicle The tunicle is a variant with the dalmatic of the *alba dalmatica*. An overgarment with sleeves, it became in the ninth century the vestment of the sub-deacon and although originally completely plain (without the clavi of the dalmatic) it followed, to a lesser extent, the chasuble and dalmatic in becoming richer and more elaborate. By the ninth century it was generally accepted as the lowest ranking vestment, but bishops sometimes adopted the practice of wearing the tunicle under the dalmatic on solemn occasions. The tunicle was clearly distinguishable as a mid-way garment between the alb and the dalmatic by the tenth century but it came to be cut on the same principle as the dalmatic. Its history, as a vestment, follows that of the chasuble and dalmatic and it has always remained in the third rank.

Turkey Gown Originally a long straight gown assumed to have come from Turkey, made in any colour cloth, especially red. As a simple gown in black it was adopted by the Puritans in the sixteenth century to replace the more usual academic gowns. 'They [the Puritan divines] appeared before his Maiestie in Turky gownes, not in their scholastical habites, sorting to their degrees' (Bishop William Barlow, Hampton Court conference ii:27, 1603–4).

Umbrella The plain black umbrella became a familiar item carried by the nineteenth-century parson. Umbrellas were especially necessary at funerals where the service was held out of doors whatever the weather. The parish accounts at St John's Chester, contain the following entries:

1729	Paid Mr George Marsh for an umbrella for the parish use	00 10 6°
1786	Paid for an umbrella for Mr Richardson to read the Burial Service under	1 6 0°

This indicates that the clergy adopted the umbrella before it became a fashionable item for gentlemen.

Unitas Fratum (also Moravians) The oldest

surviving Protestant community, the Moravian Church, formed in Bohemia in 1457. At a conference at Friedberg (17 November 1747) Zinzendorf suggested that a white robe should be worn for special occasions, to remind the Brethren of Revelations 7: 9–13 and therefore the surplice was worn for the first time at a Holy Communion, at Herrnhaag, on 2 May 1748. This is the origin of the use of the surplice by modern Moravians, and the minister generally wears it at the sacraments, at weddings and at ordinations; yet there is no reference to vestments in the regulation of the Church.

Velum   The veil placed over a nun's head at the time of her dedication.

Vestis   A gown or closed tunic girt at the waist.

Vestments   Articles of clothing worn by ecclesiastics or by certain of their assistants during divine service or special occasions. The term can mean a complete set or just the chasuble.

Vexillum (also Orarium, Sudarium)   The scarf of linen or silk affixed to the crozier or the cross staff immediately below the cross head or the crook, in use as early as the tenth century.

Vicar General

1 The title assumed by or bestowed upon the Pope, as head of the Church under Christ.

2(a) Roman Catholic – an ecclesiastical officer, usually a cleric appointed by a bishop or his representative in matters of jurisdiction or administration.

 (b) Church of England – a permanent lay official serving as a deputy or assistant to a bishop, or to the Archbishop of Canterbury or York, in certain ecclesiastical causes. (This title was given to Oliver Cromwell in 1535 as a representative of the king in ecclesiastical affairs.)

White Garments   See *Baptismal garments*.

Wig   Aopted by all the clergy in the seventeenth century in common with men of all professions and not abandoned completely until the 1830s. (NB The legal profession in Britain still retains the wig.)

Zimmara   A large thick riding cloak. It is associated with the origins of the chimere.

Zona   A narrow scarf worn by some canons.

Zone   A girdle which is fastened by a clasp rather than tied.

Notes to the Text

Chapter 1, pp. 11–12

1 'Sub Tiberio quies', Tacitus, *histories* v:9. Philo does not mention the Crucifixion in his critical analysis of the career of Pontius Pilate which he wrote not much later than AD 41.
2 *Adversus Haereses* IV:30:3.
3 E.L. Cutts, *History of Early Christian Art*, 1893, p. 9; 'Recognitions of Clement' viii:6.
4 W. Lowrie, *Art and Archaeology of the Early Church*, 1901, p. 391.
5 W. B. Marriott, *Vestiarium Christianium*, 1868, p. 194.
6 Lowrie, op. cit., p. 398.
7 Marriott, op. cit., p. 195f.
8 Lowrie, op. cit., p. 399.
9 J. R. H. Moorman, *The History of the Church of England*, 1973, p. 3.
10 Moorman, op. cit., p. 4. Moorman says the date is generally assumed to have been 304, during the persecution of Diocletian. Charles Thomas in *Britain and Ireland in Early Christian Times*, 1971, p. 72, says *c.* 250 and refers to John Morris dating it as early as 209.
11 Heiron, *Adv. Palagianos*, lib. 1: cap. 9.
12 Marriott, op. cit., p. xviif.
13 *De Habitu Muliebri*, cap. 8. Marriott, op. cit., p. 185.
14 *Paedag.*, lib. ii: p. 233. Marriott, op. cit., p. 184.
15 R. A. S. Macalister, *Ecclesiastical Vestments: their Development and History*, 1896, pp. 17, 18, quoted from Marriott, op. cit., p. 42f.
16 *Etymologiae*, lib. XIX: cap. xxii (Migne, lxxxii:635).
17 *Acta S. Cyp.*, prop. fin. (Migne, *Patrologia*, 1857, vol. iii: col. 1504).
18 Eusebius, *Ecclesiastical History* vi:3:9.
19 W. H. C. Frend, *The Early Church*, 1965, p. 202. Athanasius, *Life of Antony*.
20 Frend, op. cit., p. 203.
21 Cutts, op. cit., p. 143
22 *De Habitu Monachorum* 1:7. Macalister, op. cit.
23 Isadore of Pelusium, *Epist. Lib.* cap. 136. Marriott, op. cit., p. 50.
24 Lowrie, op. cit., p. 407f.
25 *Council Narb.* i, Labbe vol. v: col. 1030. See also Macalister, op. cit., p. 235f.
26 Macalister, op. cit., p. 208.
27 Macalister, op. cit., p. 207.
28 Macalister, op. cit., p. 40.
29 Ep. 85, Migne XXII 754. Lowrie, op. cit., p. 387.

Chapter 2, pp. 23–32

1 Marriott, op. cit., p. 68. See also Macalister, op. cit., p. 113.
2 William of Malmesbury, *De Gestis Pontificum Anglorum* (ed. N. E. S. A. Hamilton Rolls Series, III, 1870).
3 ibid. See also E. S. Duckett, *Anglo-Saxon Saints and Scholars*, 1947, p. 79.
4 W. Farquhar Hook, *The Lives of the Archbishops of Canterbury*, vol. I, 1860.
5 H. Howarth, *The Golden Days of the Early English Church*, vol. I, 1917, p. 288.
6 Howarth, op. cit., p. 352.
7 Duckett, op. cit., p. 113.
8 Duckett, op. cit., p. 63.
9 Duckett, op. cit., pp. 421, 422.
10 Marriott, op. cit., pp. 75, 76.
11 ibid.
12 Macalister, op. cit., p. 41.
13 Howarth, op. cit., p. 45.
14 *Relics of St Cuthbert*, Durham Cathedral, Bathscombe, 1956.
15 ibid. See C. Hohler, *The Iconography*.
16 A. F. Kendrick, *English Embroidery*, 1900, p. 8.
17 ibid., p. 134.
18 Duckett, op. cit. p. 81. William of Malmesbury, op. cit.
19 Duckett, op. cit., p. 400.
20 A. W. Hadden and W. Stubbs, *Councils and Ecclesiastical Documents relating to Great Britain and Ireland*, vol. III, p. 264.
21 Macalister, op. cit., p. 49f.
22 Howarth, op. cit., p. 74.
23 Macalister, op. cit., p. 93f.
24 Marriott. op. cit., p. 221, and Macalister, op. cit., p. 112f.
25 Marriott, op. cit., p. 88.
26 E. L. Cutts, *Parish Priests and their People in the Middle Ages*, 1898, pp. 66–7.

Chapter 3, pp. 33–46

1 Rt Rev. Dom Paul Delatte, *The Rule of St Benedict*, translated by Dom Justin McCann, 1921.
2 Delatte, op. cit., p. 346f.

3 ibid. *S. Greg. M. Dial* 1:11:ci.

4 ibid.

5 ibid.: 'cuculla, tunica, pedules, caligae, bracile, cultellus, graphium, acus, mappula, tabulae'.

6 ibid. (*Epist.* L:I Ep. XXVIII, PLCLXXXIX, 123).

7 Richard Winston, *Thomas Becket*, 1967, p. 216; *Materials* 11:293.

8 *The Benedictines in Britain*, British Library, p. 79.

9 Ollard and Crosse, *Dictionary of English Church History*, 1919. *Speculum Ecclesiae*, Brewers translation.

10 M. Davenport, *The Book of Costume*, vol. 1, 1948, p. 100.

11 Winston, op. cit., p. 216.

12 ibid. *Materials* 111:147.

13 Gasquett, *Henry III and the Church*, 1905, pp. 328–9; Matthew Paris, v. 275.

14 P. Compton, *The Great Religious Orders*, 1931, p. 161.

15 R. W. Southern, *Western Society and the Church in the Middle Ages*, 1970, p. 249, taken from an account of the foundation of Lanthony Abbey, W. Dugdale, *Monasticon Anglicanum*, 1830 vi, pp. 128–34.

16 R. M. Clay, *The Hermits and Anchorites of England*, 1914, p. 120.

17 Sacheverell Sitwell, *Monks, Nuns and Monasteries*, 1965, p. 131.

18 M. Gibson, *Lanfranc of Bec*, Oxford 1978; *Lanfranci Epp.* 13.

19 '1371–2 De una cappa venerabilis Lanfranci cremata et de diversis Jocalibis fusis vendetis. cxvj. li. vj. s. viij. d.' J. Wickham Legg and W. H. St John Hope, *Inventories of Christ Church Canterbury*, 1902, p. 13.

20 Gasquett op cit., p. 250; Matthew Paris iv: 546.

21 E. Bishop, *Liturgica Historica*, 1918, p. 268.

22 Bishop, op. cit., p. 274; *Chron. Monast. de Abingdon*, ed. Stevenson ii:151.

23 Bishop. op. cit., p. 267; '*De Sacr. Altaris Myst.*'

24 Bishop. op. cit., p. 269; *Gemma Animae* i:c:227.

25 Bishop, op. cit., p. 263.

26 Bishop, op. cit., pp. 265, 267.

27 D. Rock, *The Church of Our Fathers*, 1849–52, p. 41.

28 Legg and Hope, op. cit., p. 14.

29 Legg and Hope, op. cit., pp. 14, 16, 17.

30 Rev. T. A. Lacey in *St Paul's Ecclesiological Society Transactions*, 1900, vol. iv: p. 126f.

31 C. C. Rolfe, *The Ancient Use of Liturgical Colours*, 1879, p. 94.

32 Marriott, op. cit., p. 125.

33 'Sacred Vestments and Insignia' in *Gemma Animae*, lib. 1: cap. 89.

34 A. W. N. Pugin, *Glossary of Ecclesiastical Ornament and Costume*, 1868.

35 Rock, op. cit., p. 99. Millia Davenport in *The Book of Costume*, 1948, says that Clement V, 1314, first wore the tiara with three crowns.

36 Marriott, op. cit., pp. 133, 190. Hugo of Sancto Victore (1096–1140) Sermo XIV: fom 11: p. 222.

37 Legg and Hope, op. cit., p. 13.

38 Anna Maria Muthesius, 'Silks from the tomb', in BAA *Conference Transactions*, 1979; and 'On the tomb of an Archbishop recently opened in the Cathedral Church of Canterbury', W. H. St John Hope, 1893, p. 4f.

39 Rock, op. cit., p. 296f.

40 Legg and Hope, op. cit., p. 17.

41 Hope, op. cit., p. 4.

42 Rolfe, op. cit. p. 93.

43 Hope, op. cit., p. 4.

44 Pugin, op. cit.

45 Rock, op. cit., p. 53.

46 Rolfe, op. cit., p. 93f.

47 Rolfe, op. cit., p. 92.

48 Pugin, op. cit.

49 ibid.

50 Hope, op. cit., p. 6.

Chapter 4, pp. 47–61

1 *The Inventories of Christ Church Canterbury*, ed. J. Wickham Legg and W. H. St John Hope, 1902; *The Inventories of the Parish Church of St Peter Mancroft, Norwich*, W. H. St John Hope, 1901; Norfolk Record Society, *Archdeaconry of Norwich, Inventory of Church Goods temp Edward III*; Dom Aelr'ed Watkin, vol. XIX, parts 1 and 2, 1948; *St Paul's Cathedral Church Inventory* 1245; and many others quoted in Hope and Atchley, *English Liturgical Colours*, 1918.

2 Rev. T. A. Lacey, 'The Ecclesiastical Habit in England' in *St Paul's Ecclesiological Society Transactions*, 1900 vol. IV, p. 126.

3 ibid.

4 J. Carter, *Specimens of English Ecclesiastical Costume*, 1817, p. 424.

5 Sitwell, op. cit., p. 40.

6 ibid. (modernized spelling from Sitwell).

7 O. J. Reichel, *English Liturgical Vestments in the 13th Century*, 1895, p. 13ff.

8 ibid.

9 Rock, op. cit., p. 285.

10 O. J. Reichel, 'Forma Degradandi Clericum' in Maskell's *Monumenta Rituli* (ed. 1882), vol. ii, p. 333.

11 E. L. Cutts, *Parish Priests and their People in the Middle Ages in England*, 1898, p. 239.

12 Joan Evans, *English Art 1307–1461*, 1949, p. 159n.; Dugdale, *The History of St Paul's Cathedral*, 1658, ed. H. Ellis, 1818.

13 Norfolk Record Society, vol. XIX, parts 1 and 2, 1948.

14 ibid. 'Item unum bonum superpelicium manicatum, ex collacione dui Galfridi [Geoffrey Jekkes] nuper eectoris cum littera G in pectore.'

15 Matthew Paris, book IV: 546.

16 Thomas Walsingham, *Gesta Abbatum Monasterii Sancti Albani AD 793–1290*, ed. H. T. Riley, Rolls Service 1, London 1867, p. 127.

17 Evans, op. cit., p. 18.

18 ibid. p. 17, and Maud Hall, *English Church Needlework*, 1913, p. 15.

19 Hall, op. cit., p. 14.

20 Donald King, *Opus Anglicanum English Medieval Embroideries*, 1963, p. 39.

21 Eileen Roberts, 'St William of York mural in St Alban's Abbey and Opus Anglicanum' in *Burlington Magazine*,

May 1968, 110: 236–41.

22 Sitwell, op. cit., p. 39.

23 Hall, op. cit., p. 139.

24 Gasquett, *Wills, Chantries and Bequests*, p. 287ff.; *Testamenta Eboracensia* (Surtees Society), vol. iv, p. 69.

25 Legg and Hope, op. cit., p. 20.

26 Norfolk Record Society, vol. XIX, parts 1 and 2, 1948.

27 Evans, op. cit., p. 56; Dugdale, *The History of St Paul's Cathedral*, 1658, ed. H. Ellis, 1818.

28 Dr M. R. James, Magdalene College Cambridge, Ms. 1916, in the Walpole Society Journal, XIII: i, p. 7.

29 Evans, op. cit.

30 C. R. Dodwell, *The Canterbury School of Illumination*, p. 76.

31 ibid., pp. 75–7.

32 Evans, op. cit., p. 38.

33 Norfolk Record Society. Disputes in 1315 about the regulation of the worsted trade show how far this branch of the clothing industry had developed; see Cunningham, *Growth of English Industry and Commerce*, p. 193.

34 W. H. St John Hope and Atchley, *An Introduction to English Liturgical Colours*, 1918, p. 21f.

35 Hope and Atchley, op. cit., p. 32.

36 W. H. St John Hope, *The Episcopal Ornaments of William of Wykeham and of William of Waynefleet Bishops of Winchester and of certain bishops of St Davids*, 1907, p. 466.

37 Legg and Hope, op. cit., p. 101. Ornaments and jewels acquired or repaired in the time of Thomas Chillenden, Prior, 1390–1411.

38 H. J. Feasey, *Ancient English Holy Week Ceremonial*, 'Charitulary of Warwick College f.ccijb' (Public Record Office).

39 Hope and Atchley, op. cit., p. 32.

40 C. L. Feltoe and H. E. Minus, eds, *1277 Inventory of churches and chapels in Cambridgeshire in the visitation book of Ralph Walpole, Archdeacon of Ely. Vetus Liber Archidiaconi Eliensis* (Camb. Antiqu. Soc. 8vo publns., no. xlviii, 1917).

41 Hope and Atchley, op. cit., p. 28.

42 ibid.; *1220 Visitations of the prebendal churches of Salisbury by Dean William de Wanda.* Register of St Osmund, Rolls Series 78, 1. 275.

43 Feasey, op. cit.

44 Macalister, op. cit., p. 77. See also C. Hohler's article on St Cuthbert's stole and maniple.

45 Macalister, op. cit., p. 65.

46 *Vetusta Monumenta* vii, p. 4 and pl. iv.

47 *Ecclesiastical Vestments in the Middle Ages – An Exhibition*, Metropolitan Museum Bulletin XXIV, 285–317, March 1971, gift of J. Pierpoint Morgan.

48 Feasey, op. cit. *Ecclesiologist* XX: 311–13.

49 W. Andrews, *Curiosities of the Church; Studies of Curious Customs, Services and Records*, 1890, p. 2.

50 W. H. St John Hope, *Episcopal Ornaments*, p. 483f.

51 Legg and Hope, op. cit., p. 22.

52 W. H. St John Hope, *Episcopal Ornaments*, p. 474.

53 Legg and Hope, op. cit., p. 101.

54 Robert Wyst Jackson, 'Mitre and Crozier of Bishop Cornelius O'Dea of Limerick' in *Connoisseur* 171: 149–51, July 1969.

55 Rev. N. F. Robinson, 'The Pileus Quadratus – priest square cap' in *St Paul's Ecclesiological Society Transactions*, vol. v, 1901.

Chapter 5, pp. 62–68

1 *St Paul's Ecclesiological Society Transactions*, vol. III, 1895. J. Wickham Legg, 'The black scarf of modern church dignitaries and the grey almuce of medieval canons' in *Archeologia*, 1890, vol. iii, p. 214.

2 The English Prayer Book issued to supersede the Latin service books 'in the second year of the reign of King Edward the Sixth', 1549.

3 Legg and Hope, op. cit., p. 188.

4 Dr Jessup, *Parish Life in England before the Great Pillage*, 'Nineteenth Century', March 1898, p. 433.

5 F. A. Gasquett, *The Eve of the Reformation*, p. 335; *Archeologia*, vol. xli, p. 355.

6 Moorman, op. cit., p. 173ff., published in Record Commission in six volumes, 1810–34.

7 Gasquett, op. cit., p. 338.

8 Legg and Hope, op. cit., p. 186f.

9 P. H. Ditchfield, *The Old Time Parson*, p. 101.

10 Gasquett, op. cit., p. 60.

11 B. Anthony Bax, *The English Parsonage*, 1964, p. 51.

12 A. G. Dickens, *The Register of Butley Priory*, 1951.

13 A. G. Dickens, ed., *The Clifford Letters of the Sixteenth Century*, 1962.

14 A. G. Dickens, *The Register of Butley Priory*, 1951.

15 F. W. Fairholt, *Costume in England*, enlarged and revised by H. A. Dillon, vol. I, p. 264.

16 Ollard and Crosse, op. cit.

17 H. W. Cripps, *A practical treatise on the law relating to the clergy*, 6th edition, 1886, pp. 44, 49. (Note Enraght v. Lord Penzance 6. QBD 376, 7 App. Cas. 240.)

18 Moorman, op. cit., p. 184.

19 H. Littlehales, ed., *The Medieval Records of a London City Church (St Mary at Hill)*, 1905, pp. 395–403.

20 *Foxe's Book of Martyrs*, p. 396.

21 ibid., p. 325.

22 Gasquett. op. cit., p. 348. J. W. Cowper, 'Accounts of the Churchwardens of St Dunstan's Canterbury' in *Archeologia Cantiana*, 1885.

23 W. Andrews, *Curiosities of the Church*, 1890, p. 11.

24 Gasquett, op. cit., p. 342.

25 W. Andrews, op. cit., pp. 11, 12.

Chapter 6, pp. 69–76

1 Dyson Hague, *The Story of the English Prayer Book*, 1926, p. 204.

2 Wickham Legg, *Two unusual forms of linen vestments*, 1898, p. 145.

3 ibid., p. 141.

4 John Strype, *Annals of the Reformation and Re-establishment of Religion*, 1709, p. 171.

5 Strype, op. cit., p. 416f.

6 Legg and Hope, op. cit., p. 210.

7 W. Nicholson, ed., *The Remains of Edmund Grindal*, 1843, p. 5.

8 Patrick Collinson, *Archbishop Grindal 1519–1583, The*

Struggle for a Reformed Church, 1979, p. 171.

9 ibid., pp. 172, 173.

10 Fairholt, op. cit.

11 P. H. Ditchfield, *The Old Time Parson*, 1908, p. 49.

12 Dyson Hague, op. cit., p. 207.

13 ibid., p. 224.

14 Legg and Hope, op. cit., p. 237.

15 B. A. Bax, *The English Parsonage*, 1964, p. 62.

16 Legg and Hope, op. cit., p. 248.

17 Collinson, op. cit., p. 99.

18 ibid., pp. 21, 22.

19 ibid., p. 56f.

20 Collinson, op. cit., p. 167.

21 Rev. H. J. Clayton, *Cassock and Gown*, Alcuin Club Tracts, 1929, p. 7.

22 ibid.

23 H. Haines, *Manual of Monumental Brasses*, 1861.

24 Strype, *Annals*, 1:336.

25 Harding's *Confutation*, London 1570, p. 397.

26 Clayton, op. cit., pp. 1, 77.

27 P. H. Ditchfield, op. cit., pp. 313, 314.

28 Clayton, op. cit.

29 ibid.

30 Collinson, op. cit., p. 168.

31 Collinson, op. cit., p. 170.

32 A. L. Rowse, *The England of Elizabeth*, 1953, p. 500.

33 Moorman, op. cit., p. 243f.

34 Charles R. Beard, 'Liturgical Gloves in the collection of Mrs Philip Lehman' in *Connoisseur* 94: 226–30, October 1934.

35 Edith Appleton Standen, *The Bulrushes in the Waves*, Metropolitan Museum Bulletin XIV: 181–5, April 1956.

Chapter 7, pp. 77–91

1 Penelope Byrde, *The Male Image*, 1979, p. 33.

2 ibid.; and Diana de Marly, 'King Charles II's own fashion: the Theatrical Origins of the English Vest' in *Journal of the Warburg and Courtauld Institutes*.

3 Byrde, op. cit., p. 83.

4 James Woodforde, *The Diary of a Country Parson*, 5 vols. 1924–31.

5 J. Downey, *The Eighteenth Century Pulpit*, p. 86.

6 ibid., pp. 86, 87.

7 ibid., p. 210.

8 Byrde, op. cit., p. 163.

9 Fairholt, op. cit., p. 319.

10 ibid.

11 P. H. Ditchfield, *The Old Time Parson*, 1908, p. 315.

12 Fairholt, op. cit., pp. 329, 330.

13 Fairholt, op. cit., p. 327.

14 Ditchfield, op. cit., p. 315.

15 L. Tyerman, *The Life of Samuel Wesley*, p. 452.

16 Horace Walpole's letter to Lord Hertford, 12 February 1765; *Letters* vol. vi; p. 188.

17 W. Andrews, *Old Church Life*, 1900.

18 Rev. H. J. Clayton, *Cassock and Gown*, Alcuin Club Tracts, 1929.

19 J. Downey, *The Eighteenth Century Country Parson*, 1969, p. 11.

20 Henry Fielding, *Joseph Andrews*, 1742, Pan Classics 1956, p. 153.

21 Clayton, op. cit.

22 J. Wickham Legg, *Essays Liturgical and Historical*, 1917, p. 66f.

23 Clayton, op. cit.

24 Ditchfield, op. cit., p. 314.

25 Rev. Samuel Kerrich, *Memoirs of a Royal Chaplain, 1729–1763*, 1905, p. 15.

26 Ditchfield, op. cit., pp. 176, 177.

27 'The Disappointment', a play by Southern quoted by Fairholt, *Costume in England*.

28 Byrde, op. cit., p. 114ff.

29 Ditchfield, op. cit., pp. 135, 136.

30 Legg and Hope, op. cit., p. 274.

31 Legg and Hope, op. cit., pp. 302, 306.

32 J. Downey, *The Eighteenth Century Country Parson*, p. 94.

33 Wriothesley's Diary ii: 144, from Bumpus, *A Dictionary of Ecclesiastical Terms*, 1969.

34 Treasurer's Accounts 1724–5; *Officium Sacristae*, p. 69. Legg and Hope, op. cit., p. 289.

35 Bumpus, op. cit., p. 92.

36 Thoresby's Diary, quoted by Clement O. Skilbeck, *Illustrations of the Liturgy*, 1912, p. 9.

37 John Bossy, *The English Catholic Community 1570–1850*, 1975, pp. 250, 251.

38 Bossy, op. cit., p. 257.

39 Charles Chevenix Trench, *George II*, 1973, p. 154.

40 Brian Fothergill, *The Mitred Earl, an 18th Century Eccentric*, 1974 (Lord Cloncurry, *Personal Recollections*, p. 191).

41 Fothergill, op. cit., pp. 53, 97, 186, 237.

Chapter 8, pp. 92–110

1 George Eliot, *Scenes from Clerical Life*, 1858, p. 4.

2 Letter from the Archbishop of Canterbury, Thomas Secker, in 1759 to the bishops of his province, quoted by C. K. Francis Brown in *A History of the English Clergy, 1800–1900*, 1953.

3 *The Dress of the Clergy*, religious pamphlet published by Painter in the Strand. Bound in with various other pamphlets of 1840 and 1841 in Lambeth Palace Library.

4 Edward F. Carpenter and Arthur Hart, *The 19th Century Country Parson 1832–1900*, 1954.

5 Anthony Trollope, *The Warden*, 1855, p. 8.

6 S. Reynolds Hole, *More Memoirs*, p. 31, quoted by C. K. F. Brown in *A History of the English Clergy, 1800–1900*, 1953, p. 218.

7 James Laver, 'The Undress of the Clergy' in *The Country Life Annual*, 1955, p. 165.

8 Trollope, op. cit., p. 8.

9 Samuel Butler, *The Way of All Flesh*, 1903, pp. 97, 278.

10 Bumpus, op. cit., p. 30.

11 Rev. Frederick George Lee, *A Glossary of Liturgical and Ecclesiastical Terms*, 1877.

12 Trollope, op. cit., p. 18.

13 Trollope, op. cit., p. 64.

14 Trollope, op. cit., p. 41.

15 C. K. F. Brown, *A History of the English Clergy, 1800–1900*.

16 Lee, op. cit., p. 72.

17 Bumpus, op. cit., p. 55.

18 Rev. Percy Dearmer, *The Parson's Handbook*, first published 1899.

19 C. K. F. Brown, *A History of the English Clergy, 1800–1900*, p. 215.

20 P. Dearmer, op. cit., pp. 35, 136.

21 Carpenter and Hart, op. cit.

22 George Eliot, op. cit., pp. 2, 71.

23 C. K. F. Brown, op. cit., p. 217.

24 P. H. Ditchfield, *The Old Time Parson*, 1908, pp. 316, 317, also quoted by C. K. F. Brown, op. cit.

25 Samuel Butler, op. cit., p. 402.

26 Lee, op. cit., p. 391.

27 P. Dearmer, op. cit., p. 142.

28 Morris & Co., Decorators Ltd, *Catalogue of Church Ornaments*.

29 G. S. Tyack, *Historic Dress of the Clergy*, 1897, p. 64.

30 Canterbury Convocation: *Ornaments of the Church and Its Ministers*, 1908.

31 ibid.

32 Ollard and Crosse, *Dictionary of English Church History*, 1919, p. 182.

33 C. K. F. Brown, op. cit., p. 215.

34 C. K. F. Brown, op. cit., p. 216.

35 Tyack, op. cit., p. 44.

36 P. Dearmer, op. cit., p. 154.

37 J. T. Micklethwaite 'The meaning of the Ornaments Rubric so far as it affects Parish Churches' (in *St Paul's Ecclesiological Society Transactions*, vol. II, 1888, p. 324).

38 D. Hague, *The English Prayer Book*, 1926, p. 256.

39 Tyack, op. cit., p. 39.

40 C. K. F. Brown, op. cit., p. 216.

41 C. P. S. Clarke, *The Oxford Movement and After*, 1932, p. 15.

42 Georgina Battiscombe, *John Keble, A Study in Limitations*, 1963, p. 295.

43 Clarke, op. cit., p. 122.

44 Clarke, op. cit., p. 154.

45 Clarke, op. cit., p. 155. There is a chasuble made of cream taffeta lined with purple silk with a Y-shaped orphrey in yellow which belonged to Dr Pusey at the Society of the Holy Trinity, Ascot Priory.

46 Clarke, op. cit., p. 161.

47 Clarke, op. cit., p. 142, quoting from W. J. E. Bennett, *A farewell letter to his parishioners*, p. 85.

48 Clarke, op. cit., p. 162.

49 Bumpus, op. cit.

50 Clarke, op. cit., p. 138f.

51 Rev. Richard Seymour, *Diaries 1832–1873*, quoted in Carpenter and Hart, *The 19th Century Country Parson 1832–1900*, 1954, p. 116.

52 Clarke, op. cit., p. 186.

53 From a catalogue of a vestment exhibition held at St Barnabas Church, Oxford, to celebrate the 150th anniversary of the Oxford Movement, July 1983.

54 William Milton, *Sacrificial Vestments: Are they legal in the Church of England?*, 1866.

55 *Hierurgia Anglicana, Documents and Extracts illustrative of the ritual of the Church in England after the Reformation*, 1848.

56 Clarke, op. cit., p. 203f.

57 *The Ornaments of the Church and Its Ministers*, report on the Canterbury Convocation, 1908.

58 Francesca M. Steele, *Convents of Great Britain and Ireland*, 1901, describes all the habits and has many illustrations.

59 The catalogue of the vestment exhibition, held at St Barnabas Church, Oxford, July 1983.

60 *A Brief Sketch of the Morris Company* (on their 50th anniversary, 1911).

61 Anthea Callen, *The Angel in the Studio – Women in the Arts and Crafts Movement*, 1979, p. 102f.

62 ibid., p. 111.

63 Ditchfield, op. cit., p. 76.

Chapter 9, pp. 111–120

1 Quoted in A. M. Gummere, *The Quaker: A Study in Costume*, 1901, p. 5.

2 ibid., p. 64. *London Chronicle*, vol. XI: p. 167, 1762.

3 ibid., p. 7.

4 ibid., p. 68.

5 ibid.; and Alice Morse Earle, *Two Centuries of Costume in America*, 2 vols., 1903.

6 ibid., pp. 51, 52.

7 ibid., pp. 134, 135.

8 ibid., p. 43.

9 ibid., p. 14.

10 Robert Sandall, *The History of the Salvation Army*, vol. II, 1950, p. 42.

11 ibid., p. 43.

12 Reginald Woods, *Harvest of the Years*, 1960, p. 31.

13 Robert Sandall, op. cit., p. 48.

14 Janet Grierson, *The Deaconess*, 1981.

15 ibid., p. 62.

16 ibid., p. 63.

17 H. Graham Bennett, ed., *Dress worn by Gentlemen at His Majesty's Court and on Occasions of Ceremony*, 1903.

18 Tyack, op. cit., p. 111.

19 C. K. F. Brown, op. cit., p. 216.

20 R. P. Flundall, ed., *The Church of England, 1815–1948, A Documentary History*, 1972, p. 232.

21 ibid., p. 291. Moorman, op. cit., p. 403.

22 Moorman, op. cit., p. 417.

23 Alan Wilkinson, *The Church of England and the First World War*, 1978, p. 113.

24 H. Riley and R. J. Graham, eds, *Acts of the Convocations of Canterbury and York, 1921–1970*, 1971, p. 6.

25 Undated catalogue of Thomas Pratt & Sons Ltd.

26 *The Southwark Diocesan Gazette*, April 1938, p. 64.

27 Patrick Ferguson-Davie, *The Bishop in Church*, 1961.

28 ibid., pp. 7, 8.

Chapter 10, pp. 121–128

1 Walter Conan, *Ecclesiastical Dress from the French of Monsignor Barbier de Montault*, 1929.

2 ibid., p. 1.

3 Robert Lesage, *Vestments and Church Furniture*, 1960, p. 98.

4 An example of this can be found in Strangers Hall Museum, Norwich, in a cassock of the Blessed Sacrament Fathers.

5 This list is made up from two sources: Conan, *Ecclesiastical Dress from the French of Monsignor Barbier de Montault*, 1929, and Lesage, *Vestments and Church Furniture*, 1960. Where the information differs the date appears in brackets.

6 Lesage, op. cit., p. 147.

7 Lesage, op. cit., p. 148.

8 Lesage, op. cit., p. 110.

9 *The Code of Canon Law*, in English Translation, 1983, p. vii.

10 *Instructions on the Revised Roman Rites*, first published as a complete compilation in 1979, p. 136.

11 ibid., p. 137 (*Constitution of the Sacred Liturgy*, p. 128).

12 ibid., no. 305.

13 ibid., no. 306.

14 ibid., and p. 138, nos. 308, 309, 310.

Bibliography

Andrews, William, *Curiosities of the Church; studies of curious customs, services and records*, London, 1890

Andrews, William, *Old Church Life*, London, 1900

Anson, Peter, *Religious Orders and Congregations of Great Britain and Ireland*, Worcester, 1949

Ashdown, Emily, *British Costume during the Nineteenth Century (Civil and Ecclesiastical)*, London and Edinburgh, 1910

Bathscombe, *Relics of St Cuthbert*, Durham Cathedral, 1956

Bax, B. A., *The English Parsonage*, London, 1964

Bishop, E., *Liturgica Historica*, Oxford, 1918

Blunt, Rev. John Henry, *Dictionary of Sects, Heresies, Ecclesiastic Parties and Schools of Religious Thought*, London and Oxford, 1874

Bock, F., *Geschichter der Liturgischen Gewänder des Mittelatters*, 3 volumes, Bonn, 1856–71

Boutell, Charles, *The Monumental Brasses of England*, London, 1894

Boutell, Charles, *Monumental Brasses and Slabs*, London, 1847

Braun, J., *Die Liturgische Gewandung im Occident und Orient*, Darmstadt, 1964

Brown, Rev. C. K. Francis, *A History of the English Clergy 1800–1900*, 1953

Bumpus, John S., *A Dictionary of Ecclesiastical Terms*, Detroit, 1969

Carpenter, Edward, *Cantuar, The Archbishops in Office*, 1971

Carter, John, *Specimens of English Ecclesiastical Costume*, London, 1817

Christie, A. G. I., *English Medieval Embroidery*, Oxford, 1938

Clay, R. M., *The Hermits and Anchorites of England*, London, 1914

Clayton, H. J., *Cassock and Gown*, Alcuin Club Tracts, Oxford, 1929

Clayton, H. J., *The Ornaments of the Ministers as shown on English Brasses*, Alcuin Club Tracts, Oxford, 1919

Collinson, Patrick, *Archbishop Grindal 1519–1583, The struggle for a Reformed Church*, London, 1979

Compton, Piers, *The Great Religious Orders*, London, 1931.

Cripps, H. W., *A Practical Treatise on the Law relating to the Church and the Clergy*, 6th edition, London, 1886

Crockfords Clerical Directories

Cutts, E. L., *Parish Priests and their People in the Middle Ages in England*, London, 1898

Cutts, E. L., *Dictionary of the Church of England*, 4th edition, London, 1913

Cutts, E. L., *Scenes and Characters of the Middle Ages*, London, 1849

Cutts, E. L., *History of Early Christian Art*, London, 1893

Cutts, E. L., *Parish Priests and their People in the Middle Ages*, London, 1898

Darby, W. A., *Tracts on Ritual Church Vestments – an Examination*, 1866

Davenport, Millia, *The Book of Costume*, Volume 1 (Quakers), New York, 1948

Davies, J. G., ed., *A Dictionary of Liturgy and Worship*, London, 1972

Davies, J. G., *A Select Liturgical Lexicon*, London, 1965

Day, Peter D., *Eastern Christian Liturgies*, Dublin, 1972

Dearmer, Percy, *Linen Ornaments of the Church*, Alcuin Club Tracts, Oxford, 1929

Dearmer, Percy, *Ornaments of the Ministers*, London, Oxford and Milwaukee, 1920

Dearmer, Percy, *The Parson's Handbook*, 1st Edition, London 1899

Delatte, Don Paul, ed., *Dom Justin McCann: Commentary on the Rule of S. Benedict*, 1921

Dickinson, J. C., *Monastic Life in Medieval England*, London, 1961

Ditchfield, P. H., *The Old Time Parson*, London, 1908

Dodwell, C. R., *The Canterbury School of Illumination*, Cambridge, 1954

Dolby, Anastasia, *Church Vestments, their origin, use and ornament*, London, 1968

Downey, J., *The Eighteenth Century Pulpit*, Oxford, 1969

Dryden, Alice, ed., *Percy Dearmer: The Arts of the Church*, 1911

Duckett, Sir G. F., *Monastic and Ecclesiastical Costume*, 1892

Duckett, Eleanor Shipley, *Anglo-Saxon Saints and Scholars*, New York, 1947

Dugdale, *Monasticon Anglicanum*, eds Caley, Ellis and Bandina, 5 volumes, 1817

Evans, Joan, *English Art 1307–1461*, Oxford, 1949

Evans, Joan, *Pattern: A Study of Ornament in Western Europe*

1180–1900, 2 volumes, Oxford, 1931

Ferguson-Davie, P., *The Bishop in Church*, London, 1961

Gasquet, F. A., *Henry III and the Church*, London, 1905
Geldart, E., *Church Decoration and Symbolism*, Oxford, 1899
Gibson, Margaret, *Lanfranc of Bec*, Oxford, 1978
Grierson, Janet, *The Deaconess*, Oxford, 1981
Gummere, A. M., *The Quaker; A Study in Costume*, 1901

Haddan, A. W., and Stubbs, W., *Councils and Ecclesiastical Documents relating to Great Britain and Ireland*, Oxford, 1961
Hart, A. T., *The Eighteenth Century Parson*, 1955
Hart, A. T., and Carpenter, Edward, *The Nineteenth Century Country Parson*, 1954
Hope, Sir W. H. St J., 'On the Tomb of an Archbishop recently opened in the Cathedral Church of Canterbury' in Society of Antiquaries, *Vetusta Monumenta*, 1893
Hope, W. H. St J. and Atchley, *An Introduction to English Liturgical Colours*, London, 1920
Hope, W. H. St J. and Atchley, 'Ornaments of William of Wykeham and William of Waynefleet', in *Archeologia* vol lx, 1907
Howarth, *The Early English Church*, 3 vols, 1917

Jameson, Anna Brownell, *Sacred and Legendary Art*, 2 vols, London, 1874
Jones, Cheslyn, Wainwright, Geoffrey and Yarnold, Edward S. J., eds, *A Study of the Liturgy*, London, 1978

Kingsford, H. S., *Illustrations of the Occasional offices of the Church of the Middle Ages from contemporary sources*, London, 1921

Laver, James, 'The Undress of the Clergy', in *Country Life Annual*, 1955
Legg, J. Wickham, 'On two unusual forms of Linen Vestments', in *St Paul's Ecclesiological Society Transactions*, 1898
Legg, J. Wickham, and Hope, Sir W. H. St J., *Inventories of Christ Church, Canterbury*, 1902
Lesage, Robert, *Vestments and Church furniture*, 1960
Lowrie, Walter, *Monuments of the Early Christian Church*, 1923
Lowrie, Walter, *Art in the Early Church*, New York, 1947
Lowrie, Walter, *Christian Art and Archaeology*

Macalister, R. A. S., *Ecclesiastical Vestments: their Development and History*, London, 1896
Marriott, W. B., *Vestarium Christianum*, London, 1868
Menzies, A. C., *Sportsmen Parsons in Peace and War*, London, 1919
Moorman, J. R. H., *The History of the Church of England*, London, 1973

Morris & Company Ltd, *Church Decoration and Furniture*, catalogue, 1910

Neff, E. C., *An Anglican Study in Christian Symbolism*, Cleveland, Ohio, 1898
Norris, Herbert, *Church Vestments: Their Origin and Development*, London, 1949

Ollard, S. L., *A Dictionary of English Church History*, Oxford, 1919

Pinnock, W. H., *The Laws and Usages of the Church and the Clergy*, Cambridge, 1855–63
Pugin, A. W. N., *Glossary of Ecclesiastical Ornament and Costume*, enlarged and revised by B. Smith, London, 1868

Randall, Gerald, *Church Furnishings and Decoration in England and Wales*, London, 1980
Reichel, O. J., *The Origin and Growth of the English Parish*, London, 1921
Reichel, O. J., *English Liturgical Vestments in the 13th Century*, London, 1895
Rock, D., *Church of Our Fathers*, 3 volumes, London, 1849–52
Rolfe, C. C., *The Ancient Use of Liturgical Colours*, Oxford and London, 1879

Sandquist and Powicke, eds, *Essays in Medieval History*, Toronto, 1969
Sitwell, Sacheverell, *Monks, Nuns and Monasteries*, London, 1965
Skilbeck, C. O., *Illustration of the Liturgy; being thirteen drawings of the celebration of the Holy Communion in a parish church*, London, 1912
Southern, R. W., *Western Society and the Church in the Middle Ages*, London, 1970
St Paul's Ecclesiological Society Transactions, London
Stokes, Margaret, *Early Christian Art in Ireland*, London, 1887

Tyack, G. S., *Historic Dress of the Clergy*, 1897

Walker, Christopher, *Art and Ritual of the Byzantine Church*, London, 1982
Wilpert, Joseph, *Ein Cyclus Christologischer Gemälde aus der Katakombe*, Freiberg, 1891
Wilpert, Joseph, *Die Malereien der Sacraments Kapellen in der Katakombe*, Freiburg
Wilpert, Joseph, *Des Kallistus*, Freiburg, 1897
Wilpert, Joseph, *Roma Sotteranea*, Rome, 1903
Winston, Richard, *Thomas Becket*, 1967
Woodforde, James, *Diary of a Country Parson*, Oxford, 1924–31

Index

Principal text references are given in **bold** type; numerals in *italic* type indicate pages on which illustrations occur.